ADHD and Sex

This innovative workbook allows couples and individuals to explore the intersection of ADHD and sexuality and its many manifestations in a couple's sex life and relationship.

With useful and practical interventions provided to help identify and address common sexual problems, Dr. Lyne Piché provides individuals with tools to better communicate their needs to improve intimacy. Chapters discuss how to better maintain attention and focus during sex, explore grounding strategies to help individuals get in touch with their bodies and encourage individuals to confront anxieties surrounding sexual pleasure, sexual transitions and address common sexual problems. Through these exercises and discussions, individuals and couples alike can feel empowered to develop a sexual plan and outline ways to improve communication, break down barriers and discover the advantages of ADHD.

This book is essential for adults with ADHD looking to embrace their sexuality, partners of neurodivergent adults, as well as therapists, counselors and coaches who work with neurodivergent clients.

Lyne Piché, PhD, is a Registered Psychologist in British Columbia and has been a sex therapist for 25 years, working in the field of couples counselling, sexual counselling, forensic psychology and trauma therapy. In her clinical practice, she currently focuses on improving sexual health, understanding neurodiversity and exploring relationships.

ADHD and Sex

A Workbook for Exploring Sexuality
and Increasing Intimacy

Lyne Piché

Routledge
Taylor & Francis Group

NEW YORK AND LONDON

Designed cover image: Cover Original Artwork "Metamorphosis" by Nadine Kelln
www.nadinekelln.com

First published 2025
by Routledge
605 Third Avenue, New York, NY 10158

and by Routledge
4 Park Square, Milton Park, Abingdon, Oxon, OX14 4RN

Routledge is an imprint of the Taylor & Francis Group, an informa business

© 2025 Lyne Piché

Book illustrations by Chris Gardner

The right of Lyne Piché to be identified as author of this work has been asserted in accordance with sections 77 and 78 of the Copyright, Designs and Patents Act 1988.

Disclaimer
The content of this workbook is based on my clinical experience. The workbook does not constitute a client–therapist relationship. You are encouraged to seek out specific recommendations tailored to your individual situation from a qualified mental health professional in your local area.

ISBN: 978-1-032-72274-0 (hbk)
ISBN: 978-1-032-71046-4 (pbk)
ISBN: 978-1-003-42237-2 (ebk)

DOI: 10.4324/9781003422372

Typeset in Sabon
by Newgen Publishing UK

Visit ADHDsex.com for more news and information about this workbook!

Contents

Acknowledgments

This workbook is the culmination of many years of curiosity and exploration. I would like to thank all the people who have shown me love and support throughout my life. My family has shown me a tremendous amount of patience and love, for which I will be eternally grateful.

I am very thankful to the wonderful folks at Routledge/Taylor & Francis who have supported me throughout this project, as well as everyone who has helped me explore ideas, edit sections of this book and who have generally allowed me to talk in great detail about the link between neurodiversity and sex! I have had the privilege of working with fantastic colleagues and wonderful clients. Thank you: this workbook could never have existed without you!

Foreword

If you have ADHD or are in a relationship with someone with ADHD, it can feel like too much of your day is spent on putting out fires or checking off the ever-regenerating list of obligations. Sure, it's important to solve problems and prevent negative things from happening, but it's not very inspiring. A lot of managing ADHD is about reducing the negative experiences that untreated ADHD can cause – for both partners. It's a good place to start, but a bad place to end. You shouldn't aspire to only get your life and relationship to go from bad to fine. What about adding the positives – you know, the good stuff; the meaningful, exciting and maybe even restorative.

When you look at your partner, do you wonder where the good times went? When you used to have fun together? When you couldn't wait to get some time alone together? Busy lives can squeeze out the fun, and busy couples can feel like their connection gets squeezed out along with it. This is even more true when your ADHD isn't well managed or if there has been too much struggle for too many years.

It's time to get greedy and create a relationship that's really worth having. This means not just surviving the day, but to really enjoy your partner. There's more to a great relationship than great sex, but that fiery passion can protect you from the inevitable frustrations and annoyances. More importantly, it cements your connection to each other – we stand strong in the face of all the stresses and strains that life throws at us.

Making time for sex says that your partner and relationship are important. You're blocking out the outside world and just focusing on each other. You're being generous and accepting generosity. You're proclaiming, "we deserve this!".

This smart and practical workbook covers all the right topics that will teach you the skills and strategies to take your sex life to that next level and really enjoy each other. So work your way through it. Take your time and enjoy the process. Stay open to what you learn about yourself, your partner, your chemistry and even the places that you get stuck. Feel free to skip over parts and to maybe go back later. Just like a great sexual encounter, it's not about performance or checking boxes; it's about enjoying every part of the journey and being open to what happens next.

Ari Tuckman, PsyD, author of *ADHD After Dark: Better Sex Life, Better Relationship*

Introduction

Hi! Hello! Hey there! We are going to talk about Attention Deficit Hyperactivity Disorder (ADHD), sexuality and finding ways to both understand and improve your sex life as an ADHDer or as a partner of an ADHDer. If you are an ADHDer who is struggling to understand how your ADHD impacts your sex life or if you are a partner or family member of an ADHDer and want to better understand the link between ADHD and sexuality, this book is for you! In this workbook, we explore how being neurodivergent can impact your sexuality. As you know, ADHD can impact your whole life. It can have an effect on your schooling, your relationships, your time management, your money management, your emotional regulation and your sensory processing, to name only a few. This workbook addresses the intersection of ADHD and sexuality.

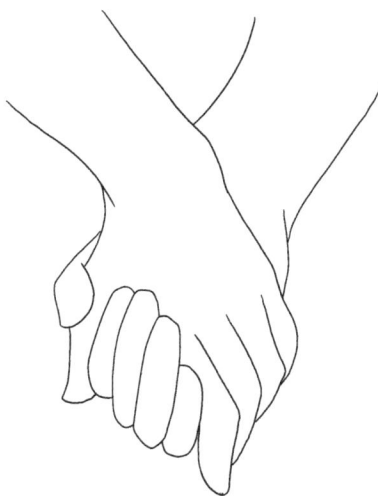

Many people with ADHD report specific struggles with their sexuality. Often, people with ADHD report attention problems and problems with their focus during sex, as well as transition problems such as getting into sex and getting out of sex. Difficulties with interoceptive awareness impede connection with your body (Goddall & Brownlow, 2022). Struggling to ground yourself into your body can lead to sexual difficulties and/or feelings of anxiety during sex. Sensory issues are also frequently reported by neurodivergent folks. Sensory issues can interrupt sexual pleasure. In addition, other ADHD symptoms can get

DOI: 10.4324/9781003422372-1

in the way of sex such as impulsivity, hyperfocus and sexual decision-making which can lead to negative long-term consequences. There are often intimacy problems identified by ADHDers that create difficulties establishing and/or maintaining relationships. As neuro-divergent people tend to mask all the ways that ADHD is impacting their lives, we will also discuss how masking can interfere with building intimacy, communicating openly and having great sex!

In this workbook, we will address:

✓ Attention problems
✓ Transition problems
✓ Sensation problems
✓ Hyperfocus problems
✓ Anxiety
✓ Sexual dysfunctions/Sexual problems
✓ Impulsivity
✓ Intimacy problems

This workbook aims to help you better maintain your attention during sex, explore grounding strategies to help you sit in your body more effectively during sex, manage transitions both in and out of sexual pleasure, manage anxiety, manage common sexual problems and reduce masking to improve intimacy with your sexual partners. Helping you identify, articulate and communicate sexual difficulties clearly, as well as finding solutions in order to help you to better navigate these realities are also important goals within this workbook.

ADHD can impact both solo sexual activities and partnered sexual activities. A quick word about solo sex vs partnered sex. Solo sex means that you are having sex on your own or with the assistance of a computer or sex toys. Partnered sex means that you are having sex with a partner or multiple partners. For ease in discussing these themes, regardless of whether you are engaged with multiple partners, in a monogamous relationship, open relationships or poly relationships, the term partnered sex will be used throughout the workbook to refer to sex with another person or persons. Whatever your relationship structure, when partnered sex or sex with a partner is identified, it means sex with another consenting adult.

This workbook is focused at helping you explore your relationship with sex and how ADHD has impacted that relationship. While you may have more questions that are specific to your unique situation, it is hoped that this workbook can help you clarify the important elements related to sex in your life and to start discussing these with your support system, your partners and/or any mental health professionals that may be working with you.

When talking about relationships, we will explore ways in which ADHD can impact your relationship through the lens of sexuality. Should you require more specialized assistance with your partnered relationship, seek out additional mental health resources in your area. If you do need couples counseling and you are in a neurodivergent relationship, it will be important to find a therapist who is knowledgeable about neurodivergence and neurodivergent relationships. Couples counseling with neurodivergent couples can be enhanced by using strategies that are informed by research and strategies specific to neurodivergent relationships (Orlov, 2010). Positively, there are more and more specialized programs available for you to access using telehealth or in person services.

Within this workbook, you will be encouraged to create a plan to improve your sexual satisfaction, your sexual communication and your sexual health. Creating this plan starts with understanding and acknowledging how ADHD impacts your sexuality. You may find it helpful to talk with your sexual partners as you work through this workbook to discuss how *YOUR* ADHD has impacted your sexual engagement. In addition, consider reaching out to trusted friends and family members for support as you explore the various themes in this workbook. People with ADHD vary, so you may be impacted by some symptoms more than others. Focus on the materials in this workbook that apply to you and leave the rest! Should you require further assistance, please find a local mental health professional who is specialized in working with ADHD to help you.

Let's explore how ADHD may be affecting your sexuality! Our journey begins in the next Chapter: Chapter 1 – What is ADHD? This chapter provides a quick overview, where we briefly explore ADHD and its impact on your overall life.

References

Goodall, E. & Brownlow, C. (2022). *Interoception and Regulation: Teaching skills of body awareness and supporting connection with others*. London: Jessica Kingsley Publishers.

Orlov, M. (2010). *The ADHD Effect on Marriage: Understand and rebuild your relationship in six steps*. Speciality Press/A.D.D. Warehouse, p. 225.

Chapter 1

What is ADHD?

A quick overview

Attention Deficit Hyperactivity Disorder (ADHD) is a neurodevelopmental disorder that impacts a portion of the population. A neurodevelopmental disorder simply means a group of symptoms that show up at some point during a child or a youth's development. It is difficult to obtain accurate statistics about how prevalent it is, owing to a lack of access to mental health professionals who are specialized in offering proper diagnosis for this disorder. We do know that features of ADHD are seen in many cultures; this is not simply a North American problem. It is most often hereditary but not always (APA, 2022).

There are three different ADHD presentations, predominantly inattentive, predominantly hyperactive/impulsive, and combined presentation (APA, 2022). In addition, people may have mild, moderate, or severe symptoms. This creates additional confusion as people with ADHD can present quite differently. The diagnostic criteria is quite rigid and, if you are working with a North American registered/licensed mental health professional, an ADHD diagnosis requires you to have the specific symptoms listed in the DSM-V-TR (*Diagnostic and Statistical Manual of Mental Disorders*, American Psychiatric Association, 2022). These include: failing to give close attention to details or making careless mistakes, difficulty sustaining attention in tasks or play, not seeming to listen when spoken to directly, not following through on instructions and/or failing to finish duties, schoolwork, chores or work, difficulties organizing tasks and activities, avoiding dislikes or being reluctant to engage in tasks that require sustained mental effort, losing things necessary for tasks and activities, easily being distracted by outside stimuli and often being forgetful in daily activities. Criteria also include often fidgeting, taping hands or feet or squirming in seat, often leaving situations where being seated is expected, running about or climbing where it is inappropriate or feeling restless, being unable to play or engage in quiet activities, often being on the go, uncomfortable or unable to be still for extended periods of time, talking excessively, blurting out answers, difficulties waiting for a turn as well as interrupting or intruding on others (see APA, 2022 for exact criteria). Not all symptoms are expected to be present in one individual, but they must cause difficulties throughout a person's lifespan (Sibley, 2021). People with ADHD can experience delays in language, motor skills, social development as well as emotional dysregulation and emotional impulsivity (APA, 2022).

DOI: 10.4324/9781003422372-2

It is apparent from information gleaned in social media that people with ADHD present with struggles that do not always fit neatly into the mental health classification system (Jones & Hesse, 2018; Ginapp, 2023; Guntuku, 2019). These struggles can cause distress and/or difficulties for people with ADHD. Positively, there has been a heightened community awareness of ADHD and neurodiversity in recent years.

Common ADHD symptoms reported by people with ADHD include many of the symptoms identified above as well as a few others. These may include:

o Impulsivity
o Emotional reactivity (quick to anger, easily frustrated, overreactive, big emotions)
o Forgetfulness
o Difficulties maintaining focus and attention
o Special interests/hyperfocus
o Too much or too little participation
o Interrupting
o Difficulties in planning
o Novelty seeking
o Restlessness
o Learning disabilities
o Performance difficulties in work and/or school

Additional symptoms related to ADHD include:

o Poor interoceptive awareness
o Difficulties feeling grounded/difficulties connecting with your body
o Social difficulties
o Anxiety
o Depression
o Sleep difficulties
o Perfectionism
o Rigidity in thought/black and white thinking
o Rejection sensitivity
o Eating disorders
o Physical variability (illnesses, autoimmune issues, food sensitivities)
o Substance use problems
o Nail biting, skin picking, tongue chewing (Body Focused Repetitive Behaviors)
o Higher rates of physical injury and/or experiencing trauma
o Obesity and difficulty managing weight

To further complicate matters, many people with Autism Spectrum Disorder also experience ADHD symptoms. There can be a large crossover in symptoms between people who have Autism and people who have ADHD (Antshel & Russo, 2019). In this workbook, we will use the term neurodivergent to encompass everyone in the group rather than trying to parcel people into specific groups.

There can be marked individual differences between neurodivergent people. In addition, when people are initially meeting a mental health professional, their tendency is often to mask their symptoms, which can make receiving an accurate diagnosis more difficult (Sibley, 2021). Finding professionals who are specialized in assessing neurodiversity can be particularly hard, although this appears to be improving with the advent of telehealth mental health services. Seek out registered or licensed mental health professionals who can offer a formal diagnosis that is accurate and who offer complete assessments that explore all aspects of your functioning throughout your life.

✓   Look at the lists above and put a check mark, a star or a funny face, beside the symptoms that apply to you!

What do you notice when you review these lists? Do you have more features of inattention, hyperactivity or both?

_____
_____
_____
_____
_____

What are the symptoms that others have noticed in you? Whether you agree with their observations or not, write down what you have been told about your behaviors:

_____
_____
_____
_____
_____

When did you start noticing these symptoms in your life? Write down some examples from your childhood, your teen years and your adult years (include your young adult years and older adult years too!).

Childhood:

_____
_____
_____
_____
_____

Puberty/Teen years:

_____
_____
_____
_____
_____

Young Adult years:

_____
_____
_____
_____
_____

Older Adult years:

_____
_____
_____
_____
_____

There are lots of great things about being neurodivergent! The good things like hyperfocus and special interests can be a lot of fun! Finding communities of like-minded people, as well as living your life in a way that suits your preferences can be a positive experience. Seeing the big picture and focusing on activities that stimulate your brain can be challenging and enjoyable! The negative aspects of ADHD, however, can get in your way. Let's explore the symptoms that get in your way most often.

What are the most difficult ADHD symptoms that you manage on a daily basis?

_____
_____
_____
_____

What ADHD symptoms consistently get in the way of your goals?

_____
_____
_____
_____

How have you tried to address these symptoms?

_____
_____
_____
_____

What has worked well to IMPROVE your symptoms? *Note: It doesn't have to be perfect but what tends to make it better?

_____

_____

_____

_____

_____

Fully exploring best practices for ADHD symptom management is your unique journey! There are many resources to assist you: see Barkley, 2021; Hallowell & Ratey, 2022; Solden, 2012; Tuckman, 2013; Sira & Hudock, 2022 for more details. Here are some strategies that research, clinicians and other ADHD folks have identified as being helpful.

Which one of these strategies do you use on a daily, weekly or monthly basis? Which ones do you never do?

Recommended way to improve ADHD symptoms	I do this daily	I do this weekly	I do this monthly	I NEVER do this one
Exercise				
Healthy food choices				
Eating regularly				
Drinking water regularly				
Taking your meds regularly[1]				
Talking to your doctor if you are unhappy with how medication makes you feel				
Visual reminders (whiteboards, notes on the fridge or mirror)				
Phone reminders				
Using a daily agenda or calendar				
Proper sleep				

Recommended way to improve ADHD symptoms	I do this daily	I do this weekly	I do this monthly	I NEVER do this one
Using a timer or specific code words to facilitate transitions				
Sticking to a schedule				
Electronic locks rather than key locks				
Regular counseling				
Coaching services				
Online support groups				
Limiting screen time				
Changing your household organizational structure (e.g. using bins, hooks)				
Creating a launchpad for your essential items for the day including medications, daily planner, keys and wallet				
Asking for help				
Hiring help				
Body doubling/joining a body doubling community				
Putting additional resources in place during monthly PMS periods and/or during hormonal transitions				

Recommended way to improve ADHD symptoms	I do this daily	I do this weekly	I do this monthly	I NEVER do this one
Making chores a game				
Balancing completing chores with your special interests				
Other:				
Other:				
Other:				

<u>ADHD is part of the entire landscape of your life</u>. You are not **YOU** without your ADHD! There are positive aspects about having ADHD and there are negative aspects about having ADHD. The good news is that the positives can outweigh the negatives! Finding activities that give you a feeling of success and accomplishment is essential when living with ADHD.

We will use the term ADHD consequences when talking about those life events that have impacted your life. While things may have turned out well with time, ADHD consequences can be difficult and can cause you significant stress. An ADHD consequence can be: an unexpected pregnancy, a tragic car accident, not completing your schooling, messing up a relationship with someone you love, losing a job that you really liked, living with bankruptcy as a result of a failed business, not paying your taxes or mismanaging your finances/bills, losing an important friend or any other consequences that can be traced back to your ADHD.

People with ADHD report higher levels of living with a sense of failure, difficulty reaching their goals, feelings of anxiety, feeling down, difficulties with studies and academic achievement, medical issues and/or illnesses, increased accidents, working too much, feeling misunderstood and drug or alcohol abuse, to name only a few (Hallowell & Ratey, 2022; Barkley, 2015; Wallin et al., 2022). There are many ways that ADHD can impact your life!

How has ADHD impacted your life? What ADHD consequences have you suffered?

_____

_____

_____

_____

When you think about the ADHD consequences in your life, how did you cope with these challenges? What did you learn from these experiences? How did you make your life better as a result of these events?

_____

_____

_____

_____

_____

_____

Despite these challenges, there are likely many ways that ADHD has improved your life or made your life better, more interesting, provided positive challenges and/or opportunities. For example, you may have tried new experiences, found success in your special interests, tackled social justice issues, achieved your goals and/or joined communities of like-minded people. How has ADHD improved your life?

_____

_____

_____

_____

_____

_____

You are strong and resilient!

Focus on the ways that you have improved your life as a result of the ADHD consequences that you have experienced.

Some people may struggle to understand ADHD and how it impacts your life. You may find that people openly criticize you or discount the difficulties you may have when living with ADHD (Hallowell & Ratey, 2022).

When someone openly criticizes you about an ADHD symptom or passes judgement on you about the impact of ADHD on your life, some things that might be helpful to say include:

- "I can set countless reminders, but my ADD brain will sometimes find a way to scuttle the mission (smiley face)!"
- "My ADD brain sometimes works against my best intentions".
- "Thanks for being patient when my mind wandered off".
- "Thanks for being willing to try new things with me, even if it didn't work out, the process was fun!"
- "My brain and I thank you for waiting; I am so glad to spend time with you".
- "My ADHD brain does not react to situations with malicious intent; this wasn't personal".
- "My ADHD is not a personal attack".
- "Moral judgments hurt me and don't reflect my reality as a person living with ADHD".

- "My intention was to express or achieve the following (clarify your intended outcome); clearly it didn't land the way I had hoped".
- "My ADHD is alive and well!"

What would you like to say when someone challenges you about an ADHD symptom or passes judgment about an ADHD consequence in your life?

_____
_____
_____
_____
_____

What specific struggles related to your ADHD symptoms would you like to communicate to others?

_____
_____
_____
_____
_____

Partnered relationship problems are frequent for people with ADHD. These can include significant difficulties such as more separations and divorce (Orlov, 2010), high conflict relationships (Barkley, 2015) and sexual issues (Tuckman, 2019). There are specific programs developed for couples where at least one partner has ADHD (see Orlov, 2010 as well as Corvelli, 2022, ND compass program, Neurodiverse Partners Institute for more details). These programs and resources can be quite helpful to address your relationship concerns. Work with a mental health professional who is knowledgeable about the impact of ADHD on relationships when seeking out couples counseling.

How do your ADHD symptoms impact your relationships with your partner(s)?

_____
_____
_____
_____
_____

According to your partner(s), how do your ADHD symptoms impact your relationships?

_____
_____
_____
_____
_____

Women present with particular differences, in terms of ADHD symptoms and symptom management (Eng et al., 2024; Young et al., 2020). Firstly, women with ADHD are often misdiagnosed with other disorders such as anxiety, depression, or personality disorders (Young et al., 2020; Solden, 2012). Secondly, hormone changes are identified as creating increased ADHD symptoms for women (Eng et al., 2024; Young, 2020). As a result, mental health professionals may not see the overall symptom patterns, as some weeks a biological female can function relatively well but other weeks they don't; there are changes in their presentation and the severity of their symptoms. Women with ADHD tend to really struggle during times when their hormone levels change such as following the start of puberty, pregnancy/childbirth, perimenopause and menopause (Solden, 2012). Premenstrual Dysphoric Disorder (PMDD) is a condition that is more often experienced in women with ADHD (Dorani et al., 2021).

In this workbook, we will strive to address issues that impact sex and ADHD for everyone. We will refer to biological females to distinguish biology from gender when it applies to our discussion[2].

As a biological female, I have experienced the following difficulties related to my ADHD symptoms:

_____
_____
_____
_____
_____

As a biological female, my ADHD symptoms have been most problematic during <u>these specific times</u> in my life:

_____
_____
_____
_____
_____

Some strategies to help manage ADHD for biological females include:

✓ Track your period/monthly cycle
✓ Speak to your health care provider about increasing ADHD medication dosage during PMS periods
✓ Communicate with your partner about the times when your ADHD symptoms are intensified
✓ Recognize and honor your periods of fatigue
✓ Work with your health care provider to address other symptoms that may be occurring in conjunction with your ADHD symptoms
✓ Discuss birth control medication options that will not create a drop in hormone levels
✓ All the other recommendations outlined earlier in this chapter

As a biological female, I plan to address my increased ADHD symptoms during specific times of hormonal change by doing the following:

_____
_____
_____
_____
_____

A quick word about sleep issues:
It is beyond the scope of this workbook to address sleep issues and neurodivergence. It is common for people with ADHD to have sleep issues (Hiscock & Sciberras, 2019; Konofal, Lecendreux & Cortese, 2010). Sleep issues will interfere with many aspects of your life. It is essential to identify and treat any sleep issues you may have. If you are struggling with a sleep issue, talk to your health provider and/or your mental health provider for specialized assistance. Addressing sleep issues is an essential part of improving your daily functioning!

Having ADHD can be hard!

Doing something about your ADHD symptoms, something that is effective and helpful, is essential. There are great books to help you improve your ADHD symptoms. See the Additional Resources section at the end of this workbook for more details.

If you want to improve your life, and you have ADHD, your best bet is to focus on symptom management. Symptom management is an important first step to improving your life, your mood, your relationships and your sexuality!

Let's continue our journey together in Chapter 2, where we explore in more detail, Why ADHD and sex?

Working towards my goals

To best manage my ADHD symptoms, I will start adding the following strategies to my daily life:

- ☐ Exercise daily
- ☐ Healthy food choices
- ☐ Eating regularly
- ☐ Drinking water regularly
- ☐ Taking my meds regularly
- ☐ Talk to my doctor if I am unhappy about how my medication makes me feel
- ☐ Visual reminders (whiteboards, notes on the fridge or mirror)
- ☐ Phone reminders
- ☐ Using a daily agenda or calendar
- ☐ Proper sleep
- ☐ Using a timer or specific code words to facilitate transitions
- ☐ Sticking to a schedule
- ☐ Electronic locks rather than keys
- ☐ Regular counseling
- ☐ Coaching services
- ☐ Online support groups
- ☐ Limiting screens
- ☐ Changing my organizational structure (bins, hooks)
- ☐ Creating a launchpad with my essential items for the day including medications, daily planner, keys and wallet

☐ Asking for help/hiring help
☐ Body doubling/joining a body doubling community
☐ Putting additional resources in place during PMS periods and/or times of hormonal changes
☐ Making chores a game
☐ Balancing my chores with my special interests
☐ Tracking my period/monthly cycle
☐ Discuss medication dosage options during PMS periods with my health care provider
☐ Communicate with my partner(s) about times when my ADHD symptoms are intensified
☐ Recognizing and honoring periods of fatigue
☐ Work with my health care provider to address other symptoms that may be occurring in conjunction with my ADHD symptoms
☐ Other:_____
☐ Other: _____
☐ Other: _____
☐ Other: _____

I LOVE my ADHD because:

_____
_____
_____
_____
_____

Notes

1 Consider carrying extra medication with you, in case you forget to take them in the morning.
2 It does not appear that there is research exploring ADHD symptoms in ADHD individuals who experience a sudden, permanent change in hormone levels for other reasons such as gender transitions and illnesses/medical interventions.

References

Antshel, K. M. & Russo, N. (2019). Autism spectrum disorders and ADHD: Overlapping phenomenology, diagnostic issues, and treatment considerations. *Current Psychiatry Reports*, 21(5). doi:https://doi.org/10.1007/s11920-019-1020-5.

American Psychiatric Association (2022). *Diagnostic and Statistical Manual of Mental Disorders* (5th edition text revision, DSM-5-TR), https://doi.org/10.1176/appi.books.9780890425787.

Barkley, R. (2021). *Taking Charge of Adult ADHD: Proven Strategies to Succeed at Work, at Home, and in Relationships* (2nd ed.). Guilford Publications.

Barkley, R. (2015). Attention-Deficit Hyperactivity Disorder: A Handbook for Diagnosis and Treatment, 4th Edition, Guilford Publications.

Corvelli, Jill (2022). ND compass program, Neurodiverse Partners Institute, www.ndpartnerscompass.com.

Dorani, F., Bijlenga, D., Beekman, A.T.F., van Sumeren, E.J.W. & Kooij, J.J.S. (2021) Prevalence of hormone-related mood disorder symptoms in women with ADHD *Journal of Psychiatric Research*, 133, 10–15. https://doi.org/10.1016/j.jpsychires.2020.12.005.

Eng, A.G., Nirjar, U., Elkins, A.R., Sizemore, Y.J., Monticello, K.N., Petersen, M.K., Miller, S.A., Barone, J., Eisenlohr-Moul, T.A. & Martel, M.M. (2024). Attention-deficit/hyperactivity disorder and the menstrual cycle: Theory and evidence. *Hormones and Behavior*, 158, 105466. https://doi.org/10.1016/j.yhbeh.2023.105466.

Ginapp, C.M., Greenberg, N.R., Macdonald-Gagnon, G., Angarita, G.A, Bold, K.W. & Potenza, M.N. (2023). The experiences of adults with ADHD in interpersonal relationships and online communities: A qualitative study. *SSM – Qualitative Research in Health*, 3, 100223.

Guntuku, S.C., Ramsay, J.R., Merchant, R.M. & Ungar, L.H. (2019). Language of ADHD in adults on social media. *Journal of Attention Disorders*, 23(12), 1475–1485. https://doi.org/10.1177/1087054717738083.

Hallowell, E.M. & Ratey, J. J. (2022). *ADHD 2.0: New Science and Essential Strategies for Thriving with Distraction--from Childhood through Adulthood*. Ballantine Books, p. 208.

Hiscock, H. & Sciberras, E. (2019). *Sleep and ADHD: An evidence-based guide to assessment and treatment*. Academic Press.

Jones, S. & Hesse, M. (2018). Adolescents with ADHD: Experiences of having an ADHD diagnosis and negotiations of self-image and identity. *Journal of Attention Disorders*, 22(1), 92–102. https://doi.org/10.1177/1087054714522513.

Konofal, E., Lecendreux, M. & Cortese, S. (2010) Sleep and ADHD, *Sleep Medicine*, 11, 652–658.

Orlov, M. (2010). *The ADHD Effect on Marriage: Understand and rebuild your relationship in six steps*. Speciality Press/A.D.D. Warehouse, p. 225.

Sibley, M.H. (2021). Empirically-informed guidelines for first-time adult ADHD diagnosis. *Journal of Clinical and Experimental Neuropsychology*, 43(4), 340–351. https://doi.org/10.1080/13803395.2021.1923665.

Sira, C. & Hudock, T. (2022). *Getting it done with ADHD: Specialized ADHD Techniques to expertly handle the overwhelm, distraction, and procrastination of accomplishing tasks, Be The Boss of Your Brain*.

Solden, S. (2012). *Women With Attention Deficit Disorder: Embrace your differences and transform your life*. Introspect Press, p. 515.

Tuckman, A. (2013). *Understand Your Brain, Get More Done: The ADHD Executive Functions Workbook*. Specialty Press/A.D.D. Warehouse.

Tuckman, A. (2019). *ADHD after dark: Better sex life, better relationship*. Routledge. https://doi.org/10.4324/9780429274671.

Wallin, K., Wallin Lundell, I., Hanberger, L., Alehagen, S. & Hultsjö, S. (2022). Self-experienced sexual and reproductive health in young women with Attention Deficit Hyperactivity Disorder: A qualitative interview study. *BMC Women's Health*, 22, 289. https://doi.org/10.1186/s12905-022-01867-y.

Young, S., Adamo, N., Ásgeirsdóttir, B. B. et al. (2020). Females with ADHD: An expert consensus statement taking a lifespan approach providing guidance for the identification and treatment of attention-deficit/hyperactivity disorder in girls and women. *BMC Psychiatry*, 20, 404. https://doi.org/10.1186/s12888-020-02707-9.

Chapter 2

Why ADHD and sex?

SEX IS PLAY!

Sex is play means that sex is fun, relaxed, without expectations, easy, flowing, connecting, pleasurable and you are present. When we are talking about sex throughout this workbook, we mean pleasure, we mean play. Sex does not necessarily equal intercourse. Sex is all the things that bring you pleasure when you are touching your body, touching someone else's body and/or touching each other. It's not dependent on your genitals. It's not dependent on having an erection. It's not dependent on having an orgasm. Sex is about following pleasure. Sex is all the things that feel good. **SEX IS PLAY!**

Imagine a group of puppies playing together: they are jumping on each other, biting each other's ears, rolling under and over, nipping at each other and engaging in lots of movement. They are enjoying what is going on and when another puppy does something they don't like, they let the other pup know right away. **This is play. This is sex.**

Play is best defined as something that is fun to do! According to Brown and Vaughan (2010), play provides many skills that are essential to our survival; but while playing is linked to our survival, when we play, it doesn't feel like we are doing an activity to survive; we are simply doing an activity for fun. **Play creates joy!**

According to Brown and Vaughan (2010), play is like oxygen, it's all around us and we don't even notice it. Brown and Vaughan (2010) set out criteria for an activity to be defined as play. According to Brown and Vaughan (2010), play is: purposeless (it's done for the pleasure of it), voluntary (we want to do it), offers inherent attraction (it's fun and makes you feel good), offers freedom from time (we lose the sense of time), creates diminished consciousness of self (we are not focused on ourselves, our bodies or our thoughts), has improvisational potential (it doesn't have to be done a certain way or a specific way; we can change it each time and, because we can do things differently each time we experience it differently) and offers continuation desire (we keep it going and want to keep doing it after we are done)[1]. There is lots to know about play, but you can simply remember that if you are having fun, you are playing!

DOI: 10.4324/9781003422372-3

What is your first thought when you think about play?

_____

_____

_____

_____

What type of play do you prefer?

_____

_____

_____

_____

There are many ways to increase play in your life! Here are only a few examples:

✓ Do one fun activity daily or weekly that brings joy to your life
✓ Play boardgames or card games with a partner or a friend
✓ Try a new activity
✓ Go for a walk while trying to spot something new or explore a new road
✓ Visit or talk to old friends
✓ Visit or talk to new friends
✓ Sing
✓ Dance
✓ Play sports
✓ Plan a trip, a staycation or a zoom meeting with someone special
✓ Go out for a date night or a get together with friends
✓ Exercise by trying something different (e.g. roller skating, ballroom dancing, kite flying, scuba diving, belly dancing, etc.)
✓ Creative activities: paint, build Lego, pottery or clay work, puzzles
✓ Build something, make something: metal work/welding projects, carpentry, renovations
✓ Engage with nature: walking trails, swim, bike, photography, collect rocks, mine for minerals, geocaching, build a garden, science projects
✓ Challenge yourself with new projects, new adventures, new thrills

Consider the impact of play both for yourself and for others in your life.

If I add more play into my life, it will improve my life by:

_____

_____

_____

_____

If I add more play into my life, it will improve other people's lives by:

_____

_____

_____

_____

_____

To increase the amount of play in my life, I want to try doing:

_____

_____

_____

_____

_____

Now... think about sex!

What is the first thought that comes to you when you think about sex?

_____

_____

_____

_____

_____

Hold that thought...

What is the most fun sexual experience you have ever had? What made it so fun?

_____

_____

_____

_____

_____

Sometimes, people have a hard time reproducing their most fun sexual experience. They can't quite seem to repeat that experience. Other times, people notice that their thoughts about sex are quite negative or they don't have many positive sexual experiences. Others have found ways for sex to be fun on a fairly regular basis.

What are your beliefs relating to sex? Are these positive or negative?

_____

_____

_____

_____

For many people with ADHD there are specific challenges that can make sex harder. We will discuss those challenges in the upcoming chapters. As you get to know these challenges, you will be encouraged to manage them in ways that work best for you. Throughout this workbook, take the information that works for you and leave the rest!

<u>Quick reminder</u>: In this workbook, we will be talking about partnered sex and solo sex. Partnered sex means that you are having sex with a partner or multiple partners. For ease in discussing these themes, regardless of whether you are engaged in a monogamous relationship, open relationships, having sex with multiple partners or in poly relationships, the term partnered sex will be used throughout this workbook to refer to sex with another person or persons. Whatever your relationship structure, when partnered sex or sex with a partner is identified, it means sex with another consenting adult.

Solo sex means having sex on your own, with your own body and this often occurs with your computer or cellphone. If you are talking or reaching out to someone through the phone or on the computer, it is no longer solo sex. Keep in mind that any sexual engagement with a partner requires consent, a partner who wants to be there, who says yes, who knows what's going on and who is of age to consent to the activities being discussed. Enthusiastic consent is essential to having good, safe and fun sex!

When you reflect on your sex life, who are your usual partners? Does your sexual activity occur in long term relationships, short casual friendships, open relationships that involve multiple people or does sex occur mostly with yourself rather than with others? If you have had many types of sexual partnerships, what type of sexual play partners do you prefer?

My sexual relationship preferences are:

☐ Long-term monogamous relationships
☐ Short-term monogamous relationships
☐ Close friends
☐ Casual partners/acquaintances
☐ Online partners
☐ Strangers
☐ Groups
☐ Myself

☐ Other: _____

Now that you have identified with whom you are engaging with or with whom you would prefer to engage with for sexual activity, what else would you like? Often ADHDers find that what they like isn't always seen as acceptable or normative in the neurotypical world. As you complete this workbook, you are encouraged to write down WHAT YOU ACTUALLY WANT, not what you <u>think</u> you should want or what other people want for you. Getting to know yourself and your sexuality means that you are taking the time to connect with yourself and your <u>actual</u> desires.

Reflecting on your sexuality and your personal preferences, let's start with frequency! Ideally, how often are you engaging in sexual activity?

If I am experiencing my ideal sex life, I am having sex:

- □ Daily
- □ Once a week
- □ 2-3 times a week
- □ Every 2 weeks
- □ Monthly
- □ Twice a year
- □ Yearly

- □ Other: _____

In your ideal sex life, what are you doing and, perhaps more importantly, what are you not doing?

If I have my ideal sex life I am doing:

- □ Solo sex exclusively
- □ Partnered sex exclusively
- □ Mix of solo and partnered sex
- □ Multiple partners – known to me
- □ Multiple partners – unknown to me
- □ Touching only
- □ Foreplay only
- □ Masturbation only
- □ Oral without penetration
- □ Penetrative sex (anal, vaginal or both)
- □ Role plays
- □ Embracing fantasy
- □ BDSM and bondage activities
- □ Pornography use
- □ The sky's the limit

- □ Other: _____
- □ Other: _____
- □ Other: _____
- □ Other: _____
- □ Other:_____
- □ Other: _____

If I have my ideal sex life, I am NOT doing:

- ☐ Solo sex exclusively
- ☐ Partnered sex exclusively
- ☐ Mix of solo and partnered sex
- ☐ Multiple partners – known to me
- ☐ Multiple partners – unknown to me
- ☐ Touching only
- ☐ Foreplay only
- ☐ Masturbation only
- ☐ Oral without penetration
- ☐ Penetrative sex (anal, vaginal or both)
- ☐ Role plays
- ☐ Embracing fantasy
- ☐ BDSM and bondage activities
- ☐ Pornography use
- ☐ The sky's the limit
- ☐ Other: _____
- ☐ Other: _____
- ☐ Other: _____
- ☐ Other: _____
- ☐ Other: _____
- ☐ Other: _____

Oftentimes, when you have ADHD, you may be very fearful of ADHD consequences and, as a result, keep yourself tightly managed and controlled (see Chapter 1 for a discussion of ADHD consequences). Being overcontrolled can interfere with building a relaxing sexual experience with yourself and with a partner.

Have you thought about trying something sexually but have not tried it yet for fear that you will get carried away?

_____

_____

_____

_____

What would make the sexual activities that you wanted to try feel safer for you?

_____

_____

_____

_____

Communicating your sexual desires to the people in your life will be something that we will tackle in Chapter 10 – Intimacy… Yikes! For now, focus on being clear within yourself about what you like and what you dislike as it relates to sexual play.

There are many ways to increase the amount of play in your life, whether by yourself or with a partner. Knowing how you like to play and what type of play interests you is an important first step. Acknowledging and communicating your playful desires to others will help increase the frequency of play and will help play become more fun!

Sex takes physical movement! Physical movement requires connecting to your body. If you are like others with ADHD, perhaps connecting with your body is difficult. You may find that you don't like your body very much; you may be carrying excess weight that is getting in your way or you may have physical limitations that make movement difficult. ADHD is associated to being overweight (Cortese & Tessari, 2017), having more body image issues (Van Eck, Morse & Flory, 2018; Bisset, Rinehart & Sciberras, 2019; Gowey et al., 2017), experiencing chronic pain or chronic health issues (Mundal, 2023; Kerekes et al., 2022; Barkley, 2015) as well as having difficulty with grounding (Kutscheidt et al., 2019; Goodall & Brownlow, 2022). Difficulties moving your body may lead you to feel less confident about your ability to please your partner. We will talk more about interoceptive awareness and feeling connected to your body in the Chapter 4 – What is that feeling? Being in your body to achieve good sex. For now, let's focus on your relationship with your body as it relates to **moving** your body.

What do you think about your ability to move your body?

My physical movement is:

- ☐ Great! – No problems
- ☐ Good – I could improve but I am on the right track
- ☐ Passable – I am not proud about how I move my body but I can improve
- ☐ Ouch! – I am feeling really stuck and struggle with my physical movement
- ☐ I have disabilities that limit my ability to move my body in certain ways

Some people with ADHD suffer physical health concerns. In fact, you may be more likely to have autoimmune difficulties, chronic pain problems or other illnesses that get in your way (APA, 2022; Kerekes, 2022; Barkley, 2015; Garcia-Argibay, 2022; Nirouei et al., 2023). Food allergies/sensitivities are also frequently reported by people with ADHD (Jiang et al., 2018; Xu et al., 2022). There are therapies designed to help you with chronic pain including Pain Reprocessing Therapy based on the book The Way Out by Alan Gordon, resources such as the Curable app, as well as specific books to help you with the distress of having a chronic illness such as *Finding Freedom in Illness* by Peter Fernando and *How to be Sick by Toni Bernhard*. If you are suffering from chronic pain, seek out additional assistance. Ask health professionals who are specialized in dealing with physical ailments and chronic illnesses for help to address your particular concerns.

If your physical movement is compromised, find ways to set yourself up for success. There are different types of sex furniture and supports that can help make sex more comfortable. Explore and search sexual aids, sexual furniture, wedges, and sexual pillows to make yourself and your partner more comfortable. You can also consult a physiotherapist or a movement specialist to help you find ways to enhance your physical comfort in sexual situations. Ensuring physical comfort during sex is a great place to start in your goal to make sex fun again!

What physical supports (for example, wedges, sex pillows, sex furniture, etc.) would help you improve your physical movement and be more successful within sexual interactions?

_____
_____
_____
_____
_____

Here are some other ways to improve your physical movement:

- Address any issues that you may have with food. There are specialists who work with ADHD and food who can help you. Look up ADHD and food specialists (e.g. *Eating with ADHD program* by Nicole DeMasi Malcher)
- Exercise daily to improve your overall mobility (with the permission of your doctor)
- Yoga (insert my self-deprecating negative comments about yoga here ☺) – yoga can be very helpful with flexibility, body movement and grounding in your body!
- Deep breathing (use deep breathing apps to guide you, place your hand on your chest when breathing, use combat breathing strategies/box breathing strategies, or put your arms up and breathe!)

- Proper medication
- Consultation with a physiotherapist, kinesiologist and/or other physical health professional that specializes in physical movement
- Deal proactively with any physical health concerns with the assistance of your doctor or health care provider

ADHD and sex – Emerging Research

When we talk specifically about ADHD and sex, we see some trends in the emerging research. ADHD folks had higher number of sexual partners, lower condom use, higher rates of condomless sex, higher STI diagnoses, higher numbers of unplanned pregnancies and more emergency contraceptive use (Rohacek et al., 2022; Hetz et al., 2022; Rokeach & Weiner, 2018). In addition, there is research suggesting that people with ADHD perceive themselves as being kinkier than people who do not have ADHD and more ADHDers have engaged in consensual non-monogamy (Tuckman, 2019). ADHDers also tend to be more fluid in their sexual experiences as it relates to sexual orientation (Young & Cocallis, 2023; Hetz et al., 2022). This means that you may have experiences with same sex and opposite sex partners in sexual situations regardless of your sexual orientation.

There is also research that suggests that people with ADHD are sexually eager, more sexually eager in fact than neurotypical folks (Young & Cocallis, 2023). ADHD people tend to masturbate more often than the average (Tuckman, 2019). To be specific, Tuckman (2019) identified that ADHD women masturbated approximately every six days and ADHD men masturbated approximately every two or three days; while non-ADHD women masturbated approximately every nine days and non-ADHD men masturbated approximately every three or four days.

We don't know why people with ADHD tend to be more sexually eager, and there may be multiple reasons that explain why this might be. Orgasm feels really good! ADHDers also really like activities with lots of stimulation, and there is lots of stimulation to be found in sexual activities, either solo or partnered. Other explanations include the fact that people with ADHD have a hard time staying focused during sex; as a result, they would require more sexual stimulation or sexual intensity than others (Soldati, 2021). There may also be a tendency for ADHDers to escape into various activities, such as reading, daydreaming and videogames, and sex can be a very effective form of escape.

Over time, being sexually eager can turn into being very invested in sex, preoccupied with sex or becoming "addicted" to sex. In this workbook, we will call this problem **hypersexuality**. Of interest, there may be a relationship between being preoccupied with sex (also known as hypersexuality) and the ADHD inattentive presentation and perhaps the combined presentation (Hetz et al., 2022; Young et al., 2023). This means that if you tend to be primarily inattentive in your ADHD symptoms, you may struggle with too much sex and transitioning out of sex, more than if you are hyperactive/impulsive in your ADHD symptoms; however, research remains very sparse on this topic. One study identified self-esteem as an important moderator in this relationship (Reid et al., 2011). For example, you may use sex to make you feel better about the things that are not going well in your life or to deal with certain emotions that you don't like such as feeling mad, sad or afraid. In contrast, there is also research that suggests that some people with ADHD are uninterested in sex (Soldati, 2020). So, having ADHD doesn't necessarily mean that you always want sex. You may have ADHD and not be interested in sex most of the time.

Divorce rates are higher for people with ADHD and there is often less stability and satisfaction in relationships (Hetz et al., 2022; Barkley, 2015). In addition, people with ADHD show higher rates of engaging in some form of infidelity (Young et al., 2023; Tuckman, 2019). All of this can ultimately impact a person's sex life.

Here are some examples that ADHDers have reported about the impact of ADHD on their sexuality:

- I am in hyperfocus over here, my special interest is taking all my time, there is no time for sex! All my energy is put into this other project
- I just can't stay focused during sex
- I lose focus during sex so I must not like my partner/this activity/sex in general
- I can't sit in my body long enough to figure out how I feel. Do I want sex? Do I want a cookie? Do I want to sleep? No idea…
- I struggle with sexual problems so there is no point in having sex
- I feel terrible about my body, I don't want to share it with someone else
- I am bothered by sounds, smells, weird sensations during sex, so forget it!
- I liked sex with my partner before but now I don't…
- I am bored during sex
- Being drunk or high is impacting my ability to maintain an erection
- I am irritable and tired; I don't want sex
- I simply don't feel like having sex unless I am on holidays
- I can't imagine sharing my sexual history with a future partner so I would rather lie about what I like to do sexually or simply be alone
- I need to be grounded INTO my body during sex and I can't get there on my own
- I am in it until I am not; I am not in it until I get into it; I was into it, now I am not
- Solo sex is easier for me than partnered sex

Distraction is frequently reported by ADHDers during sex. ADHD partners tended to struggle with distraction during sex more than non-ADHD partners (Tuckman, 2019). This problem will be tackled in its own chapter: Chapter 3 – What is that noise? How ADHD can impact your focus during sex.

In addition, being present within your body, being able to sit and feel your body, is an important prerequisite to experiencing good sexual engagement. When you aren't in your body, it is hard to experience pleasure.

People with ADHD consistently report difficulties with mind-body connection. People with ADHD report problems engaging with mindfulness and experiencing interoceptive awareness (Kutscheidt et al., 2019; Goodall & Brownlow, 2022). Mind-body connection appears essential to achieving sexual pleasure and managing your response to pleasure (for example, having genital control) during sexual interactions. These concerns will be discussed in more detail in Chapter 4 – What is that feeling? Being in your body to achieve good sex.

Sensory concerns can occur if you become distracted by specific sensations during sex. Sensations can be specific textures, smells, touches, sounds, sights or tastes. Sensory issues can interfere with sexual pleasure and your sexual interactions with others. You may prefer to avoid sex if you are struggling with difficult sensations during sex. See Chapter 8 – What is that smell? A word about sensory issues and ADHD for further details.

In addition, sexual problems (also known as sexual dysfunctions) appear to be more common in people with ADHD (Soldati, 2021). These problems will be discussed in more detail when we talk more specifically about anxiety and sex in Chapter 7 – What am I afraid of? Anxiety and ADHD.

We will talk about how impulsivity can impact your sexual health as well as your life trajectory in Chapter 9 – What have I gotten myself into? Impulsivity, sex and ADHD. Ideas on how to address hypersexuality can be found in Chapter 5 – What is going on right now? Transition problems! and again in Chapter 9 – What have I gotten myself into? Impulsivity, sex and ADHD.

As you can see, while sexual issues can be related to ADHD; there is hope! Research suggests that managing your ADHD symptoms will improve your sex life (Tuckman, 2019). In addition, managing your ADHD is an important strategy to improve your relationships (Orlov, 2010). All the strategies you use to manage your ADHD will benefit both your sex life and your relationships!

Women, ADHD and Sex

There are specific concerns reported in research about women who have ADHD as it relates to their sexuality. Premenstrual Dysphoric Disorder (PMDD) is more common for ADHD women (Dorani et al., 2021). In addition, hormone changes create increased ADHD symptoms (Eng et al., 2024). For biological females with ADHD, these monthly changes can interrupt sexual interest, sexual urges and increase conflicts in relationships which often leads to a decrease in sexual satisfaction (Wallin et al., 2022; Sanchez-Fuentes, Santos-Iglesias & Sierra, 2014).

In addition, women with ADHD report that they struggle with feeling different and have difficulties feeling sexually secure (Wallin et al., 2022). Disclosing a more varied sexual history can also result in ADHD women feeling judged sexually which can lead to having a negative image of themselves and low self-esteem (Wallin et al., 2022). The dichotomy between societal expectations, such as gender roles, what women are "supposed to like" sexually or what sexual partnerships are acceptable in comparison to a woman's actual life history, such as having had a varied sexual history or difficulties fulfilling traditional gender roles, can lead to poor communication with sexual partners and a fear of being rejected by future partners. We will discuss these themes in more detail in Chapter 10 – Intimacy… Yikes!

Themes specific to sexual victimization and sexual safety will be discussed in more detail in Chapter 11 – Neurodivergent Safety: The importance of Sexual and Relationship Safety.

Sex and Medications

It can be helpful to consider your medication use and explore if any medications you are currently taking could be contributing to your sexual concerns.

Medications can change your level of sexual interest. For example, a specific type of anti-depressants are known to create a drop in sexual desire, lower sexual thoughts and reduced sexual urges. At times, these medications can also result in sexual dysfunctions, for example, problems getting erections. Alternatively, medication may help resolve sexual problems such as hypersexuality. Specific to ADHD medications, some medications may resolve sexual problems while others might create concerns. Speak with your physician, pharmacist or health care professional to discuss the impact of ADHD medications on your sexuality.

It is noteworthy that in a survey of ADHDers by Tuckman (2019) it was reported that the timing of when ADHD medication was taken did not address or change sexual functioning in any meaningful way.

✓   Keep a journal or a log and write down changes in your sexual functioning both before and after starting any new medication to facilitate discussions with your health care provider

Medications may impact you and your sexuality. Talk with your health care provider and/or your pharmacist to learn more about the interactions between your medications and your sexuality.

Neurodiversity Grief

Grief about who you are, your ADHD and your individual needs can interfere in establishing a sex life that makes you happy! Grief is common when facing a situation that you cannot control and a situation that creates strong feelings of loss.

Address any feelings of grief you may have as it relates to your neurodiversity. Becoming comfortable with being neurodiverse can take time and it does involve purposefully exploring who you are, looking at both the positives and the negatives of how your body and brain impact you. Getting to know your strengths and weaknesses is one way to embrace your neurodiversity.

If you are struggling with grief as it relates to your journey with neurodiversity, consider joining a community of like-minded individuals who are also exploring these issues and/or an ADHD support group. In addition, reaching out to a qualified mental health professional can be a lovely way to find support, validation and assistance as you explore the impact of neurodivergence in your life[2].

Has ADHD made your sex life more fun and varied? If so, how?

_____

_____

_____

_____

_____

Has ADHD made your sex life problematic? If so, how?

_____

_____

_____

_____

_____

_____

Are there ADHD consequences that are specific to your sexuality that you have faced?

- □ Yes
- □ No
- □ I don't think so

If yes, what are they?

_____

_____

_____

_____

_____

_____

How have you made the best of things when experiencing an ADHD consequence? Were you able to turn it around and create a positive outcome or a positive learning experience for yourself and/or others?

_____

_____

_____

_____

_____

_____

Research tells us one important thing about ADHD and sex, the more you manage your symptoms of ADHD overall, the better your sex life will likely be (Tuckman, 2019). Managing your ADHD symptoms will address some of the issues highlighted in this workbook. Finding solutions that work for you to better manage your ADHD is the first key to addressing your sexual issues.

> As you go through this workbook, we will look at the different ways that ADHD impacts
>
> YOU
>
> and your sexuality

Let's continue our journey together in Chapter 3, where we explore in more detail: What is that noise? How ADHD can impact your focus during sex.

Working towards my goals

I need to practice adding more play into my life:

☐   I am doing great! Lots of play
☐   I am doing ok, could be better but there is some play!
☐   I am not having enough play in my life
☐   What is play???

To increase the amount of play in my life, I want to try:

_____
_____
_____
_____
_____

I will try these specific activities with my sexual partner to create more fun together:

_____
_____
_____
_____
_____

✓   I will post my list of fun activities on my whiteboard, reminder system or agenda so I don't forget to try them
✓   Fun activities can include anything that brings me joy such as boardgames, time together, exercise together, walks, etc.
✓   I will stay on the lookout for new ways to play that I might want to try!

When I tried new activities, I noticed that these specific activities made me happy:

_____
_____
_____
_____
_____

✓   Remember that what makes you happy today will likely change in the future. Be flexible! When it stops feeling good, try another activity.

I have identified that my ideal sex life includes the following:

_____

_____

_____

_____

_____

My most fun sexual experience taught me that the following activities, situations and/or partners are what I like most about sex:

_____

_____

_____

_____

_____

New sexual activities and experiences that I want to try or become more comfortable with include:

_____

_____

_____

_____

_____

There are other issues that I need to address that are impacting my sexuality; for example, my body movement, my sleep or other physical health issues. I will address these issues by doing the following:

_____

_____

_____

_____

_____

I have suffered ADHD consequences that continue to upset me: _____ Yes _____ No

   Dealing with ongoing problems can be addressed by:

- talking to a qualified mental health professional
- getting support from my friends/family
- joining a support group
- working through another self-help book
- asking a mentor for help

My plan to address the ADHD consequences that still upset me includes:

_____

_____

_____

_____

_____

Notes

1 See Brown, S. & Vaughan, C. (2010) *Play: How it Shapes the Brain, Opens the Imagination, and Invigorates the Soul* for more details about the science of play.
2 A qualified mental health professional is someone who is licensed or registered for practice in your area.

References

Barkley, R. (2015). *Attention-Deficit Hyperactivity Disorder: A Handbook for Diagnosis and Treatment* (4th ed.). Guilford Publications.

Bernhard, T. (2010). *How to be Sick: A Buddhist-Inspired Guide for the Chronically Ill and Their Caregivers*. Massachusetts: Wisdom Publications.

Bisset, M., Rinehart, N. & Sciberras, E. (2019). Body dissatisfaction and weight control behaviour in children with ADHD: A population-based study. *European Child & Adolescent Psychiatry*, 28(11), 1507–1516. https://doi.org/10.1007/s00787-019-01314-8.

Brown, S. & Vaughan, C. (2010). *Play: How it Shapes the Brain, Opens the Imagination, and Invigorates the Soul*. New York: Avery Press.

Cortese, S. & Tessari, L. (2017). Attention-Deficit/Hyperactivity disorder (ADHD) and obesity: Update 2016. *Current Psychiatry Reports*, 19(1), 4. https://doi.org/10.1007/s11920-017-0754-1.

Dorani, F., Bijlenga, D., Beekman, A.T F., van Someren, E.J.W. & Kooij, J.J.S. (2021). Prevalence of hormone-related mood disorder symptoms in women with ADHD. *Journal of Psychiatric Research*, 133, 10–15. https://doi.org/10.1016/j.jpsychires.2020.12.005.

Eng, A.G., Nirjar, U., Elkins, A. R., Sizemore, Y. J., Monticello, .K. N., Petersen,M. K., Miller, S.A., Barone, J., Eisenlohr-Moul, T.A. and Martel, M.M. (2024) Attention-deficit/hyperactivity disorder and the menstrual cycle: Theory and evidence. *Hormones and Behavior*, 158, 105466. https://doi.org/10.1016/j.yhbeh.2023.105466.

Fernando, P. (2016). *Finding Freedom in Illness: A Guide to Cultivating Deep Well-Being through Mindfulness and Self-Compassion*. Colorado: Shambhala Publications.

Garcia-Argibay, M., du Rietz, E., Lu, Y., Martin, J., Haan, E., Lehto, K., Bergen, S.E., Lichtenstein, P., Larsson, H. & Brikell, I. (2022). The role of ADHD genetic risk in mid-to-late life somatic health conditions. *Translational Psychiatry*, 12(1), 152. https://doi.org/10.1038/s41398-022-01919-9.

Goodall, E. & Brownlow, C. (2022). *Interoception and Regulation: Teaching Skills of Body Awareness and Supporting Connection with Others*. Jessica Kingsley Publishers.

Gordon, A. (2020). *The way out: A revolutionary, scientifically proven approach to healing chronic pain*. New York: Avery Publications.

Gowey, M.A., Stromberg, S.E., Lim, C.S. & Janicke, D.M. (2017). The moderating role of body dissatisfaction in the relationship between ADHD symptoms and disordered eating in pediatric overweight and obesity. *Children's Health Care*, 46(1), 15–33. https://doi.org/10.1080/02739615.2015.1065745.

Hertz, P.G., Turner, D., Barra, S., Biedermann, L., Retz-Junginger, P., Schöttle, D. & Retz, W. (2022). *Sexuality in Adults With ADHD: Results of an Online Survey*. Frontiers Psychiatry, 13, 868278. doi: 10.3389/fpsyt.2022.868278.

Jabalkandi, A., Raisi, S., Shahrivar, F., Mohammadi, Z., Meysamie, A., Firoozikhojastefar, R. & Irani, F. (2020). A study on sexual functioning in adults with attention-deficit/hyperactivity disorder. *Perspectives in Psychiatric Care*, 56(3), 642–648. https://doi.org/10.1111/ppc.12480.

Jiang, X., Shen, C., Dai, Y., Jiang, F., Li, S., Shen, X., Hu, Y. & Li, F. (2018). Early food allergy and respiratory allergy symptoms and attention-deficit/hyperactivity disorder in Chinese children: A cross-sectional study. *Pediatric Allergy and Immunology*, 29(4), 402–409. https://doi.org/10.1111/pai.12888.

Kerekes, N., Lundqvist, S., Schubert Hjalmarsson, E., Torinsson Naluai, Å., Kantzer, A., Knez, R., Institutionen för biomedicin, Institute of Neuroscience and Physiology, Göteborgs universitet, Gothenburg University, Sahlgrenska Academy, Sahlgrenska akademin, Institute of Biomedicine, & Institutionen för neurovetenskap och fysiologi. (2022). The associations between ADHD, pain, inflammation, and quality of life in children and adolescents—a clinical study protocol. *PloS One*, 17(9), e0273653–e0273653. https://doi.org/10.1371/journal.pone.0273653.

Kutscheidt, K., Dresler, T., Hudak, J., Barth, B., Blume, F., Ethofer, T., Fallgatter, A.J. & Ehlis, A. (2019). Interoceptive awareness in patients with attention-deficit/hyperactivity disorder (ADHD). *Attention Deficit and Hyperactivity Disorders*, 11(4), 395–401. https://doi.org/10.1007/s12402-019-00299-3.

Mundal, I., Schei, J., Lydersen, S., Thomsen, P.H., Nøvik, T.S. & Kvitland, L.R. (2023). Prevalence of chronic and multisite pain in adolescents and young adults with ADHD: A comparative study between clinical and general population samples (the HUNT study). *European Child & Adolescent Psychiatry*. https://doi.org/10.1007/s00787-023-02249-x.

Nirouei, M., Kouchekali, M., Sadri, H., Qorbani, M., Montazerlotfelahi, H., Eslami, N., & Tavakol, M. (2023). Evaluation of the frequency of attention deficit hyperactivity disorder in patients with asthma. *Clinical and Molecular Allergy CMA*, 21(1), 4–4. https://doi.org/10.1186/s12948-023-00185-4

Orlov, M. (2010). *The ADHD Effect on Marriage: Understand and rebuild your relationship in six steps*. Speciality Press/A.D.D. Warehouse, p. 225.

Reid, R.C., Carpenter, B.N., Gilliland, R. & Karim, R. (2011). Problems of self-concept in a patient sample of hypersexual men with attention-deficit disorder. *Journal of Addiction Medicine*, 5(2), 134–140. https://doi.org/10.1097/ADM.0b013e3181e6ad32.

Rohacek, A., M. Firkey, M.K., Woolf-King, S.E. & Antshel, K.M. (2022). Moderation of risks to sexual health by substance use in college students with ADHD. *Journal of Clinical Psychiatry*, 83(4), e1–e7.

Rokeach A & Wiener J. (2018) The Romantic Relationships of Adolescents With ADHD. *Journal of Attention Disorders*, 22(1):35–45. doi: 10.1177/1087054714538660.

Soldati, L., Bianchi-Demicheli, F. Schockaert, P. Köhl, J., Bolmont, M., Hasler, R. & Perroud, N. (2021). Association of ADHD and hypersexuality and paraphilias. *Psychiatry Research*, 295, 113638. https://doi.org/10.1016/j.psychres.2020.113638.

Soldati, L., Bianchi-Demicheli, F., Schockaert, P., Köhl, J., Bolmont, M., Hasler, R. & Perroud, N. (2020). Sexual Function, Sexual Dysfunctions, and ADHD: A Systematic Literature Review. *Journal of Sexual Medicine*, 17, 1653e1664.

Tuckman, A. (2019). *ADHD After Dark: Better Sex Life, Better Relationship* (1st ed.). Routledge.

Van Eck, K., Morse, M. & Flory, K. (2018). The role of body image in the link between ADHD and depression symptoms among college students. *Journal of Attention Disorders*, 22(5), 435–445. https://doi.org/10.1177/1087054715580845.

Wallin, K., Wallin Lundell, I., Hanberger, L., Alehagen, S. & Hultsjö, S. (2022). Self-experienced sexual and reproductive health in young women with Attention Deficit Hyperactivity Disorder: A qualitative interview study, *BMC Women's Health*, 22:289 https://doi.org/10.1186/s12905-022-01867-y.

Xu, G., Liu, B., Yang, W., Snetselaar, L. G., Chen, M., Bao, W., & Strathearn, L. (2022). Association of Food Allergy, Respiratory Allergy, and Skin Allergy with Attention Deficit/Hyperactivity Disorder among Children. *Nutrients, 14*(3), 474. https://doi.org/10.3390/nu14030474

Young, S. & Cocallis, K. (2023). A systematic review of the relationship between neurodiversity and psychosexual functioning in individuals with autism spectrum disorder (ASD) or attention-Deficit/Hyperactivity disorder (ADHD). *Neuropsychiatric Disease and Treatment, 19*, 1379–1395. https://doi.org/10.2147/NDT.S319980.

Young, S., Klassen, L.J., Reitmeier, S.D., Matheson, J.D. & Gudjonsson, G.H. (2023). Let's talk about sex... and ADHD: Findings from an anonymous online survey. *International Journal of Environmental Research and Public Health, 20*(3), 2037. https://doi.org/10.3390/ijerph20032037.

Chapter 3

What is that noise?

How ADHD can impact your focus during sex

Peter likes sex. He likes his partner. Peter thinks that his partner is lovely and kind. He used to think that his partner was super hot, but now Peter is having a hard time getting an erection. He is really worried! He doesn't want his partner to assume that he doesn't like him. Peter saw his medical doctor. He also saw a counsellor. Both say that there is nothing wrong with him. Peter starts wondering if he is in the wrong relationship. He thinks that maybe his partner isn't the right one after all.

Sex and attention go together! When your mind is wandering from one topic to another, it's difficult to stay focused on what is happening in the moment. To fully engage sexually, you need to be present. You need to be paying attention to what is going on in the moment to fully explore and enjoy sexual pleasure. If your mind is wandering, this can negatively impact your sex life.

ADHDers often identify sexual problems that stem from having a wandering mind (Solden, 2012). Research identifies that being unfocused and distracted can lead to sensory

DOI: 10.4324/9781003422372-4

problems which ultimately impairs the sexual response cycle (Abdel-Hamid, Basilowski & Schönfeld, 2021). These authors identify that distractibility impacts all the phases of sexual play including: sexual desire, sexual arousal/excitement, and orgasm. This is also identified by Tuckman (2019), who noted that distractibility was often reported by ADHD women during sex. In clinical practice, it is often reported that people's minds simply can't settle during sex (Solden, 2012). Unfortunately, distracting thoughts during sex are associated to experiencing less sexual satisfaction (del Mar Sanchez-Fuentes, Santos-Iglesias & Sierra, 2014).

Here are some examples of how ADHDers might identify that their focus gets distracted during sex:

✳ My mind wanders
✳ I have to have everything done on my to do list before I can even consider having sex
✳ Once I get going it is ok, but to get going, I need the house to be quiet, the kids to be in bed and the lights must be turned off
✳ I am a terrible partner because I think about sexual scenarios with other people while I am having sex with my partner
✳ Sex is boring; if it isn't off the scale, I am not interested
✳ If the fridge is running or the dog is barking, I lose my arousal
✳ I can't relax enough to have sex
✳ I was into it the other day, sex was fun, then I heard the neighbours and I couldn't keep going!
✳ Sex is easier when we are on holidays; there is nothing else to do

Does this feel familiar to you? Do you notice your mind wandering during sex?

_____ Yes _____ No

If your partner has ADHD, do you notice that their mind wanders during sex?

_____ Yes _____ No

If you believe that a wandering mind does impact you or your partner during sex, take note of <u>WHEN</u> your mind wanders in the sequence of sex.

When does your mind and/or your partners' mind wander during sex?

☐ Noticing sexual feelings – Getting my attention focused on sex, noticing that I am feeling aroused, noticing that my partner is feeling aroused, noticing that now would be a good time to engage in sex. I just don't notice.
☐ Initiating sex – Taking my clothes off, sexual touching, sexual thoughts. I have other things to do. I just don't want to go there. I don't want to be touched. I don't want to take my clothes off. I just don't want to think about it.
☐ Engaging in sex – Kissing, touching, masturbating, focusing on my body or a partner's body, sexual play. I am thinking about other things. I just can't keep my mind in the game.

- The climax – Getting close to orgasm but not coming "over the hump". My mind starts drifting when I get close to orgasm. I just can't let go enough to orgasm. I can't build enough excitement to orgasm. I don't get there.
- Cuddle time – Expectations around cuddling, time together, discussions, etc. After sex, I just want a sandwich and the freedom to move on to another activity.

Let's explore ways to tame that wandering mind!

Wandering minds get to have fun too!

Many of us have areas in our homes where we have sex most often. You may notice that a space other than your home is better for sexual engagement. For example, it might be that you used to prefer having sex at your partner's place but now that you are living together, sex in your own shared space isn't so much fun. You might also notice that if you are having sex elsewhere (e.g. sex club, hotel room, outdoors, anywhere but your bedroom really), sex becomes easier. Let's see if there are things about your home or personal space that may be getting in the way and distracting you during sex.

Sit in your usual sexual space. Breathe. Put your hand on your chest. Breathe again. What do you notice about this space? Is your space:

- Cluttered?
- Smelly?
- Noisy?
- Comfortable?
- Private?
- Convenient?
- Can you reach things that you might want or need during sex?
- Temperature? Too cold or too hot?
- Peaceful?
- Desirable?
- Sexy?
- Full of children's toys, paraphernalia and other stuff?
- Full of pet's toys, paraphernalia and other stuff?
- Full of work stuff?
- Full of other people's stuff?
- Other: _____
- Other: _____

Addressing your physical space, where you typically have sex with yourself or with others, is the first step to addressing distractions during sex. Often, clutter is the first thing that people notice about their usual sexual space. Reducing clutter can be an effective way to ensure that your space holds fewer distractions. In addition, reducing clutter can allow you to combat your mind wandering as there are less distracting items for you to focus on.

It may be time to work with a cleaning service to reduce concerns about the dirt/cleanliness of your space, and/or it may be time to hire a home organizer to assist with the clutter. There are many services that offer information aimed at reducing clutter in your home (see NAPO – National Association of Productivity & Organizing Professionals for specialized home organization assistants and/or social media channels that focus on home organization). There are also many great books to help you organize your space from an ADHD perspective (see Kolberg and Nadeau, 2016 for ideas).

Temperature

The temperature of the room also matters quite a bit. If the temperature (either being too cold or too hot) is a source of distraction, find a compromise. This may involve temporary fixes such as adding a fan or a heater for use during sexual play or resolving the issue more permanently by addressing the overall heating and cooling systems in your home. If the temperature is a source of distraction, communicate clearly about the problem so that you can find a way to address it.

Addressing the privacy of your space is also important. Do you need a way to secure the door that is safe and offers a feeling of "being away"? Do you have a door? The knowledge that a door is closed and locked can help people create distance from whatever is happening on the other side of that door. If you have young children or if you need space from the older teens/young adults who are still sharing living space with you, a privacy lock may be helpful[1].

Sound

Noises that are getting in your way should be addressed. Squeaky, loose or broken bed frames are culprits that often come up when identifying distractors during sex.

Start with identifying problematic noises:

* Is it the bed frame?
* Traffic?
* Neighbours?
* Animals?
* Appliances?
* Other household members?

As you sit in your space, what do you hear:

_____

_____

_____

_____

_____

Now that you have identified the noise problems, address them!
You can address noise in a few simple ways:

✓ Fix a broken bedframe, squeaky bed frame or a bed that is not quiet when you move in it
✓ Temporarily unplug or get rid of the noise making item
✓ Add a competing noise that will grab more of your attention
✓ Address and fix structural sources of excessive noise such as upgrading windows, adding soundproofing, moving to a quieter living space
✓ Organize childcare/outside activities for other household members and/or settle pets

There are many ways to create sound dampening and to decrease distracting noises in your environment:

☛ Explore noise dampening items (e.g. soundproofing panels, soundproofing curtains, door stoppers)
☛ Effect structural changes (e.g. insulation, caulking windows/doors, newer windows or doors)
☛ Competing sounds (e.g. music, brown noise, white noise or specific soundproofing devices)

If you cannot remove the noise distracting item or fix it, consider using competing sounds to address the problem. Take the time to fix the distractors so that they are not getting in your way!

Music can be a great way to both focus your attention and to avoid distractions. Many people have their favourite songs or playlist that they use during sexual activity. There are many songs out there, from many different genres, that are great to help focus your mind before, during and after sex. I bet that you already use this trick in other aspects of your life! Consider your workout playlist, you may have a stretching set of tunes, a cardio set of tunes and a cool down set of tunes. A sexual playlist works the same way. Find songs that help you feel sexy and get you thinking about sex, think about the songs that would connect you into sexual play and then consider songs that are all about cuddling and connecting with one another.

Take a moment to think about the music that makes you most aroused, makes you feel desirable and helps you connect with your body. Take a moment to play that song or those songs.

Right now, play it!

What do you notice? How do you feel?

_____
_____
_____
_____
_____

If your favourite songs help you feel more aroused, more in your body and more desirable, you are on the right track! If you are listening to a song and it makes you feel sad or creates a feeling of longing or yearning for something that you do not currently have in your life, this is not a good song to add to your sexual playlist. Do this exercise with a goal of creating a "starting up" sexy playlist, an "in it" sexy playlist and a connecting/cuddling "after sex playlist". You don't need more than two or three songs per category.

What category is the easiest for you to identify?

☐   My start me up sexy playlist
☐   My "In it" sexy playlist
☐   My connection and cuddling sexy playlist

If you struggle to find specific songs for each category, explore different music genres. You may find some nice options in the jazz genre, classical genre or other music that you do not typically explore. You may also want to ask friends, acquaintances, coworkers or family members for suggestions.

What are your favourite "sex songs"? Write your ideal playlist.

_____
_____
_____
_____
_____
_____
_____
_____

Now, let's explore other ways to help you create focus during the sexual activity you are having and reduce your distractibility.

The environment

Sometimes, the best way to manage distractions is to change the location where you usually have sex. If you can't reduce distractions in your space, consider moving to spaces that are less distracting for you.

Some people find that hotel rooms offer less distractions. When you are staying in a hotel, there are less competing demands and you are less likely to be sidetracked by household chores and other responsibilities. While it probably isn't realistic to pay for a hotel room every time you want to have sex, planning a "nightly getaway" on a regular basis is one way to deal with the distractions inherent to your sexual environment.

Whether alone or with a partner, there is something unmistakably intense about shower sex. The lack of distractions in the bathroom, the perceived privacy and the shower/bath can combine to be quite effective at eliminating distractions. In addition, the sound of water is extremely effective to reduce competing noises and can be quite calming for many people. Many people report similar sensations of calm, privacy and a lack of distractions whether they are in the bath or shower. Which do you prefer?

☐   I am a bath person!
☐   I am a shower person!

Touching your body and/or a partner's body when you are in the shower or the bath is one way to reduce external distractions. Positively, there aren't many competing noises, visual stimuli or competing sensations in the bathroom. If you notice yourself focusing on the caulking in the shower/tub – Stop, Call a handyman, Get that shit sorted and then go back to playing[2]

Other spaces in your home might also offer less distractions during sex. This may be another room in your home, a larger closet, a basement or a space that feels cozy, private and distraction-free. Explore other spaces and see how they feel in order to improve your focus during sex!

Timing

Timing can be tricky! Some people believe that the timing of sex is essential for them to experience good sex (e.g. "I need sex to happen only in the morning"). You might want sex to occur at a specific time, or you may want your partner to only engage with you at a specific time of the day. Some moments are not conducive to sex. If you are wanting sex with a partner and your partner is sick, unavailable, upset or focused on another task, this attempt likely won't be terribly successful.

Keep an open mind as it relates to the timing of sex in your day. What works best for you AND for your partner? Compromise! Take turns having sex timed to your personal preferences and to your partner's personal preferences. Keep track of whose turn it is so that everyone feels that the system is fair. Notice how things feel when you have sex at a less "ideal" time for you. Is it really that bad? Most likely, you will notice that sex outside of your preferred time isn't as bad as you first thought it would be.

✓   Take turns having sex at times that work best for you and at other times that work best for your partner.
✓   Try having sex at different times of the day to see if there is more flexibility than you first thought about the timing of your sexual play

What about meds and what happens when those meds have worn off? Current research is limited. ADHD medication wearing off may not significantly impact your sexuality

(Tuckman, 2019). However, partners do complain that their ADHD partner can get grumpy and irritable when their ADHD medication wears off (Orlov, 2010). This may result in sex becoming less appealing to the non-ADHD partner. Given the limited research, it is worth noticing what works best for you and/or your partner in regards to the impact of medication on your sexual timing.

Do you have more focus in the morning or in the evenings? _____ AM _____PM

Does your overall engagement with your partner improve when you are medicated?

_____ Yes _____No

Does your overall engagement with your partner decrease later in the day when your meds have worn off? _____ Yes _____No

Is sex better soon after you have taken your meds in the morning, in the afternoon or is it better once they have worn off? _____ AM _____ NOON _____PM

On holidays, what do you notice about your focus? Is it easier to engage sexually when expectations and chores aren't present? _____ Better _____Worse

If you are a shift worker, you will have to adjust your sexual timing based on your energy levels. Play with the timing of sex to see what works for you!

Intensity of touch

Physical touch is a good way to stay engaged during sex and it can help you be more present. Intense touch can create focus. Different intensity of touch such as light touch, hard touch, biting, pinching, different textures (think: feathers, lube, creams) can all enhance sexual engagement and focus attention.

Let's play a game!

Touch your hand softly, super softly. How does that feel?

_____
_____
_____
_____
_____

Touch your hand with a feather, make it tickle. How does that feel?

_____
_____
_____
_____
_____

Pinch your hand. Pinch hard! How does that feel?*

_____

_____

_____

_____

_____

Slap your hand. Slap hard! How does that feel?*

_____

_____

_____

_____

_____

* These exercises are meant to explore sensations and touch. If you have a medical condition that would make them unsafe or unhelpful to you, please skip ahead to the other exercises in this workbook.

What do you notice about your focus during each one of these types of touch? Is a soft touch focusing your attention and reducing distractions or is a hard touch focusing your attention and reducing distractions?

Now repeat the same exercise with a partner and ask them the same questions.

The type of touch that sharpens my attention is:

_____

_____

_____

_____

_____

The type of touch that sharpens my partner's attention is:

_____

_____

_____

_____

_____

The goal of this exercise is to identify what focuses your attention. The type of touch that you prefer and the type of touch that improves your attention, might be different. You may not need the type of touch that sharpens your attention all the time during sexual play. It may be that integrating the touch that enhances your attention at times throughout your sexual play is enough. Playing with more intense touch may heighten your focus during sex.

   A word about BDSM and intensity of touch. Many types of intense touch are explored in the BDSM community (e.g. touch with electricity, nipple clamps, whips, chains, ropes, etc). There are ways to explore sexual touch without establishing a submission and dominance sexual partnership. If you enjoy more intense sexual touch, there are many groups, books, videos, podcasts, community organizations and community events that can assist you to explore intense touch safely.

Play with touch!

We will talk more about touch and intensity of touch in later chapters of this workbook.

Speed

Speed is another way of heightening your attention in the present moment. Sometimes moving fast into sex can spark your attention like nothing other. Jumping in with consent (obviously!), feeling all the feels, and jumping out, can be the equivalent to standing under a cold waterfall. Fast moves can be attention grabbers!

To be clear, we are not talking about going so fast that you are feeling nothing, that would be counterproductive. The goal is to create intensity as a way to maintain focus and attention. Creating intensity is an important part of catching an ADHDer's attention!

What about going slow? If you go slow by feeling your body, this can be a good way to laser focus your attention to what is happening in the moment; however, if you are going so slow that nothing much is happening, you may find that your attention will wander right out of the room! The key to this skill is keeping enough momentum to remain engaged in the moment. There are many ways to slow down <u>and</u> maintain your attention during sex (for example, Tantric sexual practices). You may wish to explore these strategies to gain more information about how going slow might also assist you in finding and maintaining your attention during sex.

Sex toys

Sex toys are an easy way to increase focus and to reduce distractions during sex whether solo or partnered. Intensity of touch is enhanced when you are touched with a sex toy. Sex toys or vibrators offer a unique feeling that is hard to produce manually. Larger sex toys, anal toys and/or penetrative machines can offer a huge amount of intensity for you and your partner. Masturbation sleeves are another way to change the physical sensations associated with sexual play and can be purchased with vibration. There are multiple types of sexual toys including sex toys that can be used cold or warm, which produce varying sensations. Sex toys can be very effective in increasing sexual intensity.

Sex toys are not specific to one gender! Everyone can enjoy the feelings that are aroused by playing with various sex toys.

What do you notice about the sexual intensity created by sex toys?

_____

_____

_____

_____

_____

If you are not willing to try sex toys to enhance intensity and focus attention, what are your concerns?

My concerns about sex toys include:

_____
_____
_____
_____
_____

Is there a compromise that would allow you to explore this topic from a more playful perspective?

_____
_____
_____
_____
_____

Talk with your partner to explore how you might address these concerns in more detail.

Words/mental imagery/visualization/erotic stories

Staying in the moment can be tough. Use words and mental imagery to stay in the moment!

What do you notice when your partner talks to you during sex?

☐   I enjoy sexual words; they keep me in the moment
☐   I dislike sexual words; they distract me and take me out of my body

Words that focus on sexual arousal, sexual energy and sexual play can maintain your attention and keep that spark going! Alternatively, some words can be very distracting. Focus your words on enhancing pleasure rather than about the mechanics of what you are doing. Careful not to use so much humor that sexual play becomes distracted by your use of humor. Use words to keep things feeling sexy!

Thinking about sex can also help you focus on the moment. While this seems easy, it actually can be quite difficult to stay focused on sexual thoughts during sex. If you notice your attention drifting, bring yourself back to specific sexual thoughts or sexual fantasies to help you stay focused.

Sexual stories are another way to stay focused on sexual thoughts. If you like words and stories, try to share sexual thoughts and/or stories during sex. Can you get into the story and make it fun?

✓   Some ways to use words would be to talk softly, talk slowly, talk with intensity and talk with passion
✓   Tell a story rather than simply thinking about sexual thoughts

✓ Make your story engaging, add details, add personalities or maybe make your stories about sensations and touch rather than about people
✓ Include you and your partner in the story
✓ Ensure that your stories are arousing to your partner by asking for feedback later on or asking them ahead of time what fantasies they might enjoy

Words and stories can help build a fun, playful and relaxed sexual encounter[3].

Auditory cueing

Auditory cueing means a word, a sentence or a command that gathers your thoughts automatically to one place. An auditory cue may be a word that you use to remember your own strength (e.g. sexy) or a command that a partner uses to keep you focused (e.g. squeeze your butt). Using auditory cues is one way to enhance focus during sex.

Examples of auditory cues:

✓ Come now
✓ Contract your (fill in the body part)
✓ Relax your face
✓ Calm your legs
✓ Let go
✓ Breathe
✓ Lick

Do auditory cues help you stay focused? _____ Yes _____No

What do you notice when you <u>receive</u> auditory cues?

_____
_____
_____
_____
_____

Does giving auditory cues to others help you stay focused? _____ Yes _____No

What do you notice when you <u>give</u> auditory cues?

_____
_____
_____
_____
_____

What words can you use to cue yourself and/or your partner to the sexual nature of your interactions?

_____

_____

_____

_____

_____

_____

Use specific words that help you and/or a partner stay in the moment!

Visual or auditory pornography

Pornography, either audio or visual porn, is a quick and easy way to keep your mind focused on sex. People often turn towards pornography to create sexual arousal. This can be quite useful as a tool to help reduce distraction.

If pornography is the only way you use to create focus before sex or during sex, this can be quite limiting. Sometimes pornography isn't available or sometimes, it isn't convenient to watch porn. In addition, sexual partners can feel badly if you need to watch porn prior to engaging in sexual activity with them. Talk openly with your partner about your difficulties with sexual focus and your use of pornography. Practice expanding your skills by adding other ways that can also help you to create focus.

If you are uncomfortable using pornography to increase your focus during sex, consider ethical porn sites as an alternative. You may also like audio pornography if the visual stimulation becomes too intense, too bothersome or if the sounds are enough to sharpen your focus during sex.

Sexual games

There are sexual games that you can purchase or create yourself to add focus and make sex more fun.

Explore boardgames, sexual card games, sexual dice and/or other sexual games to assist you in creating a fun, light, sexual play with a partner or with yourself. Playing a sexual game does not require you spending money. You can create your own games by writing sexual ideas and placing them in a jar or by writing a sexual fantasy together. Creating sexual challenges for each other is another way to play with your partner and increase your focus.

Try different sexual positions! Changing sexual positions is another way to remain engaged in sexual play. Make exploring different positions a game!

What do you notice when you try different types of sexual activities?

_____

_____

_____

_____

_____

What do you notice when you try different sexual positions?

_____
_____
_____
_____
_____

What do you notice when you give or receive a sexual challenge?

_____
_____
_____
_____
_____

Try different ways to engage sexually and notice how they impact your attention and focus during sexual play!

Following pleasure

Pleasure is a tricky sensation. Pleasure feels good. It is sensory in nature. Sometimes you expect to experience pleasure, but you don't; and, sometimes you don't expect to experience pleasure and you do. What is happening here?

Consider your favorite meal. Imagine eating that meal, slowly, with joy. What do you notice in your mouth? Maybe you notice your saliva. Maybe you can actually taste your favorite food. If you try to break down the exact ingredients in your favorite food, it likely won't accurately describe the joy and the pleasure that you feel in that moment.

Following pleasure means that you follow the positive sensations that are occurring during sexual touch. Focusing on the body part that you are touching, sucking, feeling, caressing is one way to follow pleasure.

Place your attention on a body part, whether by looking at it, thinking about it, talking about it, smelling it and/or touching it as a way to maintain your attention during sex. When your attention wavers, move to another body part! This process holds true whether you are focused on your body parts or someone else's body parts. When your mind wanders, refocusing on a particular body part can be a very helpful way to refocus your attention.

What do you notice as you place your attention on one body part?

_____
_____
_____
_____
_____

Take note of your whole body. What is it about each body part that you enjoy?

When focusing on _____ body part, I enjoy _____

_____

_____

When focusing on _____ body part, I enjoy _____

_____

_____

When focusing on _____ body part, I enjoy _____

_____

_____

When focusing on _____ body part, I enjoy _____

_____

_____

When focusing on _____ body part, I enjoy _____

_____

_____

Take note of a partner's whole body. What is it about their body parts that you enjoy?

When focusing on _____ body part, I enjoy _____
When focusing on _____ body part, I enjoy _____
When focusing on _____ body part, I enjoy _____
When focusing on _____ body part, I enjoy _____
When focusing on _____ body part, I enjoy _____

There may be some body parts that are distracting to you, that you do not like or that take your attention away from sex. As noted in Chapter 2, people with ADHD have a higher likelihood of eating disorders and concerns about their bodies (Van Eck, Morse & Flory, 2018; Nazar et al., 2016). For people who struggle with gender dysphoria, this may also be of particular concern.

Are there parts of your body that you do not like and/or do not enjoy having touched?

_____ Yes _____No

When focusing on _____ body part, I do not enjoy _____
When focusing on _____ body part, I do not enjoy _____
When focusing on _____ body part, I do not enjoy _____
When focusing on _____ body part, I do not enjoy _____

It can be helpful to communicate your concerns about your body to a partner, trusted friend or family member. If your discomfort is related to body sensations, we will talk more about sensory issues in Chapter 9. You may also experience concerns related to your body as a result of experiencing trauma which we will discuss in Chapter 11. Consider talking with a qualified mental health professional to discuss your specific struggles as it relates to your body.

Engaging with yourself and/or a partner to stay focused during sex!

Are you an engaging sexual partner?

Are you a fun sexual partner?

Do you play with your partner?

Key ingredients:

✓ Play!
✓ Communication!

Play is the first ingredient! Sex that is only focused on genitals, penetration and/or orgasm can lack engagement and playfulness. Please review your answers in Chapter 2, when we explored your fun sexual experiences in the past. Reflecting on what used to be fun can help you remember how to become more sexually engaged.

Communication is the second ingredient. Sexual engagement requires communication – you need to talk about sex with your partner. Talking about sex is essential! It is a very important way to engage with someone sexually. Some people hold gender beliefs as it relates to sex such as biological females don't talk about sex or initiate sex. Engaging sexually with a partner implies that all partners contribute to creating sexual play. Be willing to engage with your partner!

At times, people get stuck on what they think they "should" be doing rather than what IS sexually engaging for them. Being open and honest with your partner and yourself about what you like is the first step to creating positive sexual engagement. We will talk more about sexual communication in Chapter 10 when we talk about intimacy.

Sexual engagement also means paying attention to your partner. Do you notice yourself paying attention to your partner? If not, what is getting in your way? We will talk more about the things that get in the way of paying attention to your partner in Chapter 6 – I'm busy! Hyperfocus and pleasure.

What are two things you could do to enhance the sexual engagement with yourself or a partner?

_____

_____

_____

_____

_____

If you don't feel comfortable engaging sexually with yourself or your partner, what is getting in your way? Address any issues that you may have about sexual engagement by considering your thoughts and beliefs about sex, body image and pleasure. You may wish to talk about these issues in more detail with a qualified mental health professional.

Sexual expectations

Being unclear about your sexual expectations or your partner's sexual expectations can interfere with your focus. If you are wondering how things will go, what they use for contraception, if they have any other partners, their STI status, your STI status, what you want, what they want, what might happen as a result of your sexual encounter or any other concerns that you have about engaging in sexual activity, these can take you out of the moment and contribute to a loss of focus.

Sexual expectations don't interfere as often during solo sex. People who prefer solo sex will often acknowledge that solo sex is more enjoyable as it offers less stress and fewer expectations. You are only expected to focus on yourself and your genitals. Creating that same sensation during partnered sex is the goal!

Sit in the present rather than thinking about the future helps create a sharpened focus during sex. Being able to sit in the present means that you have enough information to dismiss any future concerns. In addition, sitting in the present means that you are not preoccupied, angry, bitter or resentful about past events. If you have experienced past conflicts with your current sexual partner, you may not have forgiven them for their past choices, behaviors or words. Those events require resolution so that you can focus on what is happening right now, rather than the past or the future.

Ensure that you have:

✓ Enough information to feel comfortable about the sexual play that you are engaging in
✓ Accurate information about their health status as well as your own
✓ Clear understanding of any expectations that are held about the sexual play
✓ Address past events that may be leaving you preoccupied, angry, bitter or resentful
✓ A mindset that facilitates being in the present rather than the past or the future

Focus on clear communication about your sexual expectations and your partner's sexual expectations. Get the information you need so that you are not concerned about future events and address past events that continue to upset you. We will talk more about being present in your body in Chapter 4 – What is that feeling? Being in your body to achieve good sex.

Condoms, IUDs, Dental Dams and other distracting things

Attention can be hyjacked during sex due to items useful for sex but which may be distracting, for example: spicy lube, condoms (smells, textures, use of) as well as IUD's and other interfering items.

Condom-associated erection problems (CAEP) can occur for males (Mallet & Fraser, 2020). This simply means that it becomes hard to maintain your focus and attention during sex due to unpleasant sensations created by condom use. Condoms get in the way if they are too small, too tight, too big, too smelly, bothersome to you or your partner and/or if you experience a loss of sensation using condoms. At times, condom use can also create anxiety.

There are ways to address CAEP including using tailored for size condoms. Adressing this problem involves finding condoms that fit your specific penile size. These can be ordered online. Some examples are "They fit", "My Size" or "MyOne" condoms. You may also want to practice masturbating with a condom on in order to become familiar with the sensation of wearing a condom during partnered sex (Mallett & Fraser, 2020). Other suggestions include waiting until you are FULLY erect to put on a condom (see Mallett & Fraser, 2020 for details on how to manage CAEP).

Some condoms can add more stimulation and interest (e.g. ribbed, flavoured or textured condoms). Exploring different condom styles can be a fun activity and may help you find a condom that feels good despite those initial distracting sensations.

How does condom use affect your sensations and ability to stay focused during sex?

_____

_____

_____

_____

_____

For biological females, some birth control items can also create distractions. Barrier methods of birth control can interrupt sexual play and/or create distractions that leave you unfocused. Find methods that are less distracting for you. If you are experiencing pain or discomfort with an IUD or other barrier methods of birth control, speak with your physican or a medical health professional for assistance.

Sexual Pain

If you are experiencing sexual pain, it will certainly impact your ability to stay focused in the moment. Sexual pain must be taken seriously. Sexual pain can occur regardless of your gender. Do not continue to have sex if you are experiencing pain.

There are resources to help you navigate sexual pain such as Goldstein et al.'s book *When Sex Hurts* (2023). Contact your physician, speak to a urologist, consult a pelvic floor physiotherapist, talk to a qualified mental health professional, or talk to a qualified physical health professional to address physical pain. While you work on resolving symptoms of sexual pain, don't continue to engage in pain producing activities, focus on elements of the sexual experience that you enjoy!

If you don't trust your partner not to engage in pain producing activities, it is time to talk about your concerns with a therapist or a couples counsellor to ensure that trust is re-established and/or maintained within your relationship.

You can find ways to improve your focus during sex!

Sex requires attention. Difficulties staying focused during sex could explain the higher sexual desire, higher masturbation and higher use of pornography in some ADHD folks (Soldati, 2021). Sexual skills for ADHDers must involve learning how to stay focused during sex in the same way that you learn to stay focused during other important activities in your life (e.g. at school or work).

Create intensity, reduce outside distractions and have fun! These are essential sexual skills for people with ADHD.

We will continue our journey by exploring other issues that may be impacting your ability to stay focused during sex. These issues can get in your way, making it harder to remained focused during sex. Join me in Chapter 4 as we discuss being physically present in your body!

Working towards my goals

To battle my distraction during sex, I will:

☐ Address my physical space

To improve my physical space, I will:

_____

_____

_____

_____

_____

☐ Address sounds and noise

My sexual playlist includes songs from the start-up sexy playlist, the "in it" sexy playlist and the connecting/cuddling after sex playlist. This is my sexual playlist:

_____

_____

_____

_____

_____

_____

This is my plan to address distracting noises that occur in my space:

_____

_____

_____

_____

_____

I will increase intensity during sex by adding:

- ☐ Sexual touch
- ☐ Sexual stories
- ☐ Sexual toys
- ☐ Sexual imagery
- ☐ Sexual speed
- ☐ Auditory cueing
- ☐ Words/mental imagery/visualization/erotic stories
- ☐ Visual or auditory pornography
- ☐ Sexual games

If I rely on pornography to maintain my attention before sex and/or during sex, I will expand my skills by adding the following strategies to help focus my attention:

_____
_____
_____
_____
_____
_____

To increase sexual engagement, I will try these <u>two</u> new ways to engage with my partner and/or myself:

_____
_____
_____
_____
_____
_____
_____
_____
_____
_____

These problems interfere with my ability to maintain my attention during sex:

- ☐ Difficulties with contraception
- ☐ Sexual pain
- ☐ Poor sexual engagement
- ☐ Other: _____
- ☐ Other: _____

I will address interfering problems by doing the following:

_____
_____
_____
_____

Notes

1 Any form of privacy lock must allow people to easily leave the space without assistance and should not be easily triggered by a child or a toddler accidentally. Find a way to secure your space that allows for the safety of all the members in your household!
2 Caution: Ensure that your space is safe! Do not engage in any activity that could lead to physical harm to yourself or others. If your shower/bath is not equipped with safety equipment such as anti-slip pads, grab handles and/or if there isn't space to safely be two or more in there, don't do it!
3 A quick note about consent, ensure that the sexual stories you discuss are legal and include elements of consent.

References

Abdel-Hamid, M., Basilowski, M., Schönfeld, B, Bartels, C. et al. (2021). Sexual dysfunction in patients with adult attention deficit hyperactivity disorder: A pilot study. *The Canadian Journal of Human Sexuality*, 30(1), pp. 106–113. https://doi.org/10.3138/cjhs.2020-0036.

del Mar Sánchez-Fuentes, M., Santos-Iglesias, P. & Sierra, J.C. (2014). A systematic review of sexual satisfaction. *International Journal of Clinical Health Psychology*, 14, 67–75.

Goldstein, A., Pukall, C., Goldstein, I. & Krapf, J. (2023). *When Sex Hurts: Understanding and Healing Pelvic Pain* (revised and updated). Da Capo Lifelong Books.

Kolberg, J. & Nadeau, K. (2016). *ADD-Friendly Ways to Organize Your Life: Strategies that Work from an Acclaimed Professional Organizer and a Renowned ADD Clinician* (2nd ed.). Routledge.

Mallett, S.J.J. & Fraser, R. (2020). Condom associated erection problems (CAEP) in heterosexual young men (under 40): A systematic review and qualitative synthesis. *The Canadian Journal of Human Sexuality*, 29(2), 228–239. https://doi.org/10.3138/cjhs.2020-0008.

Nazar, B.P., Bernardes, C., Peachey, G., Sergeant, J., Mattos, P. & Treasure, J. (2016). The risk of eating disorders comorbid with attention-deficit/hyperactivity disorder: A systematic review and meta-analysis. The International journal of eating disorders, 49(12), 1045–1057. https://doi.org/10.1002/eat.22643.

Soldati L, Bianchi-Demicheli F, Schockaert P, Köhl, J., Bolmont, M., Hasler, R. & Perroud, N. (2020). Sexual Function, Sexual Dysfunctions, and ADHD: A Systematic Literature Review. *Journal of Sexual Medicine*, 17, 1653e1664.

Solden, S. (2012). *Women With Attention Deficit Disorder: Embrace your differences and transform your life*. Introspect Press, p. 515.

Tuckman, A. (2019). ADHD After Dark: Better Sex Life, Better Relationship (1st ed.).

Van Eck, K., Morse, M. & Flory, K. (2018). The role of body image in the link between ADHD and depression symptoms among college students. *Journal of Attention Disorders*, 22(5), 435–445. https://doi.org/10.1177/1087054715580845.

Chapter 4

What is that feeling?

Being in your body to achieve sexual pleasure

Being present and attending to your body can be hard for ADHD folks! Connecting to your body, feeling your body and finding pleasure within your body is the first step to establishing a positive and fun sex life. Before we get started, take a moment and breathe... inhale 1–2–3–4, exhale, and repeat, inhale 1–2–3–4, exhale. Phew! Breathing is such an easy skill but finding the time to breathe and connect to your body can be a struggle.

Pleasure is a sensation. It's like other bodily sensations that you experience. When you think of a bodily sensation, you might first think of a feeling of hunger or thirst. You may also consider the sensation of having chills or feeling sweaty. Pleasure is a sensation that feels good in your body. Pleasure is simply one way that your body is communicating with you.

Think about something that creates a sensation of pleasure for you. This can be a drink, a type of food, that feeling when you first stretch your body in the morning, the warmth you experience when you hold someone's hand or it can be an experience, such as getting a backrub or a massage, or perhaps it is that sense of freedom when you are wandering in a new city or exploring a new country.

Take a moment and sit in a past memory where you experienced pleasure.

I have felt the sensation of pleasure when I was doing the following:

_____
_____
_____
_____
_____

Remember that past feeling of pleasure and consider the questions below.

What do I first notice when I feel a sensation of pleasure?

_____
_____
_____
_____
_____

DOI: 10.4324/9781003422372-5

When I feel a sensation of pleasure, I tend to remember it and cherish it:

☐ Yes
☐ No
☐ I am not sure

When I feel a sensation of pleasure, I notice these specific changes in my body:

_____

_____

_____

_____

_____

_____

Let's explore the feeling of pleasure as it relates specifically to your body and sex!

What is it that my body likes about sex? For example, is it the touching part, the buildup tension, the orgasm part, the post sex release? Or is it getting ready for sex (the flirting, the fantasizing, wearing something special and tending to your personal hygiene) also known as the pre-sex games with a partner, the post-sex games with a partner (the cuddling, the time together, that warmth feeling in your body), or is it something else entirely?

My body likes these parts of sex:	✓ Check the ones that apply
Getting ready for sex	
• The flirting	
• The fantasizing about sex	
• Wearing something special	
• The hygiene part or "getting my body ready" part	
The touching part	
The buildup tension	
The orgasm part	
The post-sex release	
Post-sex games with a partner	
• Cuddling	
• Time together	
• Feeling warmth in my body	
Other:	

Pleasure is best experienced alone _____ Yes _____ No

Pleasure is best experienced when I am with a partner _____ Yes _____ No

Pleasure is more comfortable for me when I am alone because:

_____
_____
_____
_____
_____
_____

Pleasure is more comfortable for me when I am with a partner because:

_____
_____
_____
_____
_____
_____

Does my body like sex? _____ Yes _____ No _____ It depends:

_____
_____
_____
_____
_____
_____

I notice positive sensations and/or positive thoughts when I feel pleasure in my body. These include:

_____
_____
_____
_____
_____
_____

I notice negative sensations and/or negative thoughts when I feel pleasure in my body. These include:

_____
_____
_____
_____
_____
_____

For some people, pleasure can feel uncomfortable for many reasons including past trauma, negative beliefs about pleasure (e.g. if I feel good, bad things will happen to me), feelings of anxiety (e.g. overthinking the feeling rather than enjoying the moment) or a negative belief about yourself (e.g. I do not deserve to experience pleasure).

Keep in mind that pleasure is a sensation like any other sensation, it is not good or bad. If you notice negative feelings associated to feeling pleasure or the memory of experiencing pleasure in your life, take the time to talk with a qualified mental health professional about those negative feelings.

How do we notice the communication that we receive from our bodies? Interoception is our perception of the internal state of our body. This 8th sense is becoming more widely discussed and researched as there are differences between people as it relates to interoceptive awareness (see Goodall & Brownlow, 2022 for more details). Neurodivergent folks can struggle with interoceptive awareness; they can have a hard time identifying what is going on in their bodies. People with ADHD report problems engaging with mindfulness and experiencing interoceptive awareness (Kutscheidt et al., 2019; Goodall & Brownlow, 2022). When you struggle with interoceptive awareness, you struggle to notice how your body feels. For example, is it hard to know if you are tired and it is time to go to sleep? Do you notice when you are edgy or bored?

How good am I at noticing how my body feels?

- ☐ I am super good; I can always tell when I am hungry, thirsty, tired, anxious or mad
- ☐ I am good; I can mostly tell when I am hungry, thirsty, tired, anxious or mad
- ☐ I am just ok when communicating with my body
- ☐ I am inconsistent; sometimes I can tell but sometimes I can't
- ☐ I am not great; mostly I can't tell
- ☐ I am really bad at noticing when I am hungry, thirsty, tired, anxious or mad. It's easier when other people tell me or I use a fixed schedule or an external monitoring device (e.g. I check my heartrate) so I don't miss it!

If you are tired, angry or overwhelmed but don't know it, it will be hard for you to find pleasure either by yourself or with a partner. It is outside the scope of this book to help you assess and improve your interoceptive awareness. If interoception is difficult for you, there are some resources available including a workbook by Kelly Mahler[1] to help you improve your interoceptive awareness (see Additional Resources list for more details). Improving your overall awareness of your body's communication, your body's feelings and your body's needs is the first step to fully enjoying pleasure.

In this workbook, we will call being connected and aware of your body, being "seated" in your body. Taking the time to connect to your body is one key to feeling "seated" in your body.

There are many ways to accomplish this goal.

- ✓ Mindfulness exercises are a good way to connect to your body
- ✓ Exercise helps focus attention on your muscles, blood flow and breath work which are all helpful to enhancing connection to your body
- ✓ Calming exercises such as deep breathing, hot baths or sitting quietly in a peaceful place can help you achieve this goal
- ✓ Creative and artistic pursuits such as dance and singing can also be a good way to connect with your body

There is no right or wrong way to connect with your body! We will now explore ways to enhance feeling seated in your body.

When you consider how you feel "seated" in your body, do you prefer becoming seated with activity (moving your body) or with stillness (sitting quietly or mindfully)?

- ☐ I prefer active movement to feel seated in my body
- ☐ I prefer stillness to feel seated in my body
- ☐ I am not sure

What type of activity creates the most seated feeling for you?

- ☐ Cardio exercises
- ☐ Strength exercises
- ☐ Flexibility exercises
- ☐ Walking
- ☐ Playful exercises
- ☐ Being still
- ☐ Meditation
- ☐ Mindfulness practice
- ☐ Heat (baths, saunas, etc.)
- ☐ Cold (cold showers, snow and winter activities, etc.)
- ☐ Dance
- ☐ Art
- ☐ Singing or playing music
- ☐ Yoga/Pilates/Martial arts
- ☐ Breathwork
- ☐ Other: _____
- ☐ Other: _____
- ☐ Other: _____

My favorite activities for feeling seated in my body include:

_____

_____

_____

_____

_____

Moving your body is one way to feel seated in your body. When we sit for hours and watch streaming entertainment, we miss out on connecting to our bodies. Passive activities such as shows, videogames and movies, while enjoyable, don't help us feel connected to ourselves. Excessively engaging in passive activities can be used as a form of escape.

When you are exploring movement activities, remember that these can be done fast or slow. For example, Tai Chi a type of martial art, is renowned for using slow movement to achieve connection with the body; conversely, running sprints is a way that uses speed to achieve connection with your breath and your muscles. There are many specific movements that can help with feeling seated in your body; some examples are: yoga, pilates, martial arts, dance, stretching and walking in the woods, to name but a few.

We talked about enhancing your level of physical movement in Chapter 2. How are you doing at improving or maintaining your level of physical movement?

☐ Great!
☐ Pretty darned good!
☐ So-So
☐ Could be better
☐ I haven't thought about it yet!
☐ Other: _____

Has your physical movement improved recently? _____ Yes _____ No

- If yes, what did you do to achieve your goal?
- If no, what do you need to do to keep working towards your goal?

_____

_____

_____

_____

_____

Deep breathing is another way to feel seated in your body. Deep breathing is free, easy, quick and comfortable for most people to do. There are many different breathing exercises, breathing apps and specific strategies to enhance deep breathing.

Here are some ways to practice deep breathing:

✓ Box breathing (in four seconds, hold four seconds, out four seconds, hold four seconds)
✓ Pressured breathing (two short inhales in and long exhale out)
✓ Put your hand on your chest and breathe
✓ Hands up in the air and breathe (my favourite one! ☺)
✓ Download a deep breathing app
✓ Download a meditation app
✓ Download an emotional first aid kit

Let's practice!

Sit in your body for two to three seconds and simply breathe. What do you notice?

_____
_____
_____
_____

What changes do you notice in your body when you breathe deeply for two to three seconds?

_____
_____
_____
_____

Here is another way to practice deep breathing that can include a partner:

Version 1: Sit face to face. Put your hand on their chest. Ask them to put their hand on your chest. Breeeeathe. Inhale, 1–2–3–4, exhale 1–2–3–4, breathe again, inhale, 1–2–3–4, exhale 1–2–3–4 and a third time, inhale 1–2–3–4, exhale 1–2–3–4. Look into each other's eyes if that is comfortable and repeat the breathing exercise.

Version 2: Sit back to back. Press your back against your partner and have them push back towards you. Hold hands if you can. Breeeeathe. Inhale, 1–2–3–4, exhale 1–2–3–4, breathe again, inhale, 1–2–3–4, exhale 1–2–3–4 and a third time, inhale, 1–2–3–4, exhale 1–2–3–4. Squeeze each other's hands or fingers and repeat the breathing exercises.

What do you notice when you breathe with a partner?

_____
_____
_____
_____

Is it easier to breathe deeply when you are alone or with a partner?

_____
_____
_____
_____
_____

The purpose of becoming seated in your body is to feel a connection to your body in order to notice feelings of pleasure and perhaps feel more inclined to engage sexually with yourself or a partner. Enhancing your connection with your body can also help you feel enticing and sexy prior to starting sexual play.

Meditation and mindfulness training are key skills that can help you feel seated in your body. Mindfulness practice has been shown to be a helpful way to manage ADHD in your daily life (Sánchez-Soto & Sánchez-Suricalday, 2023). Regularly practicing meditation or mindfulness can improve your connection with your body. There are many ways to practice mindfulness and a plethora of resources that can help you improve these skills.

Keep it simple or make it as intricate as you like (e.g. sitting with your eyes closed for a few moments and feel your heartbeat or participating in a multi-day meditation retreat). One resource specific to mindfulness and sexuality is Dr. Lori Brotto's book *Better Sex Through Mindfulness: How Women can cultivate desire*. This gendered book is dedicated to help biological females explore their connection to their bodies and improve sexual engagement.

There are simply too many resources that target mindfulness and meditation to name them all in this workbook. A few examples of other resources that focus on mindfulness and/or meditation include: programs provided by MARC – UCLA Mindful Awareness Research Center, the Finch app (I love my little bird!), the Headspace app, various mindfulness apps (of which there are plenty), regular yoga practice, Tai Chi practice, DBT therapies (developed by M. Linehan, see Linehan, 2014 for details) the Irest program for PTSD (by R. Miller, www.irest.org), as well as various spiritual practices.

Find and apply a mindfulness practice that works for you and that connects you positively to your body!

Let's see how this might work in practice. How seated in my body am I right now?

☐ Total shutdown: dissociated, not present, gone – but not in a good way
☐ Edgy
☐ Can't feel my body, can't feel my toes! Am I breathing?!?
☐ Breathing, I am breathing
☐ I am here
☐ I am here and I can feel my body
☐ I am here and I am IN my body
☐ Peaceful cohabitation with my body
☐ Me and my body are rocking it out: I can feel the flow – it's like magic!

Your connection to your body matters. If you find yourself often on the higher levels of this scale or if you tend to dissociate, it may be time to work with a qualified mental health provider[2] to address current life events or past traumas that are getting in your way.

Now, let's take this connection to your body and apply it to sex! When you are entering a sexual situation that involves only yourself, which level of the scale is more conducive to positive sexual energy and pleasure?

When you are entering a sexual situation that involves you and a partner, which level of the scale is more conducive to positive sexual energy and pleasure?

I prefer to engage sexually when I am: (Use a checkmark to identify the column that most applies to you)	Me alone	Me and a partner
Total shutdown: dissociated, not present, gone – but not in a good way		
Edgy		
Can't feel my body, can't feel my toes! Am I breathing?!?		
Breathing, I am breathing!		
I am here		
I am here and I can feel my body		
I am here and I am IN my body		
Peaceful cohabitation in my body		
Me and my body are rocking it out; I can feel the flow – it's like magic!		

We have talked about deep breathing, movement and mindfulness as ways to help you get seated in your body. There are other things that you can do prior to engaging sexually with yourself or a partner to enhance your feeling of being seated in your body.

Let's explore other ways to get you into your ideal sexual state prior to engaging in sexual pleasure!

In Chapter 3, we talked about how having sex in the shower or bath can be a helpful way to reduce distractions and to focus your attention during sexual activity with a partner. Sitting in water and/or washing your body can be a great way to connect with your body and to feel seated in your body. Many people enjoy bathing for this exact reason. In addition, using water to feel seated into your body can also resolve any distracting thoughts about hygiene that you may have prior to engaging in sexual activity with a partner. This can be a nice way to get connected and seated into your body.

✓ Feel the water travel down your body while washing your skin!

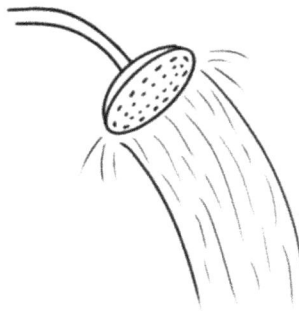

Try this exercise:
Stand or sit in the shower and find a temperature that feels nice on your body. Allow the water to drip over your head, down your body and off your fingers. Focus on the dripping sound as the water passes over your body and down onto the ground. Breathe. Notice your bodily sensations as the water is passing over you. If you are feeling comfortable, rub your nipples as you feel the water on your chest. You can also use soap to massage your upper body. Notice how that feels. Now move to your toes and feet. Rub your feet slowly and carefully. Notice each toe. Trail your fingers up your legs. Caress your legs as the water flows over you. How do you feel? Are you more seated in your body?

A similar exercise can be done in the bathtub. Sit or lie in the tub allowing the water to lap onto your body. Notice your upper body and chest. Touch your arms and dip your fingers into the water. Play with your nipples. What feels good to you? Now focus on your genitals. Touch them and notice how they feel with the water running over them, near them, on them. Allow the touch of the water to caress your body. Does your body enjoy this sensation? Move a part of your body out of the water and then return it to the water. Notice the sensation; how does this change feel?

You can also try these exercises with a partner present allowing them to hear and see what feels good for your body and watch how you like to touch your body when you are feeling more seated in your body. If you are sensitive to soaps or suffer dry skin, you may find alternative ways to explore your skin without water such as using a massage oil while lying in bed or sitting in a chair. You can also complete a similar (but perhaps slightly less erotic version of this exercise) in a swimming pool.

Being seated in your body with the assistance of a warm shower or allowing cool water to drip down onto your skin, are both lovely ways to explore connecting with your body. If you do not like to transition into water based environments (e.g. you dislike taking showers or baths) focus your attention on the transition in and out of the water (e.g. wet skin feels cold, it feels different to be wet rather than dry and vice-versa) rather than the feeling of the water itself. Do the sensations that you experience during these transitions help seat you in your body?

Other ways to feel seated in your body can include touch. Touch is a very good way to feel seated in your body.

Let's explore touch!

Stand or sit naked and take a moment to close your eyes. Breathe for 1-2 seconds. Now touch every part of your body, starting with your head and working your way down your body. Once you are done touching your body down to your toes, work your way back up! Touch every part of your body from your toes to your head.

What do you notice when you take the time to touch your body?

_____

_____

_____

_____

_____

Using touch can be a helpful way to become seated in your body. Hard touch is often identified as being helpful for neurodivergent people to enhance grounding as it is reported to facilitate interoceptive awareness (see Amythest@neurowonderful, May 2021, and The Five Neurodivergent Love Locutions, 19 April 2022, Stimpunks.org and Bogdashina, 2016, for details). Hard touch, consensual bondage, consensual rough sexual play are all ways that can help you get seated in your body.

Massages are another way to use touch to feel seated in your body. You can use a massage oil or a body scrub to help you focus on each part of your body. A hand massager is an alternative way to introduce touch. Explore different strategies to become more seated in your body!

Want to explore a non-partnered way to engage your limbs? Consider progressive muscle relaxation. This strategy involves contracting and relaxing each muscle group in your body, one muscle group at a time. This can be an excellent way to become seated in your body!

Rubbing your feet or your hands is another way to use touch to enhance your connection to your body. Focusing on touching or rubbing particular parts of your body can be very helpful to get seated into your body.

Let's reflect on sexual touch!

To feel seated in my body, I enjoy touch that is:

- ☐ Hard
- ☐ Soft
- ☐ Both

My partner gets me seated in my body most often when they touch me in the following way:

_____
_____
_____
_____
_____

I would like to ask my partner to provide the following types of touch to help me become seated into my body:

- ☐ Hard
- ☐ Soft
- ☐ Both

I would like to discuss my preference for this type of touch by saying:

_____
_____
_____
_____
_____

I would like to ask my partner to touch <u>this particular body</u> part more often to help me become seated in my body:

_____
_____
_____
_____
_____

A word about kissing and hugging: Hugging and kissing are lovely types of touch that can be very helpful to seat people into their bodies. While we will talk more about kissing in the chapter on transitions, it is worth mentioning that kissing and/or hugging can be a very useful partnered exercise to become seated in your body.

Some people will use intoxicants to become seated in their bodies. While using alcohol or recreational drugs to engage sexually is not necessarily problematic, this can become an issue if it is the only way for you to feel seated and comfortable in your body. It can also make you more vulnerable to sexual victimization. If you are becoming reliant on having sex while intoxicated, try alternative ways to enhance the connection with your body. Finding alternative ways to facilitate pleasure during sex can provide more flexibility in your sexual play.

This same caveat applies to pornography use. Are you using porn to make it easier to connect to your body?

What ways do I use to get myself into my ideal sexual state?

_____
_____
_____
_____
_____

Are these healthy habits for me? _____ Yes _____ No _____ Seems Ok

   People with ADHD can have more difficulties with body focused concerns, body dysmorphia and body image (Van Eck, Morse & Flory, 2018; Bisset, Rinehart & Sciberras, 2019; Gowey et al., 2017). Problems related to body image can impact people with ADHD of all genders (Van Eck, Morse & Flory, 2018). There is a wonderful resource by Dr. Hillary McBride called *The Wisdom of Your Body: Finding healing, wholeness and connection through embodied living* that may be a helpful resource to explore your relationship to your body in more detail. Your relationship with your body matters as it relates to becoming seated in your body.

Do you like your body? _____ Yes _____ No

What parts of your body do you love?

I love the following body parts:

_____
_____
_____
_____
_____

I would like to improve the following body parts:

_____
_____
_____
_____
_____

If your list of things that you would like to improve includes areas of your body that are not easily changed, a longstanding dissatisfaction that is not going away or if your list of things to improve is much longer than the things that you love about your body, it's time to consider that you may benefit from specialized assistance to address your relationship with your body. Work with a qualified mental health professional to address your body image concerns, particularly if these body image concerns interfere with your efforts to become seated in your body.

Sex is play! It's easier to play when you feel seated in your body; you can feel your body and can interact with someone else's body. This is an important skill to help you find and maintain sexual pleasure (Brotto, 2018). Sitting and connecting to your body can be hard when you have ADHD.

If you notice that other elements such as anxiety or specific sensations are getting in the way of being seated in your body, don't fret! We will address those specific concerns in Chapter 7 – What am I afraid of? Anxiety and ADHD and Chapter 8 – What is that smell? A word about sensory issues and ADHD. If getting seated into your body is fairly easy if you are alone but becomes very difficult when a partner is present, we will talk more about concerns specific to intimacy in Chapter 10 – Intimacy... Yikes!

Let's continue our journey and explore transitions both getting in and out of sexual pleasure.

Working towards my goals

Pleasure in my life means:

_____

_____

_____

_____

_____

I will add pleasure to my life by trying:

_____

_____

_____

_____

_____

I will practice finding pleasure in both sexual and non-sexual ways by:

_____

_____

_____

_____

_____

I like to do this every day to embrace my body and feel seated in my body:

- ☐ I like to move or exercise daily
- ☐ I like to meditate daily
- ☐ I like to engage in mindful practice daily
- ☐ I like to use deep breathing
- ☐ I like to put my hand on my chest and breathe
- ☐ I sit quietly and listen to my heartbeat
- ☐ I like to use touch
- ☐ I like to use progressive muscle relaxation, contracting and releasing each muscle group one at a time
- ☐ I like to use massage oils or body scrubs to connect myself to my body
- ☐ I like to use showers or bathing as part of my practice of engaging with my body
- ☐ I like to use a body massager to help me connect with my body
- ☐ I like to dance, sing or engage in other creative endeavors
- ☐ I like to use my spiritual practice
- ☐ I like to work with my favorite app to keep me on track
- ☐ I like to go outside and feel the ground beneath my feet
- ☐ I like to walk in a peaceful place

Do I rely on external ways to get seated into my body that are not useful for me, such as alcohol, drugs or pornography use?

- ☐ Yes, I do this a lot
- ☐ Yes, I do this a little
- ☐ No, not really
- ☐ No, this is not my issue

I would like to practice engaging with my body in a different way to increase my ability to become seated in my body. I will try:

_____

_____

_____

_____

_____

Practice taking note of your level of engagement with your body every day.

Right now I feel:

- ☐ Total shutdown: dissociated, not present, gone – but not in a good way
- ☐ Edgy
- ☐ Can't feel my body, can't feel my toes! Am I breathing?!?
- ☐ Breathing, I am breathing!
- ☐ I am here
- ☐ I am here and I can feel my body

□ I am here and I am IN my body

□ Peaceful cohabitation in my body

□ Me and my body are rocking it out, I can feel the flow – it's like magic!

If I find myself in total shutdown before or during sex.

✓ I will stop and allow myself a break to discuss what is happening with a safe support person or with a partner

I will consider talking with a qualified mental health professional for further assistance

Notes

1 Mahler, K, Rothschild, C. & Alma, J. (2019). *My Interoception Workbook: A guide for adolescents, teens and adults*. www.kelly-mahler.com.

2 A qualified mental health professional is someone who is licensed or registered for practice in your area.

References

Amythest@neurowonderful (May 2021) and Stimpunks Foundation (19 August 2022). The Five Neurodivergent Love Locutions, Creative Commons Attribution-ShareAlike 4.0 International license, Stimpunks.org.

Bisset, M., Rinehart, N. & Sciberras, E. (2019). Body dissatisfaction and weight control behaviour in children with ADHD: A population-based study. *European Child & Adolescent Psychiatry*, 28(11), 1507–1516. https://doi.org/10.1007/s00787-019-01314-8.

Bogdashina, O. (2016). *Sensory Perceptual Issues in Autism and Asperger Syndrome: Different sensory experiences – different perceptual worlds* (2nd ed). London: Jessica Kingsley Publishers.

Brotto, L.A. (2018). Better Sex Through Mindfulness: How Women can cultivate desire. Vancouver, BC: Greystone Books.

Goodall, E. & Brownlow, C. (2022). *Interoception and Regulation: Teaching skills of body awareness and supporting connection with others*. London: Jessica Kingsley Publishers.

Gowey, M.A., Stromberg, S.E., Lim, C.S. & Janicke, D.M. (2017). The moderating role of body dissatisfaction in the relationship between ADHD symptoms and disordered eating in pediatric overweight and obesity. *Children's Health Care*, 46(1), 15–33. https://doi.org/10.1080/0273961 5.2015.1065745.

Linehan, M.M. (2014). *DBT Skills Training Manual* (2nd ed.). Guildford Press.

Mahler, K., Rothschild, C. & Alma, J. (2019). *My Interoception Workbook: A guide for adolescents, teens and adults*. www.kelly-mahler.com.

McBride, H. (2021). *The Wisdom of Your Body: Finding healing, wholeness and connection through embodied living*. Michigan: Brazos Press.

Miller, R.C. (2015). *The iRest Program for Healing PTSD, A Proven-Effective Approach to Using Yoga Nidra Meditation and Deep Relaxation Techniques to Overcome Trauma*. New Harbinger Publications.

Sánchez-Soto, L. & Sánchez-Suricalday, A. (2023). The impact of mindfulness therapy in individuals with Attention Deficit Hyperactivity Disorder (ADHD): a systematic review (El impacto de la terapia mindfulness en personas con Trastorno por Déficit de Atención/Hiperactividad

(TDAH): una revisión sistemática). *Journal for the Study of Education and Development*, 46,3, 529–556. doi: 10.1080/02103702.2023.2191427.

Siebelink, N.M., Asherson, P., Antonova, E., Bögels, S.M., Speckens, A.E., Buitelaar, J.K. & Greven, C.U. (2019). Genetic and environmental aetiologies of associations between dispositional mindfulness and ADHD traits: A population-based twin study. *European Child & Adolescent Psychiatry*, 28(9), 1241–1251. https://doi.org/10.1007/s00787-019-01279-8.

Van Eck, K., Morse, M. & Flory, K. (2018). The role of body image in the link between ADHD and depression symptoms among college students. *Journal of Attention Disorders*, 22(5), 435–445. https://doi.org/10.1177/1087054715580845.

Chapter 5

What is going on right now?

Transition problems!

It's been a big day, kids to daycare, signing up one kid for dance class and the other for martial arts. You worked. You answered emails. You found food hiding at the back of the fridge and made a good enough meal. There was some complaining about the food that you provided the family but overall it was edible! You still have to deal with the dishes, the cat's litter box and that funky smell coming from downstairs. You look over and your partner is looking at you with a glint in their eyes. WHAT IS THAT GLINT ABOUT? Perhaps they have lost their minds?!? You react with irritation, frustration and anger. They are hurt. They feel rejected. The next day is more of the same. The transition to sex never happens.

A transition is the process of moving from one condition or state to another. For example, a transition can be going from being dry to being wet which happens when you take a shower or jump into a swimming pool. Transitions can be uncomfortable. A sexual transition refers to how you move towards sexual activity and how you move out of sexual activity. Relationship difficulties can occur for people who struggle to transition towards sex and who struggle to transition out of sex. Transition problems can create significant relationship friction.

Difficulties transitioning towards sex may be one reason why some people don't have sex. They are not sure how to get there, how to start focusing on sexual pleasure and/or how to create feelings of pleasure in their body. Sexual transitions may feel easier if you are alone rather than with a partner. Alternatively, it might be easier to transition towards sex when a partner initiates sexual activity.

We often assume that sexual desire (also known as feely horny or feeling aroused) will simply appear like hunger does throughout the day. Sexual desire doesn't necessarily show up without an invitation. There are many good reasons why your sexual arousal does not simply appear on command, including the impact of certain medications, biological or hormonal changes, long term sexual partnerships (Perel, 2007) and/or differences in spontaneous vs responsive sexual desire (Nagoski, 2021)[1]. According to some authors, we learn the signals of being hungry, thirsty and even going to the bathroom through co-regulation (Goodall & Brownlow, 2022). If you apply the co-regulation theory to sex, it would follow that feelings of arousal might appear more easily by engaging sexually with a partner, than they would without a sexual context or a sexual initiation by another person. It is important to keep in mind that sexual desire is something that you create in your life; simply waiting for it to appear is not very effective.

Addressing how you transition towards sex may help you overcome a lack of interest in sex.

DOI: 10.4324/9781003422372-6

Some people with ADHD do not like sex, avoid sex and/or prefer not having sex. If you have this problem, and it occurs outside of general relationship problems, this may suggest that anxiety is a concern for you. Other times, sensory issues lead someone to not want sex. Note that both problems can be exacerbated by engaging in partnered sex. When you are exploring sexual pleasure alone, as in solo sex, there is typically less anxiety and you will naturally avoid any sensory issues that may be of concern to you. As a result, you may find that partnered sex is difficult for you in ways that you cannot easily explain. Hyperfocus problems may also lead to some people not wanting to have sex. If these issues apply to you and interfere with your willingness to transition towards sex, do not fear; we will address them in more detail in the upcoming chapters of this workbook. Consider transitions as the first step to re-establishing a sex life that is adjusted to your needs.

The flip side of this problem is that transitioning out of sex can also be a concern. Staying in a state of sexual arousal for too long, neglecting responsibilities or becoming overly focused on sex are all things that signal a difficulty transitioning out of sex. You may also find that partners become upset or irritated by the fact that you are not transitioning out of sex. Addressing how you transition out of sex will help you create a healthier balance between sexual activity and the other activities in your life. We will talk more about transitioning out of sex in the later parts of this chapter.

Let's start to explore transitions TOWARDS sexual play!

Learning to start

Let's explore ways to improve your ability to transition towards sex and get sexual play started in your life!

You may notice that sexual feelings occur more frequently when someone else is cueing those feelings by their physical presence, their physical touch or their communication. Having a partner who is interested in initiating sexual contact can be very helpful to get things started. After all, someone has to get the ball rolling! This said, people sometimes complain that their partners transition towards sex too abruptly. They are grabbed, pinched or touched in sexual or sensitive areas of their bodies with no warning. Grabbing a partner suddenly can happen, owing to impulsivity, lack of forethought or a mistaken belief that a partner would find this type of touch sexually inviting. Initiating sex takes some style and finesse. Impulsivity can get in the way of your sexual transitions.

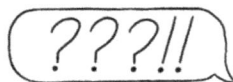

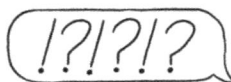

Managing your ADHD symptoms, including your impulsivity, matters! If you find that you're impulsively grabbing a partner and they are not responding positively to you, consider that you're being too abrupt. Dr. John Gottman teaches about using soft start ups when discussing conflicts or conversations that are emotionally heavy (Gottman & Silver, 1999). This same principle applies to initiating sexual contact. Saying something first, informing a partner that you are interested in sexual play and/or creating an invitation to sexual play, before touching your partner, can be a good habit to start practicing!

What do I typically do to get the ball rolling when I want to engage sexually with a partner?

_____

_____

_____

_____

_____

What are the outcomes of these attempts?

☐ Works well
☐ Works sometimes
☐ Doesn't work

When your attempts <u>do</u> work, when do they work best?

_____

_____

_____

_____

_____

Have an honest conversation about how you initiate sexual play. If you have concerns about your initiation attempts which are related to your level of impulsivity, focus on getting your ADHD symptoms better managed. This may assist you to regulate your actions and slow down your initiation[2].

We create sexual energy. For many people, sexual arousal is simply not "there" with no effort. Sexual energy needs a context, and it needs encouragement. Sexual thoughts, sexual fantasy, sexual communication and prioritizing sex are all important ways to establish a vibrant sex life. You achieve this by putting in some effort! Without effort, transitions towards sex don't happen easily.

Let's look at an example that explores the concept of effort in more detail!

You want to have some fun and decide to go outside to play ball. It's nicer to play ball with a partner so you invite them to join you!

Scenario 1: You play ball with a partner, you both run after the ball, try to throw it straight, make mistakes, maybe someone falls, maybe someone throws it too far or not far enough, you both try, you both laugh, you are relaxed, and it is a fun afternoon!

Scenario 2: You play ball with a partner. You or your partner does not try. There is no effort put into playing ball. Someone throws the ball, but the other person does not try to catch it. The other person won't run to catch the ball or they let it land in front of their feet without trying to catch it. Some weak effort is made to play ball, but no real effort is made. You feel like you did in middle school gym class when no one wanted to try for fear of looking silly or breaking into a sweat! There is no sustained effort that is made. It is not a fun afternoon, and you feel like you wasted your time.

Scenario 3: You play ball with a partner. You or your partner is taking everything very seriously. You must make the perfect throw. You can't drop a ball without becoming upset about getting it wrong. You or your partner needs the ball to soar perfectly. It's competitive and everyone is focused on doing things right. The game becomes very tense as you or your partner are trying to make it perfect. There is no room for error or mistakes. It's a high stakes game. If the ball does not go where you wanted it to go, you don't want to play anymore; you pout or you throw a tantrum. There is so much effort made that it takes all the fun out of things. It is a tense afternoon, it is not fun, and it feels like the game made your life worse, not better.

Apply these scenarios to your sex life!

What scenario do you currently have in your sex life?

- ☐ Scenario 1: Fun and Playful!
- ☐ Scenario 2: Lack of effort
- ☐ Scenario 3: It's all too serious

What scenario would you rather have in your sex life?

- ☐ Scenario 1: Fun and Playful!
- ☐ Scenario 2: Lack of effort
- ☐ Scenario 3: It's all too serious

Remember that sex is PLAY! Ideally, when you throw a partner a ball, they are able to pick it up and send it back to you. Then, it is your job to send the ball back to them. This back-and-forth game can transition you towards sex quite nicely and easily. Reciprocity is an important part of playing together!

When I toss the sexual ball to my partner to play with them, they...

- ☐ Toss it back
- ☐ Toss it back too hard
- ☐ Toss it back too softly
- ☐ Ignore it
- ☐ Try to make the throw perfect
- ☐ I have no idea as I never toss a sexual ball to my partner!

Reciprocity is an important feature for gaining a partner's attention. It is a signal that you are choosing to transition towards sexual activities. Notice the word choice. We all have a right to choose. Our choices dictate how our day goes, what we do, what we don't do and the goals that we achieve on any given day. While ADHD can certainly get in the way of accomplishing your goals, you continue to have agency in your choices. If you are not reciprocating a partner's advances, what is happening that you are choosing not to transition towards sex?

I do not transition towards sex because:

- ☐ I do not like how my partner initiates sexual play with me
- ☐ I do not like how my partner acts during sex with me
- ☐ I am bored during sex with my partner
- ☐ I am angry with my partner for other reasons
- ☐ I believe that I should feel arousal prior to engaging in sexual play, if I am not already aroused, I don't try
- ☐ I am distracted by projects, goals, to do lists, screens and/or other priorities
- ☐ I do not like the fact that my partner focuses on the frequency of our sexual activity rather than other parts of our sexuality
- ☐ Other: _____
- ☐ Other: _____
- ☐ Other: _____

Some important things to remember in order to create sexual transitions include:

- ✓ Drop the expectation that sexual desire must exist before you engage in sexual play
- ✓ Stop waiting for arousal to happen without any help or encouragement
- ✓ Start sexual talk by texts, audio messages, social media messaging and/or voicemails earlier in the day
- ✓ Accept that transitioning towards sex may take a bit of time and attention; it just doesn't happen without some effort
- ✓ Consider that sexual engagement with yourself and/or with a partner is an important goal to achieve during your week

✓ Rather than being focused on sexual frequency, explore sexual transitions
✓ Address your anger
✓ Resolve longstanding grievances, disputes and resentments
✓ Communicate what you want and what you don't want sexually
✓ Give yourself and your partner feedback about how your sex life is going and make adjustments following these conversations

Sometimes people actively resist the transition towards sex when sexual play has become overly focused on sexual frequency. We will talk more about sexual frequency and what happens when sexual frequency becomes a focus of sexual dissatisfaction in the next chapter. If you are choosing not to engage sexually with a partner, and this pattern continues despite having worked through this workbook, it may be time to seek couples counselling or individual counselling with a qualified mental health professional to discuss this problem in more detail.

Kissing, hugging and initiating sexual touch!

We often think of hugging and kissing as precursors to sex for good reason. They are bonding activities that usually feel very good. Transitioning towards sex often involves hugging and kissing a partner. Hugging and kissing can be one of the best parts of partnered sex! Kissing is often recommended as a way to enhance relationships (see Gottman Institute, 2016, *Small Things Often: How to build a Lasting relationship* for more details). In addition, kissing can be an effective way for people to feel seated into their bodies. Take the time to kiss a partner! It is a great way to facilitate a sexual transition.

What do you notice when you hug and kiss a partner?

_____
_____
_____
_____

If you have access to a partner, try this exercise:

Approach your partner and ask them if it is ok to kiss for a bit.
Kiss them for one second.
Kiss them for three seconds.
Kiss them for ten seconds.
Kiss them for one minute.
What do you notice about your sexual interest?

_____
_____
_____
_____

Kiss longer than necessary as a way to transition towards sex[3]. It is a quick and easy way to move from "I am not thinking about sex" to "I might be interested in sex".

There are multiple love languages in relationships (see Gary Chapman's book, *The Five Love Languages*, for details). There are also love languages identified for neurodiverse relationships (see *The Five Neurodivergent Love Locutions*, April 19, 2022, Stimpunks.org for details). If a partner appreciates gifts as a language of love and affection, small tokens of affection can be a useful way to transition towards affectionate play. If your partner prefers words of affirmation and/or sharing of information then love notes, romantic texts, a particular passage from a book, sending interesting information and/or verbalizing your love and affection for a partner can be helpful to facilitate transitions towards sex. Addressing your partner's needs as a way to express your affection and respect for them can be a nice way to transition towards sexual activity.

Lighting is another way to introduce a sexual transition. Mood lighting including table lamps, candles, soft lightbulbs or other ways to change the lighting in your home may help identify that it is a time of transition towards sexual play.

There are other ways to create a signal that can cue your partner about a transition. Essential oils, specific objects, emoji's and/or code words can all be used to send a SEXUAL SIGNAL to your partner. Don't rely on eye contact or non-verbal signals to initiate a sexual transition. These can be too easy to miss, particularly if you or a partner is sitting in hyperfocus.

☛ Let's play a game: Create your own codeword that can serve to transition towards sex!

Sheila, Mike and Coby like to play together; however, they can mistake cues and miss signs that someone is interested in sexual play. They agree on Purple Giraffe as a code word to signal sexual interest. Coby even found a plush purple giraffe toy that they could place on the kitchen table when sexual interest was present. They found that if one partner expressed an interest and pulled out the giraffe, the other partners would generally start thinking about sex too. It made communicating about transitions towards sex more playful, less serious and more fun!

✓ If talking about sex is hard for you, agree on a sexual signal that identifies a desire to transition into sexual play
✓ Consider sexual signals such as an emoji, a code word, a sentence sent by text or an object in your home such as a candle, pillow, plush toy, fridge magnet, etc. A sexual signal can even be a particular chore that is accomplished!

Verbal foreplay says it all! Consider a loving pet name and/or sexting (messages with sexual flirting or sexual undertones) to give you and a partner time to transition towards sex.
Use words to set the tone – it can be very impactful.
Sexual stories can be stories that you read or stories that you make up. Reading a sexual story to your partner or sending them a passage from an erotic novel can be a great way to transition towards sex[4]. There are many sexual tales out there!

Creating a sexual story together can be fun!

Try this exercise: Start a story and either tell it to a partner or send it to them. Finish your part of the story with …. **Your turn!** Your partner can say or send their addition to the story back to you. You can play this game together for as long or as little as you both like!

This exercise can also be done using music. Start a song, …. continue the song, …. then keep going! You can cover a particular song that you both like or create your own tune. Both ways can be fun!

Chores can be boring, distracting and just not fun. The difficulty that ADHDers have with chores can be overwhelming. Sadly, it turns out that doing chores around the house can be an aphrodisiac (Carlson, Miller & Sassler, 2018). If you do more chores, particularly biological men doing the dishes, you get more sex. Well darn! Since ADHDers tend to struggle with completing chores, this is a real problem. It's such a significant problem that chore division and chore management is generally included as a part of neurodiverse couples' programs, such as the program developed by Melissa Orlov (2010).

☛ As a general rule: if you are the identified male partner, pitch in, clean up and help with chores; this will be helpful to transitioning to sex more easily. As the identified female partner, do less, let things go and prioritize your sexual engagement (Tuckman, 2019).

Recommendations surrounding chores are likely true within all relationships. Take note! One way to transition towards sex is getting those chores out of the way!

Tim wants to create some space for him and a partner. They just had a baby, and he is not sure what would be the best way to move himself and his partner towards some time alone together. He looks at the pile of dishes in the kitchen and says to himself: "I don't want to do this chore but if I do, I will open up more time for us to engage sexually on our own or with each other".

Part of an effective sexual To-do list includes:

✓ Get those chores done
✓ Help your partner complete household chores
✓ Do a chores list together to determine if the chore distribution is fair
✓ Create a list of the chores that you will take on and schedule these in your planner
✓ Set reminders to complete chores
✓ Associate chore completion with creating sexual space

It can feel absolutely awesome to finish your To-do list and your plans for the day! The To-do list can feel very addictive and can become a hyperfocus. In my clinical experience, this appears to be particularly salient for biological females with ADHD. Addressing the To-do list as a hyperfocus will be discussed in more detail in the next chapter, but for now consider that sex belongs on your to do list too!

Time blindness… ya well, ADHD folks do struggle with time blindness. There was time and now there is no time. This definitely interferes with transitioning towards sex. Time blindness means that there is less time to start sexual activity. You know what I am saying here, right?!?

You just woke up. You didn't sleep great. You grab your phone. You are playing a rousing game of _____ (fill in the blank with your favorite game…). You look up and it's suddenly 11am! The morning is gone. You notice that your partner came, went and left you a coffee. You didn't notice. You run into the shower because now you are very late for work!

Time blindness means that your opportunities to transition towards sex are lost and nothing got started even if there would have been time to get something started. You also leave a partner with the impression that sex is not very important to you.

Some quick fixes for time blindness include:

✓ Schedule time for sex in your calendar or in your planner
✓ Take advantage of days where there is more time available to you, such as statutory holidays, vacations, days off, etc.

✓ Use timers to help you manage activities that tend to grab your attention and don't let go
✓ Create space for sex in your life
✓ Have sex earlier in the day rather than as the last thing to do in your day
✓ Manage those ADHD symptoms! Take your meds regularly and work with an ADHD coach or a therapist to improve your overall symptom management

Even if you are only finding a small amount of time in a week or even in a month to connect sexually with a partner or with yourself, creating that space matters! Tackling time blindness will help you create a better relationship with yourself and better your relationship with a partner.

Important note!

Scheduling simply creates the OPPORTUNITY to engage in sexual play! It is not an obligation or a forced choice. What you do with that time can vary. You are simply creating time and space to engage with either yourself or with a partner. You ultimately decide what to do with that time. Ensuring that you are not creating feelings of obligation and/or expectation for this time that provides SPACE for intimacy in your life, is essential.

   Rather than using the words, "scheduled sex", it may help to call it something else, such as scheduling intimate time, our time, intimacy breaks, time for us, time for love, life break or personal time.

What would you prefer to call this time?

✓ I will schedule time together rather than scheduling sex
✓ I will schedule intimacy breaks with a partner rather than scheduling sex
✓ I will schedule time for love rather than scheduling sex

Do not let scheduling the opportunity for sexual play move you away from the joy experienced when you simply spend intentional time together!

Transitioning from being dressed, serious and "busy" to being naked, playful and allowing yourself time, can feel unpleasant. It can feel hard. Focus on the rewards that come from completing the transition. Feeling that orgasm, being close to a partner, being close to yourself and/or feeling that post-sex glow! By focusing on the reward and the positive feelings that you have when having sex, you can ease this transition[5].

Think about a prior sexual experience. It doesn't have to be an experience that was overly exciting or anything close to perfect. Simply think about the last orgasm you had within a consensual sexual encounter. How did your body feel?

_____

_____

_____

_____

_____

How did you feel in the days after that experience?

_____
_____
_____
_____
_____

Was the experience positive enough for you to want to repeat it?

_____
_____
_____
_____
_____

If the experience wasn't positive enough to want to repeat it, what was the ultimate deal-breaker for you and how can you address this issue moving forward?

_____
_____
_____
_____
_____

While it may seem overly simple, asking to engage in sex is an easy, straightforward way to engage sexually. Communicate your interest! This can be as easy as asking. Be careful not to show any disappointment or upset if your request is not granted. We will talk more about the Sexy Communication Scale later in this chapter. If you don't want to ask outright, you can refer to that scale if you want to communicate your sexual interest in a very clear and straightforward way.

A quick note of caution: At times, ways to transition towards sexual activity can be perceived by a partner as a manipulative tactic to "secure" sex or as a way to "get" sex. In addition, if your efforts lead to a partner being hurt or upset, it will destroy trust (Tuckman, 2019). Communicate your efforts to transition towards sex from a place of interest, caring and respect.

Trust is an important part of all sexual partnerships. If the trust has been damaged for any reason, sexual transitions may trigger feelings of anger or contempt. Should your approaches not be received positively, it is best to discuss your efforts in the context of couples counselling with the assistance of a qualified mental health professional.

The need for novelty may explain why people with ADHD report having more diverse sexual experiences, more non-monogamous sexual experiences, more gender fluidity and more bisexual experiences even if they do not identify being gay (Tuckman, 2019; Young & Cocallis, 2023; Hetz & al., 2022; Young et al., 2023). For people with ADHD, getting stuck in the same sexual routine might not maintain your attention. This can create other problems in your relationship. It is notable that Tuckman (2019) reported that individual differences may be more important as it relates to novelty than having ADHD; however, in his survey, ADHD men did report more interest in having sexual variety in their lives than non-ADHD men.

Sexual novelty and ADHD often go together. If you are finding sex boring, transitioning towards sex can be uninspiring and even unpleasant. Address the issues that are leaving you sexually uninspired!

Sexual intensity can create more interesting and novel sexual experiences. The following strategies can enhance intensity:

- Intensity of touch
- Variety of touch
- Intensity of sexual storytelling
- Intensity of your gaze
- Focusing on one particular body part
- Using noises and sounds
- Creating variety in your sexual activities

Sounds can be extremely useful to create intensity. Allow yourself to express pleasure with sound. Pay attention to your partner's sounds when they are experiencing pleasure[6].

Sound is good!

If you are concerned about a lack of privacy, sounds can be quietly shared, or you can use touch to enhance the knowledge that you are both experiencing pleasure. Listening to the noises that you make and the noises that others make when they are experiencing sexual pleasure can increase sexual intensity. Intensity matters!

Other ways to improve sexual transitions with intensity include:

✓ Think about what you like sexually
✓ Think about what you want to try sexually
✓ Talk about what you like and want to try sexually with a partner
✓ Research sexual themes and ideas
✓ Talk about sex more often with your partner
✓ Discuss wants, desires, fantasies and preferences for sexual expression
✓ Surprise your partner with a different sexual transition
✓ Sit and gaze at your partner
✓ Focus on a part of your partner's body that you like and give it your full attention
✓ Exchange massages
✓ Sex toys/sexual roles plays/sexual games[7]

Claudine has been in a monogamous relationship for 20 years. She and her husband are quite happy. They both work hard to bring sexual novelty into their relationship. This is a relationship expectation that has kept their sex life rocking over the years. A few months ago, it was Claudine's turn to spice things up. She rented a pool at the local hotel for them to use privately. The swim and hotel stay spiced things up for them quite nicely! The care she demonstrated in making sex a priority, finding something creative to do as well as the novelty of the situation itself and the expectation that they both contribute to making sex an important part of their relationship, has kept things going strong for years!

You can create sexual novelty by imagining or creating sexual situations that might be quite different from your usual sexual experiences. You might fantasize about various sexual scenarios and/or plan various sexual scenarios[8]. You can explore sexual pursuits that are outside of your usual activities. If you are going to explore novel sexual activities, research and knowledge are important first steps[9]! Try new things such as adding anal play, using restraints, going to a sexy community event or playing with sexual power dynamics. When exploring new activities communicate clearly and openly with your partner about all aspects of the anticipated play[10]. If you are struggling for ideas to try, you might also want to explore different sexual scenarios online or ask someone you trust for suggestions.

Using surprise to your advantage is another way to transition towards sex. Engaging in sexual surprises or transitioning towards sex when it is unexpected can be a nice way to create novelty. It doesn't always work, particularly if a partner needs time to prepare, but it certainly can be another way to make things spicier.

Let's explore how you feel about sexual novelty in your life!

Overall, how do you experience sex when you or a partner creates novelty?

_____
_____
_____
_____
_____

Do I accept my need for sexual novelty? Is sexual novelty acceptable?

_____ Yes _____ No

Does my partner accept my need for sexual novelty? Is my need for sexual novelty acceptable to my partner?

_____ Yes _____ No

What belief(s) hinder you to feel more comfortable with sexual novelty?

_____
_____
_____
_____
_____

What would you rather believe about sexual novelty?

_____
_____
_____
_____
_____

How would you like to communicate with a partner about your need for sexual novelty? Do you have any fears about introducing sexual novelty into your life?

_____
_____
_____
_____
_____

Sexual transitions can be facilitated by engaging in activities that incorporate sexual and/or romantic themes such as attending sexy shows, burlesque, dance classes, massage classes, clubbing, pole dancing, nudist communities or sexual communities to name only a few. Find safe communities where you can explore sexual intensity in a positive way. Engaging in community activities also means that you are taking time to make sexual play a priority for you!

> Creating time for sex + engaging in an activity that will help transition you towards sexual play is a win-win!

Do you remember the first time you drove somewhere new? It seemed far. Maybe the drive was interesting or maybe it was simply confusing, but there was lots to see. The drive sustained your attention. Once you had driven that same road a few times, maybe even 200 times if it was your route to work or school, it was no longer exciting.

There is simply less intensity when we do the same thing over and over again. Learning to transition towards sex follows the same principles. If you always start the same way, sex may lose its interest; it can become too predictable, and you may find that you no longer want to transition towards sexual play.

Let's explore how you typically transition towards sex!

I typically start sexual play with myself or with a partner by doing the following:

_____
_____
_____
_____
_____

I am open to trying other ways to transition towards sex:

____ Yes ____ No

If I am not open to trying other ways, what is getting in my way?

□ My partner won't respond well to my advances
□ I need something (a medication, an environment, a context, a person) to feel safe
□ I think that my way works well; I have received no complaints
□ I don't think that I should initiate sex
□ I don't want someone to think badly about me if I transition towards sex
□ Other: _____
□ Other: _____

Transitioning towards sex means that you are choosing to engage in sexual activity. At times, cultural beliefs, spiritual beliefs, family values and/or sexual education may encourage people not to transition towards sex. For example, it may be that sexual transitions are only allowed in very limited or specific contexts. You may also have been taught that sexual transitions are not your responsibility because of your gender.

How does choosing to engage in sex align with my spiritual, cultural or personal beliefs?

_____
_____
_____
_____

What do I prefer to believe about the role of sexuality in my life?

_____
_____
_____
_____

What do I want to say to myself and/or others about the choice that I have made to engage in sexual activity?

_____

_____

_____

_____

_____

Place reminders in your home that reflect your choice to transition towards sex. These reminders can assist you to remember your goals and the importance of sexuality in your life!

Finding the right words

Introducing the Sexy Communication Scale! This scale can help you communicate how much sexual pleasure you are feeling in the moment. Sexual pleasure will impact your willingness to transition towards sex. Your level of communication about your transition towards sex can be helpful to identify where you are at in the moment and; to communicate that information concisely to a partner.

> Jonathan was working in his workshop. He had been thinking about sex on and off for a few hours. Sexual thoughts were slowly seeping into his mind. His partner had been frustrated with Jonathan's various projects which took lots of time, money and his attention. At that moment, Jonathan was feeling some sexual desire and was considering transitioning towards sex. His partner was not aware of this change in Jonathan. They came to the workshop, put a cup of coffee down quickly and left seemingly irritated. Jonathan thought it maybe wasn't such a good idea to transition towards sex. They missed an opportunity to come together.

The Sexy Communication Scale was created to help identify sexual feelings. The goal is to increase your own awareness of your sexual urges and to let your partner know your level of sexual pleasure. This can be especially useful if you struggle with verbalizing sexual interest, sexual desire and/or if you tend not to transition towards sex easily.

Use the Sexy Communication Scale to:

✓ Notice your level of sexual desire
✓ Communicate with a partner how you are feeling in the moment
✓ Drop a hint that your sexual desire is building
✓ Track your overall sexual patterns, such as when you tend to be more interested in sex
✓ Identify what works to build or stifle your sexual interest
✓ Communicate if your sexual desire gets sidetracked during sexual play
✓ Notice improvements in your sexual interest when you use these skills!

A partner can use the Sexy Communication Scale to:

✓ Share their sexual interest with you
✓ Express sexual interest without words that may trigger feelings of obligation or expectations
✓ Ask for feedback about how you are feeling in the moment
✓ Get clear information about how you are responding to their sexual advances

My Sexy Communication Scale – Gradients of sexual pleasure

0 – I'm not into it, like absolutely not; I could not pull it off even if I tried

1 – I am not into it, but I am not opposed to sex; it's just not really where I am at right now

2 – I am aware that I am a sexual being, but I have not thought about engaging in sex

3 – I am distracted by other things (tired, hungry, chores, etc.), but I feel that sex could exist if there was space for it

4 – I am thinking about sex on occasion, but I don't have any specific plans or thoughts about doing anything about it

5 – I could have sex or not have sex; I can be moved up the scale or down the scale. I am neutral, but it is an openminded neutral

6 – I am thinking more often about sex

7 – I am thinking more about sex, and I am starting to think about how I might engage in sex

8 – I am thinking about sex, and I have developed a plan to have sex

9 – I really want to have sex; I am excited to have sex

10 – I am there, I am into it, my sexual interest has become a hyperfocus, I could not do anything else right now but have sex. The urge is very strong

Learning to Stop – Exploring transitions OUT of sex!

Learning to stop means having the ability to transition out of sex and back into your life. There has been much said about the ways that people can get stuck in sexual thoughts and activities. It is often labelled sexual addiction, hypersexuality or sexual preoccupation. Transitions out of sex can be problematic for neurodivergent folks. Whether you call it addiction, hypersexuality or sexual preoccupation, not transitioning out of sex can create problems in your life and in your relationships.

> Jayden is a wonderful person with lots going for him. He enjoys his family, his work and his sports. When Jayden has sex, it feels great! This feeling is so much better than how he feels when he is dealing with other parts of his life. When he has sex, it feels amazing and he wants to keep that feeling going. He would have sex every day, multiple times a day, if he could. Once he gets going, he keeps the fire going strong. He keeps talking about sex, thinking about sex, fantasizing about sex. He doesn't transition back to his real life. This is starting to create problems for him and his family.

Transitioning out of sex means that you:

✓ Allow for other things in your life to have priority
✓ Tolerate the realities of your life that are less pleasurable or fun
✓ Accept that you cannot feel as good as "sexually good" all the time
✓ Focus on other feelings that are different from the feeling of sexual pleasure
✓ Focus on thoughts that are not related to sex
✓ Engage in other areas of your life
✓ Create and maintain life goals

One way to transition out of sex is to refocus on other parts of your life and reflect on your life's goals.

Remind yourself about who you want to be and the long term benefits of transitioning out of sex. Visualize the feeling of doing something positive for yourself and the benefits that you will experience in your life by choosing to do another, more productive, activity. Feel that positive feeling that will come from achieving your dreams. Visualize yourself succeeding!

If you do not have goals, it can be hard to transition out of sexual pleasure. Ensure that you develop short-term goals and long-term goals for yourself. If you don't know what these goals are just yet, that's ok – just pick something! You can always change your goals over time.

✓ What do you want to be proud of in one week, one month, three months, six months, five years and ten years?
✓ On my deathbed, I want to have achieved.....

What are your goals in life?

_____
_____
_____
_____
_____

What are the goals that you have already accomplished?

_____
_____
_____
_____
_____

What is a short-term goal that you are currently working on (in the next 3–6 months)?

_____
_____
_____
_____
_____

What is a moderate term goal that you want to achieve (in the next 1–3 years)?

_____
_____
_____
_____
_____

What is a long-term goal that you want to achieve (in the next 3–5 years)?

_____

_____

_____

_____

_____

If the questions above were difficult for you to answer, take some time to create some goals!

You <u>do not</u> have to create the "right" or the "perfect" goal for you. You <u>do not</u> have to be certain that this goal will make you happy or content. You simply have to choose to do something, anything really, to give your life meaning and purpose[11]. Your goals can and will change over time!

Create a visual reminder of your chores, tasks and other priorities so you can clearly see them throughout your day. Set reminders to help you focus on your other responsibilities. Find ways to make your other life priorities matter to you!

Focus on other priorities to transition out of sex:

✓ Maintain a visual reminder of your tasks, priorities and things to do!
✓ Set reminders on your phone or use apps to remind you of other priorities/responsibilities
✓ Ask someone to be an accountability partner to help you stay on track
✓ Work with an ADHD coach!
✓ Attend an ADHD support group!
✓ Participate in a workshop to improve your executive functioning

Make it a game!

If you are really struggling to transition out of sex, put alternative activities on small pieces of paper in a jar. For example, rather than sitting in my sexual pleasure, I could: go cut the lawn, walk a neighbour's dog, cook a meal for myself or others, volunteer, help an elder in the community, join a sports team, focus on a work project, clean my house, talk to a friend, go clean someone else's house, play a videogame, research a new project, go for a walk, ride my bike, go for a swim or learn a new language.

☛ Create a list of alternative tasks, activities and responsibilities that work for you!
☛ Put all these suggestions in a jar.
☛ After you have sex or experience an orgasm, draw a piece of paper from the jar.
☛ Remind yourself that it is now time to transition to another activity. Commit to doing the activity written on the piece of paper, even if you don't really feel like doing it.

Transitioning out of sex is easier when you focus on something else that is non-sexual. Most times, your arousal levels will decrease once you get involved in completing another task.

What do you notice when you force yourself to engage in an alternative activity to transition out of sex?

_____
_____
_____
_____
_____

Over time, does your sexual interest:

☐ Increase
☐ Stay the same
☐ Decrease

In addition, you can focus on other body parts rather than on your genitals/erogenous zones. Take the time to seat yourself back into your ENTIRE body, not just your genitals.

Transitioning out of sex means that you focus on other body parts:

✓ How do my feet feel right now?
✓ How do my hands feel right now?
✓ How are my fingers feeling right now?
✓ How is my back?
✓ How are my legs?
✓ How does my head feel right now?
✓ How about my neck?

Stretch your body! Move your body. Go for a walk. Dance[12].

What do you notice when you engage your body in different ways to transition out of sex?

_____
_____
_____
_____
_____

Managing your ADHD with medication is a very important step to help you transition out of sex! When your symptoms are not managed well, you are more impulsive and likely not noticing the extent of your hyperfocus. It can be more difficult to transition out of sex. If you are still struggling with transitions, talk with your health care provider to review your medication options and optimize your symptom management.

Keeping a sex log or a sexual journal of your urges is an important step in understanding why you are stuck and not transitioning out of sex. Use the Sexy Communication Scale to evaluate how high your sexual interest is throughout the day. Take note of the time of day and the context: what is going on at that time?

Try this exercise:

Right now, on the Sexy Communication Scale I am:

Number: _____ Date/Time of day: _____ Context: _____
Number: _____ Date/Time of day: _____ Context: _____
Number: _____ Date/Time of day: _____ Context: _____
Number: _____ Date/Time of day: _____ Context: _____
Number: _____ Date/Time of day: _____ Context: _____
Number: _____ Date/Time of day: _____ Context: _____
Number: _____ Date/Time of day: _____ Context: _____
Number: _____ Date/Time of day: _____ Context: _____
Number: _____ Date/Time of day: _____ Context: _____
Number: _____ Date/Time of day: _____ Context: _____

What do you notice about the pattern of your sexual urges? When are they the highest? When are they the lowest? In what context do they occur the most?

_____
_____
_____
_____
_____

Find ways to fill the time when your sexual urges are the highest with more purposeful activities. If you are often feeling a strong urge at night, what would be more helpful to help you transition towards sleep? If you are often feeling a strong urge at work, what is the context that is leading you to think about sex during work hours (e.g. bored, stressed, frustrated)?

_____
_____
_____
_____
_____

What else can you do to stay connected with your other life responsibilities at those times?

_____
_____
_____
_____
_____

There are many community groups that can assist you in your quest to transition out of sex[13]. In addition, you may want to talk to a qualified mental health professional for help. Bring in your log, show them your daily numbers and talk with them about your difficulty transitioning out of sex.

Asking for help can be an effective way to manage this concern. Ask for help if this continues to be a worry for you! We will continue to talk about transitions out of sex and sexual impulsivity in Chapter 9 – What have I gotten myself into? Impulsivity, sex and ADHD.

Learning to transition towards sexual pleasure and to transition out of sexual pleasure are skills. **You can learn these skills!**

There are many other things that can get in the way of sexual transitions. Is sex a priority for you? Are you ADHD tired? We will talk more about hyperfocus and how it can impede sexual engagement in the next chapter, Chapter 6 – I'm busy! Hyperfocus and pleasure.

Let's continue our journey exploring ADHD and sex!

Working towards my goals

The biggest issues that I have getting started sexually include:

- ☐ Impulsivity: I go too fast and upset my partner
- ☐ Chores: I don't do enough around the house and my partner is busy doing all the tasks
- ☐ Time blindness: I lose track of time and never get around to it
- ☐ Lack of effort: I don't try
- ☐ Lack of novelty: I get bored
- ☐ Relationship issues: I am angry
- ☐ Lack of communication: I don't talk about it
- ☐ Lack of touch: We don't hug, kiss or touch frequently
- ☐ Hyperfocus: I am too busy and I forget how good it feels
- ☐ Personal beliefs/values: I don't believe I should do it
- ☐ Other: _____
- ☐ Other: _____
- ☐ Other: _____

Here are three things that I want to try to better transition towards sex:

1) _____
_____
_____
_____
_____

2) _____
_____
_____
_____
_____

3) _____
_____
_____
_____
_____

✓ I will remember the importance of putting effort into my sexual transitions
✓ I will remember that sexual interest won't just appear out of nowhere
✓ I will communicate to learn what sexual transitions are most effective for my partner

In order to notice where I am at sexually and to communicate this information to a partner, I will use the Sexy Communication Scale to track my sexual interest once or twice daily. I will record my answers in a log.

My sexual interest on:

Monday: am _____   pm _____
Tuesday: am _____   pm _____
Wednesday: am _____   pm _____
Thursday: am _____   pm _____
Friday: am _____   pm _____
Saturday: am _____   pm _____
Sunday: am _____   pm _____

My sexual interest on:

Monday: am _____   pm _____
Tuesday: am _____   pm _____
Wednesday: am _____   pm _____
Thursday: am _____   pm _____
Friday: am _____   pm _____
Saturday: am _____   pm _____
Sunday: am _____   pm _____

My sexual interest on:

Monday: am _____   pm _____
Tuesday: am _____   pm _____
Wednesday: am _____   pm _____
Thursday: am _____   pm _____
Friday: am _____   pm _____
Saturday: am _____   pm _____
Sunday: am _____   pm _____

My Sexy Communication Scale – Gradients of sexual pleasure

0 – I'm not into it, like absolutely not; I could not pull it off even if I tried

1 – I am not into it, but I am not opposed to sex; it's just not really where I am at right now

2 – I am aware that I am a sexual being, but I have not thought about engaging in sex

3 – I am distracted by other things (tired, hungry, chores, etc.), but I feel that sex could exist if there was space for it

4 – I am thinking about sex on occasion, but I don't have any specific plans or thoughts about doing anything about it

5 – I could have sex or not have sex; I can be moved up the scale or down the scale. I am neutral, but it is an openminded neutral

6 – I am thinking more often about sex

7 – I am thinking more about sex, and I am starting to think about how I might engage in sex

8 – I am thinking about sex, and I have developed a plan to have sex

9 – I really want to have sex; I am excited to have sex

10 – I am there, I am into it, my sexual interest has become a hyperfocus, I could not do anything else right now but have sex. The urge is very strong

✓ I will use the Sexy Communication Scale to communicate with a partner about where I am at and I will ask them where they are at on the scale
✓ I will post the Sexy Communication Scale to encourage more communication about sex
✓ I will share my log with my partner on a daily or weekly basis so they know where I am at on the scale
✓ I will use the log to track what helps me transition towards sex
✓ I will use the log to track what helps me transition out of sex

I can use these activities to help me transition OUT of sex if I get stuck:

_____

_____

_____

_____

_____

To improve my transitions OUT of sex, I will:

☐ Talk to my health care provider to optimize my medications
☐ Focus on other priorities and tasks
☐ Maintain a visual reminder of my other activities, tasks and priorities
☐ Add more satisfying tasks to my daily life
☐ Find more joy in my daily life
☐ Take the time to get seated into my body after sex by connecting with all my other body parts (all my other senses)
☐ Engage in basic self-care such as ensuring that I am eating, drinking and sleeping enough
☐ Attend an ADHD support group and/or work with an ADHD coach
☐ Ask for help

If things don't get better, I will commit to asking for help

_____ Yes _____ No

If things don't get better, I will reach out to this person, organization or group for help:

_____

_____

_____

_____

_____

What are my life goals?

Very short-term goals: (4–6 weeks):

_____

_____

_____

_____

Short-term goals (3–6 months):

_____

_____

_____

_____

_____

Moderate term goals (1–3 years):

_____
_____
_____
_____
_____

Long-term goals (3–5 years):

_____
_____
_____
_____
_____

✓ I will remember my goals and who I want to be in this life
✓ I will remember my goals and what I want to achieve in this life
✓ I will find sexual balance by learning to transition IN and OUT of sexual pleasure

Notes

1 See E. Nagoski (2021) *Come As You Are: Revised and Updated: The surprising new science that will transform your sex life*, for more information about spontaneous and responsive sexual desire.

2 We will talk about consent and sexual safety in more detail in Chapter 11 – Neurodivergent Safety: The importance of Sexual and Relationship Safety.

3 Take the time to ask your partner if there is anything about the way you kiss together that they would like to change or improve.

4 Of the many erotic stories out there, one that is particularly playful and allows you to choose the flow of the story was written by Alina Reyes, a French writer. For more details see *Derrière la porte: Une aventure dont vous êtes le héros* which was translated into English as *Behind Closed Doors*.

5 If you are experiencing pain or discomfort during sex, if sex does not feel good physically or emotionally, it is time to ask for help! Contact a qualified mental health professional for further assistance.

6 If noise creates a sensory issue for you, we will tackle that topic in Chapter 8.

7 Sex toys are not all created equal. Find sexual toys and games that offer safety, fun and satisfaction for both yourself and a partner. There are multiple options available and these can be purchased either online or in a store. Explore the ones that you might like best!

8 As long as these fantasies involve legal themes and consensual persons, sexual fantasy is a good way to increase sexual novelty. Following through and doing the planned sexual scenario is not required. Sometimes, the fantasy is enough!

9 OMGYES! Is a website dedicated to sharing information about female masturbation. If you are engaging sexually with a biological female or if you are a biological female, knowing additional strategies to enhance pleasure for yourself and/or a partner can be particularly helpful.

10 There are some good books to help you navigate alternative sexual activities. For BDSM exploration, an oldie but a goodie is, *Screw the Roses, Send me the Thorns: The romance and*

sexual sorcery of sadomasochism by Devon & Miller (1995). If exploring anal play is new for you, try Dr. J. Morin's book (2010) *Anal Pleasure & Health: A guide for men, women and couples* for additional information and exercises to explore.

11 There are many books that discuss goal setting and finding purpose in your life. Two examples of books that can help you explore your life goals by Dr. R. Paterson are: *How to be Miserable: 40 strategies you already use* and *How to be Miserable in Your Twenties: 40 strategies to fail at adulting*. Caution: these books might not work well for you, if you interpret words literally and/or do not detect sarcasm easily.

12 If you are struggling with chronic pain, and moving your body does not help you transition out of sex, simply choose another sensory element to focus on such as a particular smell, sound, taste or a specific image/visual picture.

13 There are different organizations that offer support for people who struggle with too much sex. Some organizations are more conservative than others. Find a group that suits you! One example might be https://saa-recovery.org.

References

Amythest@neurowonderful (May 2021) and Stimpunks Foundation (19 August 2022). The Five Neurodivergent Love Locutions, Creative Commons Attribution-ShareAlike 4.0 International license, Stimpunks.org.

Carlson, D.L., Miller, A.J. & Sassler, S. (2018). Stalled for Whom? Change in the Division of Particular Housework Tasks and Their Consequences for Middle- to Low-Income Couples. *Socius*, 4. https://doi.org/10.1177/2378023118765867.

Chapman, G.D. (2009). The Five Love Languages: The secret to love that lasts. Moody Publishing.

Devon, M. & Miller, P. (1995). Screw the Roses, Send Me the Thorns: The Romance and Sexual Sorcery of Sadomasochism. Mystic Rose Books.

Goodall, E. & Brownlow, C. (2022). Interoception and Regulation: Teaching skills of body awareness and supporting connection with others. London: Jessica Kingsley Publishers.

Gottman, J. & Silver, N. (1999). The Seven Principles for Making Marriage Work. New York: Three Rivers Press.

Gottman Institute (2016). Small Things Often: How to build a lasting relationship. Washington: The Gottman Institute.

Hertz, G.P., Turner, D. & Retz, W. (2022). Sexuality in ADHD: Empirical data concerning hypersexual and paraphilic fantasies and behaviors in adults with ADHD. *European Psychiatry*, 65(S1), S283–S283. doi:10.1192/j.eurpsy.2022.725.

Morin, J. (2010). *Anal Pleasure & Health: A Guide for Men, Women and Couples*. Down There Press.

Nagoski, E. (2021). *Come As You Are: Revised and Updated: The surprising new science that will transform your sex life*. Simon & Schuster Publications.

Orlov, M. (2010). *The ADHD Effect on Marriage: Understand and rebuild your relationship in six steps*. Speciality Press/A.D.D. Warehouse, p. 225.

Paterson, R.J. (2019). *How to be Miserable: 40 strategies you already use*. New Harbinger Publications.

Paterson, R.J. (2020). *How to be Miserable in Your Twenties: 40 strategies to fail at adulting*. New Harbinger Publications.

Perel, E. (2007). *Mating in Captivity: Unlocking erotic intelligence*. New York: Harper.

Reyes, A. (1994*). Derrière la porte*. Paris: Robert Laffont.

Tuckman, A. (2019). *ADHD After Dark: Better Sex Life, Better Relationship* (1st ed.). Routledge.

Young, S. & Cocallis, K. (2023). A systematic review of the relationship between neurodiversity and psychosexual functioning in individuals with autism spectrum disorder (ASD) or attention-Deficit/Hyperactivity disorder (ADHD). *Neuropsychiatric Disease and Treatment, 19*, 1379–1395. https://doi.org/10.2147/NDT.S319980.

Young, S., Klassen, L.J., Reitmeier, S.D., Matheson, J.D. & Gudjonsson, G.H. (2023). Let's talk about sex... and ADHD: Findings from an anonymous online survey. *International Journal of Environmental Research and Public Health*, 20(3), 2037. https://doi.org/10.3390/ijerph20032037.

Chapter 6

I'm busy! Hyperfocus and pleasure

Now, I understand. I really really do understand. Asking anyone to cease a hyperfocus activity truly sucks. Let's be clear: it blows, it sucks, it is awful, it is painful, it is emotional torture, it is awful like all the things you hate combined into a huge stinky ball of goo.... When you are in hyperfocus, your hyperfocus is the only thing that matters. It is the only thing that has meaning, worth and interest. The rest of the world is boring, terrible, tedious, predictable. The world doesn't offer anything of interest outside of your hyperfocus. Hyperfocus is like an orgasm; it's an experience that you can't describe. It's tension producing, soothing, teeth grinding and fantastic all at the same time! There isn't much better in life than an orgasm, except perhaps being in hyperfocus. Hyperfocus is a close second to an orgasm and, for some, it's first. Orgasmic pleasure IS hyperfocus pleasure!

So, let us be clear... simply asking someone to pause their hyperfocus is a tad ridiculous. It's unlikely to work. It creates resentment. It breeds irritation. It is the one ADHD symptom that offers a huge advantage but comes at quite a cost. The cost of hyperfocus is its cost to your relationships, your work, your other life goals and other life priorities that matter, such as your physical health (exercise, food choice, hydration, sleep and overall movement), intellectual health (learning new things, completing your schooling, trying new skills, purposeful tasks), financial health (balancing your bank accounts, keeping your spending in check, setting financial goals), environment (cleaning, organizing, nesting) and spiritual health (mindfulness, meditation, spiritual practice).

Hyperfocus can get in the way of your sexual time, whether you are engaging in solo sex or partnered sex. When you are engaged in solo sex, you may not receive complaints about your hyperfocus; however, it can limit your time with yourself and your connection to your body.

Partners, particularly non-ADHD partners, just don't "get" hyperfocus. If you have an ADHD partner, they themselves may get lost in hyperfocus, but the timing of their hyperfocus and your hyperfocus might not always align. Hyperfocus can create differences in sexual expectations between partners.

> Tensions rise as people try to get your attention, fail to secure your attention, and inevitable feelings of rejection creep in. Hyperfocus can poison relationships!

DOI: 10.4324/9781003422372-7

Jenna is talking with her ADHD support circle. She tells the group "My partner hasn't changed their inability to greet me when I come in the door; that must mean that they aren't interested in me!" The circle reminds her about the power of hyperfocus. They encourage her to challenge this belief and to consider a more realistic conclusion. Jenna acknowledges "My partner hasn't changed their inability to greet me when I come in the door, they must be hyperfocused on their videogame". With this perspective, Jenna is less angry and is better able to problem solve with the support circle, ultimately, she can discuss the issue with her partner in a calmer way.

People with ADHD may not notice that they are in a hyperfocus cycle. Identifying when you are in hyperfocus is an important skill. If you do not notice the hyperfocus you may become defensive about your hyperfocus or try to deny it, making it very difficult to have an effective conversation with a partner.

My hyperfocus <u>typically</u> involves these types of activities:

☐ Work projects
☐ School projects
☐ Learning a new skill or a new language
☐ Relationships (falling for a person hard, making them your hyperfocus)
☐ Exercise and physical fitness
☐ Bodily reactions, your body and/or your health
☐ Animals
☐ Art
☐ Travel
☐ Creating new and novel experiences for yourself or others
☐ History
☐ The future
☐ Social justice and/or environmental issues
☐ Sex
☐ Scheduling/organizing
☐ Shopping/acquiring things
☐ Food
☐ Other: _____
☐ Other: _____
☐ Other: _____

When you are in hyperfocus, do you notice it?

☐ I do not identify my hyperfocus.
☐ I identify my hyperfocus and I become defensive about it
☐ I deny or minimize that I am in hyperfocus
☐ I expect others to participate in my hyperfocus
☐ I expect others to appreciate and/or love my hyperfocus activity/interest

When interrupted in a state of hyperfocus, some people can become irritable, grumpy and/ or angry, particularly when the interruption interferes with accomplishing their goals. This can lead to a partner walking on eggshells, fearing to interrupt you and/or fearing to disagree with you, because of your hyperfocus.

When I am interrupted in a state of hyperfocus, I typically respond by being:

☐ Pleasant and kind
☐ Dismissive: I simply ignore the interruption
☐ Angry and irritable
☐ Contemptuous: I put the other person down for interrupting me
☐ Abusive: I yell and scream
☐ Other: _____
☐ Other: _____

When I am in hyperfocus and someone wants to engage with me, I would prefer to respond in the following way:

_____
_____
_____
_____
_____

Hyperfocus is something that is special. It is precious and important. People will risk relationships, physical health and other important aspects of their life to complete their hyperfocus activities. A hyperfocus is time-limited and it will come and go. It can be difficult or even impossible to explain why a hyperfocus becomes so very important in that moment. A hyperfocus might mean a lot to you in the moment, yet it can become meaningless over time.

A special interest is something that is very important to you, and it can last in one form or another for a very long time. A special interest tends to define you. In the autistic literature, a special interest is used to define a longstanding hyperfocus or interest[1].

Even if others do not understand the appeal,
a hyperfocus or a special interest is very important
to the person that is experiencing it!

In this workbook, we aren't going to simply suggest that you stop the hyperfocus. I mean, really, has that ever worked?!?

The goal is BALANCE!
BALANCE means that sex and relationships are priorities that are included in your overall list of life priorities.

With this idea in mind, let's explore ways to tame that hyperfocus!

Jim tends to hyperfocus on building projects. He loves them! The local hardware store is a fantasy warehouse of potential projects, new tools and awesomeness! When he starts on a new project, it is typically quite impulsive. Something catches his eye, and he must get it done. Jim has been upfront with his new partner about this tendency. They have developed a budget to cover his hyperfocus activities and his partner appreciates the additional value that these projects add to their home. Jim has also been careful to include his partner by completing some projects that his partner would like to see finished. Sometimes, building projects take over so much that Jim forgets to eat, forgets to wash and is physically exhausted. Sex doesn't even enter the picture. Generally, his partner is ok with this and will engage in masturbation or stay busy with their own projects until he is done. This time Jim has taken on a six-month building project. He is losing steam, and his partner is losing patience. What can Jim do to create BALANCE for himself and his relationship?

What are your thoughts about Jim? Can Jim do things differently?

_____
_____
_____
_____
_____

What might Jim be worried about? For example, Jim might be worried that if he stops, he will lose his hyperfocus and the project will never get done. What else might Jim be concerned about?

_____
_____
_____
_____
_____

If Jim asks himself honest questions about his level of hyperfocus, Jim will likely find that he isn't as excited about this project as he was at the beginning. As time goes on, he has slowed down and he is less passionate about the whole thing. He is tired. Jim can reset! He can achieve his goals without negatively impacting his relationship.

Jim may want to consider these other options:

✓ Ask for help
✓ Sit down with his partner and create a new plan
✓ Plan a short holiday where he can reconnect with his partner and give himself some rest away from the project – if he doesn't see it, he will likely be able to focus on something new for a couple days
✓ Set due dates for certain elements of the project and then plan dates with his partner after each due date so that throughout the project, there is scheduled time for connection
✓ Remember that his hyperfocus and passion for this project will return; all is not lost if he rests

✓ Create a visual reminder of the project flow so that his partner is aware of his progress, and they can both see the small accomplishments along the way
✓ Set a reminder on his phone to offer words of affection to his partner by text or verbally
✓ Set a reminder on his phone to offer small gifts of thanks to his partner
✓ Exchange backrubs once a week to ensure physical connection
✓ Create a visual reminder of his target if he remains worried that he will lose focus and not complete the project if he takes a break

What else would you suggest to Jim to improve this situation?

_____

_____

_____

_____

_____

One trick is to make sure that your hyperfocus is something positive, that it allows for breaks, that a partner or friends can join you along the way (even if it is only in some small way) and it leaves room for other important parts of your life like your physical health, emotional health, general self-care as well as your sexuality. If your hyperfocus is not a detriment to your overall life and personal safety, it is much easier to negotiate elements of hyperfocus with loved ones[2].

Does your hyperfocus:

✓ Lead to positive or neutral outcomes?
✓ Leave room for others to join in if they choose to do so?
✓ Allow you to complete your basic self-care?
✓ Create any negative long-term consequences for you?
✓ Allow you to maintain financial stability?
✓ Negatively impact your health or safety?

Honour and acknowledge difficulties inherent to shifting hyperfocus. By honouring the importance of the hyperfocus, we are less likely to create anger, agitation and a reduced satisfaction in relationships. This being said, I am not suggesting a complete free-for-all that encourages every and all hyperfocus that comes along. This would be counterproductive. We are going to find ways to achieve balance between hyperfocus and fulfilling other life goals. The BALANCE that you find by ensuring your sex life and honouring your hyperfocus will likely lead to more positive results.

Let's explore this idea for a minute.

Neurotypical advice regarding sexual frequency sounds like this: "Try to ensure that you have sex regularly with your partner, at a frequency that works for you both, maybe once or twice weekly". There is a predictability and sustainability in this goal; however, it seems counterintuitive when you are neurodiverse.

Let's consider an alternative. Does this idea feel better? "Rotate sex into your life priorities, so that when you feel like having it, you have lots of it and when you feel like having it less, that is ok because you had lots of it a little while ago". In both options, sex remains a priority; however, how you think about it may make your goal more attainable.

Let's start by exploring frequency:

How often do you want to have sex?

- ☐ Daily
- ☐ Every 2–3 days
- ☐ Every week
- ☐ Every 2 weeks
- ☐ Every month
- ☐ Every 2–3 months
- ☐ Every year
- ☐ Impossible to say!

People generally say that they want lots of sex, but when you explore their lives and what they are actually doing on a daily basis, other activities and priorities (and yes, other hyperfoci or is it hyperfocuses.... let's move along lest we get stuck down this particular rabbit hole!) appear to be more important.

Let's try the question this way:

If you have sex daily for four or five days, do you typically take a break and move on to other activities for a while?

_____ Yes _____ No _____ Sometimes

If you have sex regularly, are you satisfied enough to enjoy your hyperfocus activity without longing for sexual activity?

_____ Yes _____ No _____ Sometimes

Imagine creating a goal of BALANCE in your sexual frequency!

Some people get stuck on the idea of sexual frequency. Sexual frequency can actually become the hyperfocus. In this case, the number of times you have sex is conflated with sexual satisfaction. Sexual frequency becomes prioritized instead of the quality of sex you experience. To avoid this common pitfall, make sure that your hyperfocus on other tasks, projects and priorities do not interfere with maintaining sexuality in your life. If sex is never or very rarely prioritized, for example, if you engage in sex every three to six months, you are not achieving sexual balance. If you are prioritizing sex and there is no time for any other interests in your life, you are not achieving sexual balance. If your partner is unhappy with the sexual balance in your relationship, it is time to reflect on your balance. Create a rotation in your hyperfocus activities so that sex has a place in your life that allows you to maintain positive relationships with yourself and with a partner.

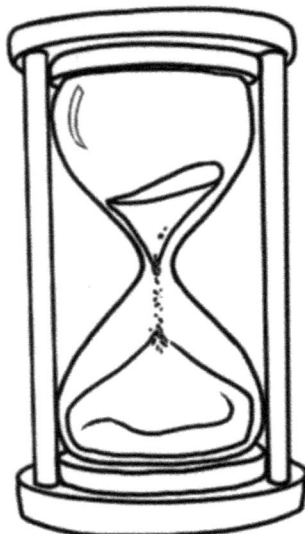

Taming hyperfocus means engaging in effective time management. Without the application of basic time management skills, there will simply be no time for sex.

✓ Get to know time management strategies
✓ Use a calendar and plan your week and/or your day ahead of time
✓ Morning sex may help when your time management is poor; it starts off your day before other projects get in your way
✓ Set timers to keep your daily activities and daily schedule on track
✓ Ensure that you are following a visual reminder system (whiteboard or an agenda/daily planner) that you can SEE throughout the day to keep you on track
✓ Create a to do list that has time for sex and/or time for connection as part of the schedule

One way to manage hyperfocus is to schedule your life priorities, including work, finances, sex, time with friends, as well as scheduling time for your hyperfocus. Schedule time in your day/weekly schedule for your hyperfocus. It can have a place in your calendar. You know that you will get to it within your day, or you can schedule a whole day or a whole week to indulge your hyperfocus. It can be the reward that gets you through the day! When your hyperfocus activity becomes part of your weekly/daily calendar, it obtains a recognized place in your life.

We discussed the idea of scheduling time for physical connection in Chapter 5; if that idea does not feel good to you, consider moving sex to an earlier time slot in your day. Often people prefer to have sex later at night, but by then there are a million other tasks, events and unexpected changes throughout your day that leads to sex being "bumped" to another day. In addition, fatigue can really get in the way!

Can sex be energizing? Does sex always make you tired? If you only have sex at the end of the day when you are tired, you might find that you hold the belief that having sex leads to rest and sleep. Having sex doesn't have to signal the end of your hyperfocus, it can simply be a nice break. Play around with your sexual schedule. You might find that sex can be energizing!

Consider:

✓ Morning sex
✓ Lunch time sex
✓ Early afternoon sex
✓ Coming home from work sex
✓ Weekend sex

It may take some time to find a routine that works for you, but finding an alternative time in your day or week that is more conducive to sexual play can avoid creating a tug of war between your hyperfocus and your other life priorities!

While we are on the topic of time management, let's discuss the "after work time drift"! You are scheduled to finish work at 5pm. Somehow, your time blindness means that you don't seem to ever get home until 7pm. Remember to schedule transition time in your calendar, particularly as you move from one activity to another. In addition, you can set timers to stay on schedule and reduce the "after work time drift"! Realistically, it can become harder to stay on track as your fatigue increases and your medication wears off.

✓ Try to get home on time; stick to the schedule as much as you can
✓ Schedule hyperfocus into your calendar

There are time management courses available to you either online or in your community. Many ADHD conferences and ADHD educational programs discuss the basics of time management. In addition, you can search for executive functioning workshops, classes and/or support groups to assist you!

Mary checked off all the things on her list for today! This made her feel powerful, motivated, strong and efficient. It felt great! Throughout her day, the to-do list is the most important thing in Mary's mind. The to-do list runs her schedule and her life. It is a priority. If something is important and must be done, it is on the to-do list. Sex isn't on Mary's list, so it doesn't get any attention.

Many people love their to-do lists. They have scraps of paper with notes, things to do, things to try, activities to explore and the daily (and perhaps dreaded) to-do list for each day. The problem is that to-do lists have a habit of morphing into other lists and additional daily obligations that will steal all your time. If your hyperfocus is the joy of checking things off the to-do list, simply add sex to the to-do list! While this may feel contrived, sex is truly an important goal, isn't it?

- ✓ Ask for help with the to-do list so that you can feel freer when it comes to sex
- ✓ Create an agreement within your household about the tasks that are essential and those that aren't
- ✓ Note what is priority #1, #2, on the to-do list and what can wait until tomorrow, next week or next month

You will likely not agree on the priority levels of the various activities that are placed on your to-do list. Keep an open mind, compromise and communicate the underlying belief or value that is attached to the activities on your list, particularly those activities that are not a priority for your partner.

We are all afraid of losing our edge! At times, creative folks, project folks, to-do list folks, artistic folks, hyperfocus folks... all get stuck in the mindset that if they stop, they will lose their hyperfocus. Let's face it, ADHD is something that gives you an edge in the world.

Trust that you will get your hyperfocus back if you take a small break! In fact research, albeit not specific to neurodivergent folks, demonstrates clearly that if you take a rest, you will retain more information, you will study more effectively and your body and mind will work better together (Biwer et al., 2023; Albulescu et al., 2022; Largo-Wight et al., 2017; Sammonds, Mansfield & Fray, 2017). There isn't any research about whether this holds true for neurodivergent folks in regard to hyperfocus; however, it does not seem likely that if people take a short break, they will lose their passions that easily. While you may be afraid of losing your hyperfocus and don't feel that you can control when, and if, it shows up again, there are ways to help it return. The things that matter to us do come back around. Things that make us feel good, motivate us and that we find enjoyable, come back around every time!

How can you prove to yourself that your hyperfocus will come back around?

- ✓ Ensure that you are properly medicated

It is possible that fears about losing hyperfocus come from years of trying to manage ADHD symptoms without the proper medication. If you are not properly medicated, your fears about forgetting a project, moving to another project without completing the first one, losing your hyperfocus and/or losing your edge may well increase.

✓   Maintain appropriate lists, visual reminders and specific goals related to your hyperfocus.

If you are always trying to remember the hyperfocus or afraid of forgetting it, it will be harder for you to let go of that hyperfocus for a brief time. Remember: If I have a reminder and I have a realistic schedule for myself, I can trust myself to get it done!

✓   Be honest with yourself about where you are in the project's life cycle

It can be difficult to maintain hyperfocus 24/7. It is typically not possible unless it is a smaller project or a series of smaller projects that lead to a larger accomplishment. Your interest does wax and wane, even within the hyperfocus. When you notice the waning, take note about whether it comes back or not. Once you have rested, eaten or drank something, it will most likely return. Tending to your self-care can help your hyperfocus return with renewed passion!

When you stop, sleep, rest or take a short break, you may notice that your brain has found its way through a problem that you were having or finds various new paths of investigation for you to explore. Use the secondary benefits of taking small breaks to your advantage!

What is a partner to do?!? Some tips for partners!
Secondary to time management, one way to get a partner's attention who is in hyperfocus is to put your hand quietly on them and wait for them to notice your presence. This strategy can be quite peaceful and relies on the heat of your hand to cue them. Take note: if you tend to have cold hands, this strategy may not work as well for you!

Touch their leg, their back or their arm. Try not to touch a body part that is required for their current task as it may feel restricting. Simply sitting beside them, without touch, can also cue your partner to your presence.

✓   Ask your partner what body part they would prefer you touch when signaling that you would like to engage with them during a period of hyperfocus

If your partner does not respond to you, wait and try again, perhaps asking when a better time would be to talk. Alternatively, leaving a written note or an agreed upon object to cue them that you would like to speak with them is another great way to peacefully interrupt hyperfocus.

Coby and Kye both have ADHD. They enjoy their times of hyperfocus. They agreed to use a code object when they wanted each other's attention. They chose a cute emoji that they also purchased as a plush toy. If they wanted their partner to respond to a text message, they would put that emoji in the message to cue their partner that it was an important message and required a timely response. They used the same image when they wanted a bit of time. While it sometimes provoked frustration, they could typically break from their hyperfocus long enough to negotiate a better time to talk or to restructure the family schedule. It allowed for more peaceful transitions out of hyperfocus and kept tensions low!

Nagging, yelling, repeating yourself, throwing things, making excessive noise and/or slamming doors are not good ways to gain the attention of a partner in hyperfocus. You won't get your needs met with any positivity. Kindness, patience and grace are better tools to interrupt hyperfocus! If you are struggling with your patience, it may be time to participate in an ADHD couple's seminar or neurodivergent couple's counselling sessions for further assistance.

Phones, videogames, laptops and other devices

Tech is a problem. It can create hyperfocus for everyone, not just neurodivergent folks! Screens can be wonderful! They offer entertainment, friendships, sex, information, schedule our activities – in short, screens are a part of our life!

It is likely that you have not found balance as it relates to your screen use in your daily life. We need screens, we want screens but they grab our attention and won't let go. It's very hard to experience balance!

Is your tech getting in the way of:

- ☐ Your relationships?
- ☐ Your life goals?
- ☐ Your parenting?
- ☐ Your exercise and physical health?
- ☐ Your digestion?
- ☐ Your sleep?

- ☐ Other: _____
- ☐ Other: _____
- ☐ Other: _____

Limiting screen time is an essential goal to address a hyperfocus that isn't positively contributing to your life in a tangible way[3]:

- ✓ Delete games that do not fill you with anything positive
- ✓ Ask for feedback about how often you are using screens and the impact of your screen use on others in your life
- ✓ Set scheduled access times for your computer use
- ✓ Add automatic shut off times for electronic devices (also known as schedule downtime)
- ✓ Only go online if you have a specific task, goal or question that you wish to resolve
- ✓ Limit or delete social media

Visual timers are another nice way to address hyperfocus. If you have scheduled time with a partner and you require a bit more time to finish your current task, negotiate a set amount of time to complete the current task. Use a visual timer, agree on the amount of time needed and set the timer together. Create a visual reminder of the time you have left after which you will be agreeable to transition into the planned activity.

Often hyperfocus leads to one partner going to sleep much later than another. Going to sleep together is an effective way to tame hyperfocus. Winding down your day at the same time as a partner, allows some time away from your hyperfocus and time focused on them. Different bedtimes and less sleep can negatively impact many aspects of your life, including your sex life. Sleep schedule differences can impact sexual satisfaction for people with ADHD (Kooij, 2018). Transitioning to bed without your partner can inadvertently send a message that you are not interested in spending time with them. Sleep problems can make you grumpy and tired which can also interfere with your relationship. Address any outstanding sleep issues with a health care professional.

If you are a shift worker or if you struggle with sleep and need your own sleeping quarters, consider taking naps with a partner, if possible, and focus on planning joint activities together to ensure that there is quality time spent with your partner.

✓ Acknowledge that your sleep schedule matters to your sex life
✓ Go to bed at the same time as your partner at least a few times a week
✓ Compromise by cuddling with a partner and then getting up after an agreed upon time if your sleep schedules don't align
✓ Plan one joint activity together on a daily or weekly basis

There is tired and then there is ADHD tired!
Trying to get through a day without making a mistake, paying attention to everything, looking for things that you may have missed and working much harder than others to accomplish the same tasks – this is ADHD tired. When you are ADHD tired, it can feel like a different level of exhaustion.

ADHD tired tends to happen more:

☛ When you are non-medicated or not optimally medicated and struggling to get through your day
☛ If you are a parent or caregiver
☛ If you are in a period of hyperfocus
☛ If you are experiencing sleep problems
☛ If you are not prioritizing sleep
☛ During your PMS period

Being ADHD tired will impact your sex life!

✓ Optimize medication
✓ Ensure that you are applying effective ADHD management skills
✓ Focus on taking care of your chores earlier in the day, so that you can get more sleep
✓ Ask for help

Hyperfocus can create tired and exhausted people; this can impact your sexuality! While this may be considered an ADHD tax, it can be easier to prioritize sex if you build regular holidays into your schedule. These can be staycations, trading houses with a friend or planning both local or international holidays. When you are ADHD tired, you may benefit from taking short breaks monthly, quarterly or bi-yearly. A yearly holiday that is longer in length can also be a good way to achieve this goal[4].

ADHD Parenting!

Parenting is less a hyperfocus and more of a lifetime responsibility. As we are exploring activities that take time and attention that could otherwise be spent on exploring our sexuality, including parenting here seems to fit.

Infants and children require much time, focus and attention. Parenting is an activity that distracts from other priorities for many years – in fact, a lifetime. The attention that is required to raise children can very easily eclipse your sex life. Let's be real, during some periods of child raising, sex will simply not be a priority. Holding realistic expectations for yourself and for a partner when you are raising children is essential. Being kind to yourself, engaging your partner from a place of grace and acknowledging the overall level of overwhelm that you and your partner are experiencing is an important consideration when communicating about sexual balance[5].

Sex does change after having a baby!

• Increased ADHD symptoms post-partum for the biological female with ADHD can significantly impact relationships leading to relationship strain and subsequent sexual difficulties[6]
• Parenting challenges are enhanced when you have ADHD
• There is less time to fulfill your own needs
• ADHD parents are very often raising neurodivergent kids

To address parenting challenges, stay realistic!

✓ Focus on creating structured time together
✓ Be forgiving if plans change as a result of the children's needs
✓ Prioritize stay-at-home holidays (also known as Staycations)
✓ Organize sleep overs or playdates with trusted friends and family members
✓ Secure additional childcare supports
✓ Engage in small gestures of play and fun amidst the responsibilities and chores
✓ Create quick, short, sexual moments amidst the chaos
✓ Schedule structured time with your partner (e.g. playing cards together, talking while doing the dishes, folding laundry together or cuddling for a few minutes)
✓ Use gratitude daily to express your appreciation for your family

Set reasonable sexual goals for yourself and for a partner if you are raising children. Children do become more independent and with time it will be easier to focus on your relationship.

Too much work!

Jamal is very excited about his new job. After a few months, he gets into a new routine and there is space for other things in his life. He joins a special group project at work. This project is time limited and he enjoys the goals that they are implementing as a team. Once that project is done, there is a secondary project that he leads to improve work flow in the office. Once that task is completed, it is time for the yearly budget to be done. After 4 years, Jamal has accomplished a series of work priorities which have felt very beneficial to him; but he has not invested any time into his relationship goals.

Finding purpose is essential in life! No one can evaluate the importance of your hyperfocus outside of yourself. The key is ensuring that your time management is consistent with your goals and your life purpose. The essential element is whether you are pleased with your choices over time, or not. If your hyperfocus is getting in the way of your relational goals, you have some decision-making to do about finding BALANCE.

> You live alone and love the single life! Family members and friends are frequently reminding you that going out with friends, dating and trying new activities may be something that you might want to try. When they bring it up, you agree that it would be fun to go out and do a few more things. In your typical day, you come home from work, eat, watch a show. You enjoy the shows that are available on multiple streaming services. You usually like watching _____ (fill in the blank with your favourite streaming show/network). Next thing you know, it's midnight. The next day is more of the same.

BALANCE is hard! The right balance can include periods of intense hyperfocus and periods of rest. It can also include making small steps towards your goals. Many ADHDers prefer intensely focusing on one thing and then not focusing on it at all. If your priorities are so far out of balance that you are not engaging sexually with yourself or others on a somewhat consistent basis, over time, your relationships will likely struggle.

Discuss your hyperfocus with yourself, your partner, your friends and other people in your life. How do they feel about your balance?

☐ They like my balance; I am getting it right!
☐ They don't have an opinion one way or another – they recognize that my life is up to me!
☐ They dislike my balance – I am too busy with other projects!
☐ Other feedback:

_____

_____

_____

_____

_____

At times, family and friends will criticize your balance, based on the fact that they themselves do not experience intense hyperfocus, they have a different type of hyperfocus and/or they do not have the same amount of energy that you do. The question of balance is not so much about what you do; rather, it's more about the ratio between your personal activities and the activities related to your relationships. If the balance conversation becomes focused on what you are doing, for example, that your hyperfocus is unimportant or concerning[7], stop and talk about this issue with a support person. If what you are doing in regards to balance works for everyone, great! Clearly communicate your projects, plans and timelines so that people around you know what to expect.

What balance do I want to achieve between my hyperfocus and my relationships with friends, family and loved ones?

_____

_____

_____

_____

_____

What balance do I want to achieve between my hyperfocus and my sexuality?

_____

_____

_____

_____

_____

I will create balance by:

✓ Adding sexual goals to my daily, weekly or my monthly plans
✓ Scheduling time for sex on a regular basis
✓ Considering sex in my time budget, the same way that I consider financial costs, time commitments and needed resources when I explore the feasibility of a new project
✓ Communicating with a partner about timelines, expectations and needs
✓ Following the plan that I created to ensure that my agreed upon priorities are maintained despite my hyperfocus

Identify your sexual goals and hyperfocus priorities for the next six months. In the next six months, I would like to prioritize the following objectives:

_____

_____

_____

_____

_____

Coaching services and/or ADHD support groups can be very effective ways to help tame your hyperfocus and get additional assistance to structure your life priorities. There are body doubling groups that can assist you with finding body doubles, which are other people who are working on similar tasks and can do it parallel to you, as a way to stay on track. Rotate your priorities. Ask for help as needed!

Some people with ADHD don't like sex, they avoid sex, they don't want it and they would prefer not having it. For some, this happens when their hyperfocus becomes more important than sex. If your special interest or hyperfocus is something that takes time, energy and has consumed you, there are likely many other things that won't maintain your attention. When hyperfocus happens, sex can be one of those things that you simply do not want to do!

For other people, the hyperfocus is about NOT having sex. Some people with ADHD will hyperfocus on avoiding sex, avoiding sexual pleasure and avoiding physical contact.

There are many reasons why this hyperfocus may occur, but like all the other hyperfoci (or should I say hyperfocuses?!?) out there, it is up to you to decide whether it is helpful to you or whether it is limiting your life. If your hyperfocus is not to have sex in your life, you might not be reading this workbook, but if you are, consider that BALANCE may be a more helpful approach!

If your hyperfocus is about avoiding sex:

✓ What information would you need to feel more comfortable with your sexuality?
✓ What concerns do you maintain about your sexuality that you are choosing to avoid?
✓ What belief underlies your choice to avoid sexual expression with yourself and/or with a partner?
✓ How would your life change if you modified your relationship with your physical body?
✓ Would balance help you achieve a sensation of comfort with yourself?

You can adapt to hyperfocus and it does not have to run amuck in your life. Finding ways to integrate hyperfocus peacefully is your goal! Include your partner in your hyperfocus, give them information about your plans, explain the appeal, share your excitement. While a partner might not get it, they can respect that the project has appeal for you. As a partner, respond positively as much as you can. Weigh the costs and benefits of the hyperfocus (is it benign or is it dangerous?). If it feels dangerous to the person in hyperfocus or to the household, find compromise and discuss these concerns openly. Keep those lines of communication open!!

Let's continue our journey exploring ADHD and sex!

Working towards my goals

What is my favorite type of hyperfocus?

_____
_____
_____
_____
_____

Is my hyperfocus congruent with my goals?

☐ Yes
☐ No
☐ Only sometimes

Do I communicate with my friends, family and partner about my hyperfocus?

☐ Yes
☐ No
☐ Only sometimes

Do I prefer my hyperfocus activities and do not wish to prioritize sexuality?

☐ Yes
☐ No
☐ Only sometimes

My preferred sexual schedule to accommodate my hyperfocus includes:

_____
_____
_____
_____
_____

When I die, will I be happy with the choices I have made about how I am spending my time? Explain if yes or no:

_____
_____
_____
_____
_____

What is my plan to address the impact of hyperfocus on my life and my relationships?

_____
_____
_____
_____
_____

I am ADHD tired. I will address being ADHD tired by doing the following:

_____
_____
_____
_____
_____

To address being ADHD tired I can:

✓ Schedule monthly breaks
✓ Talk to a physical health professional to ensure that I am healthy and well
✓ Reduce my expectations of myself and others
✓ Consider that my hyperfocus may be having a negative impact on my health and wellbeing
✓ Schedule breaks to coincide with my menstrual cycle
✓ Ask for help

As an ADHD parent, I will do the following to balance my childcare responsibilities with my sexual needs:

☐ Try one new activity over the next month to increase balance
☐ Hire childcare for one hour in the next month to increase balance
☐ Trade with another parent for one hour in the next month to increase balance
☐ Talk to my partner about ways to increase our balance
☐ Focus on a mindfulness or calming activity to add more calm to the household
☐ Organize activities that will fulfill myself and my family members
☐ Plan short breaks for myself and/or my family to increase balance
☐ Practice gratitude daily to offer appreciation for my family

☐ Other: _____
☐ Other: _____
☐ Other: _____

Notes

1 While there is some debate about the use of the label "special interest", this concept is meant to describe the level of importance that the interest holds for someone. Perhaps Important and Awesome Interest would be a better term!

2 If you are finding that you are only thinking about sex, often seeking sex and/or if your hyperfocus is sex, Chapter 5 – What is going on right now? Transition problems! and Chapter 9 – What have I gotten myself into? Impulsivity, sex and ADHD both explore themes related specifically to hypersexuality.

3 My humble apologies to the YouTubers for whom screen time has moved their lives forward in very positive ways; however, for many of us, tech gets in the way of our daily goals, rather than enhancing them.

4 The length of holidays will vary with your personal situation, some people like many mini breaks throughout the year while others enjoy taking a full month off to reset. Do what feels right for you!

5 The struggles of parents who have ADHD is real! While this struggle is very pertinent to ADHDers, it is beyond this workbook to explore parenting and ADHD in much detail.

6 There is very little information about the impact of ADHD medications on pregnancy and breastfeeding (Jiang et al., 2019). Note that hormonal mood disorders such as post-partum depression are only now being explored in ADHD women (see Dorani et al., 2021, for more details).

7 If friends or family have concerns about the type of hyperfocus you are engaging in and find that it is a safety concern to yourself or others, take the time to discuss their concerns. You may find that discussions with a trusted mental health professional can help you navigate these situations thoughtfully.

References

Albulescu, P., Macsinga, I., Rusu, A., Sulea, C., Bodnaru, A. & Tulbure, B.T. (2022). "Give me a break!" A systematic review and meta-analysis on the efficacy of micro-breaks for increasing well-being and performance. *PloS One*, 17(8), e0272460–e0272460. https://doi.org/10.1371/journal.pone.0272460.

Biwer, F., Wiradhany, W., oude Egbrink, Mirjam, G.A. & Bruin, A.B.H. (2023). Understanding effort regulation: Comparing 'Pomodoro' breaks and self-regulated breaks. *British Journal of Educational Psychology*, 93(S2), 353–367. https://doi.org/10.1111/bjep.12593.

Dorani, F., Bijlenga, D., Beekman, A., van Someren, E., & Kooij, J. (2021). Prevalence of hormone-related mood disorder symptoms in women with ADHD. *Journal of psychiatric research*, 133, 10–15. https://doi.org/10.1016/j.jpsychires.2020.12.005.

Jiang, H., Zhang, X., Jiang, C. & Fu, H. (2019). Maternal and neonatal outcomes after exposure to ADHD medication during pregnancy: A systematic review and meta-analysis. *Pharmacoepidemiology and Drug Safety*, 28(3), 288–295. https://doi.org/10.1002/pds.4716.

Kooij, JJS (2018). Attention-Deficit Hyperactivity Disorder (ADHD), Intimate Relationships and Sexuality. In: Jannini E.A. & Siracusano, A. (Eds), *Sexual Dysfunctions in Mentally Ill Patients*. Cham: Springer International Publishing, pp. 75–82.

Largo-Wight, E., Wlyudka, P.S., Merten, J.W. & Cuvelier, E.A. (2017). Effectiveness and feasibility of a 10-minute employee stress intervention: Outdoor booster break. *Journal of Workplace Behavioral Health*, 32(3), 159–171. https://doi.org/10.1080/15555240.2017.1335211.

Sammonds, G.M., Mansfield, N.J. & Fray, M. (2017). Improving long term driving comfort by taking breaks – how break activity affects effectiveness. *Applied Ergonomics*, 65, 81–89. https://doi.org/10.1016/j.apergo.2017.05.008.

Chapter 7

What am I afraid of?

Anxiety and ADHD

Anxiety and ADHD often go together, and anxiety can negatively impact your sex life. Research identified a 25 percent comorbidity rate between ADHD and anxiety disorders (D'Agati et al., 2019). Other sources report an even higher rate of comorbid anxiety disorders for folks with ADHD (Adler et al., 2007). Some people experience anxiety on a daily basis and in multiple situations, while others feel anxiety more acutely during certain activities or events. Often people struggling with anxiety do not realize how much their anxiety is impacting their lives, their relationships and their sexuality.

Anxiety can be one reason why some people don't want sex. Exploring pleasure without knowing exactly how sexual activity will unfold can create anxiety. You may also have anxiety about how your body will perform and whether your sexual response will occur as you planned.

> Robbie is kind and joyful. He does not believe that he is anxious. Guys don't worry! Just be strong and do things without complaining, is how Robbie was taught to get through life. Robbie gets very distracted during sexual activity with a partner because he thinks about the state of his erections. He tends to avoid partnered sex because he worries that he won't obtain or maintain an erection. Robbie doesn't realize these thoughts are signs of anxiety.

There are many beliefs and thoughts about sex that will increase sexual anxiety. Identifying anxiety-producing thoughts and changing them by telling yourself a more helpful thought, is the first step to better managing feelings of anxiety. Other strategies to address anxiety, such as calming your body with the use of deep breathing, mindfulness or exercise, and other ways to create safety in your environment, will be addressed later in this chapter and are discussed in other areas of this workbook[1].

Anxiety is an emotion, and like all emotions, their role is to help us out. Anxiety tells us if there is a threat. It is an emotion necessary to our survival. We will explore your fears in this chapter and help you evaluate fearful situations in more helpful ways.

Let's explore and challenge some common thoughts that create anxiety in sexual situations!

DOI: 10.4324/9781003422372-8

"I won't know what to do" or "I will do the wrong thing"

Sex is play! By framing your sexuality as a time for play, it may be easier to find a more peaceful and fun way to engage sexually. Mechanical sex (a.k.a. repetitive and often boring sex) happens when sex is expected to follow certain rules and patterns (for example, what comes first, then second and then third). It can also happen when you want things done a certain way with very little flexibility (for example, "You must touch me in this exact way"). Sex that is overly predictable lacks fun, passion and spontaneity!

Challenge this belief with: "There is no right or wrong way to have sex; sex is supposed to be fun!"

This unhelpful thought applies to me:

☐ True
☐ False
☐ Sometimes, not always
☐ Does not apply (N/A)

I will replace this thought with a more helpful thought. My replacement thought will be:

_____

_____

_____

_____

_____

"I am not a good lover, I don't do things right" or "I will not satisfy a partner"

If you are concerned about what you know vs what you do not know about sex, have a frank conversation with a partner. Learn together! There are many resources that can be helpful where you can learn more about sexuality; however, there is no replacement for practice and exploring your sexual needs, either alone or with a partner.

Learning new skills can help resolve this anxiety! Communicate your interest to try new things. Some additional resources as noted in the Appendix of this workbook include: *Lesbian Sex Secrets for Men* (Goddard & Brungardt), OMG Yes website, *She Comes First* (Kerner), *Come As You Are* (Nagoski) and *Anal Pleasure & Health* (Morin). There are also specific apps that offer sexual information and sexual mindfulness exercises, such as the Kerly app.

Challenge this belief with: "I will learn some new tricks that a partner might enjoy!" or "I will communicate with a partner to see what they would like me to improve".

This unhelpful thought applies to me:

- ☐ True
- ☐ False
- ☐ Sometimes, not always
- ☐ Does not apply (N/A)

I will replace this thought with a more helpful thought. My replacement thought will be:

_____

_____

_____

_____

_____

"My mind will drift", "I will be thinking about other things" or "I will be bored"

Sexual desire is about sexual "wanting". We explored sexual intensity and sexual novelty in previous chapters to help improve your ability to notice and maintain your sexual interest[2]. Your mind drifting may simply indicate a lack of intensity or novelty; it is not necessarily reflective of your relationship or your interest in sex. If you are bored or worried about being bored, talk with a partner about ways to increase sexual intensity during sex. Communicate your interest in having fun together – I want to be interested in sex!

Challenge this belief with: "I can make sex interesting by talking openly with a partner about what is interesting to me" or "Honest communication can create space for more interesting sexual play!"

This unhelpful thought applies to me:

- ☐ True
- ☐ False
- ☐ Sometimes, not always
- ☐ Does not apply (N/A)

I will replace this thought with a more helpful thought. My replacement thought will be:

_____

_____

_____

_____

Body image

There are many concerns about body image that can create sexual anxiety. As we discussed in Chapter 4, ADHDers often present with concerns related to body image. Body image concerns can be exacerbated by being overweight, experiencing food issues and/or having a hyperfocus on a particular body part. Body focus concerns are common for people with ADHD and impact all genders (Van Eck, Morse & Flory, 2018; Bisset, Rinehart & Sciberras, 2019; Gowey et al., 2017). Eating disorders occur more frequently in people with ADHD (including obesity) (Young et al., 2020; Ravi & Khan, 2020). According to Nazar et al. (2016) there is a moderate association between ADHD and eating disorders. They found that the risk of ADHD individuals also having an eating disorder is increased three-fold and the risk of eating disordered individuals also having ADHD is increased two-fold. As such, your physical image and self-concept are essential aspects to explore when discussing your sex life.

ADHD bodies are human bodies! Not perfect, but perfectly acceptable. Ensuring that you have a good enough body is a common source of anxiety for many people. Getting stuck on your body image is one reason that people experience sexual anxiety. There are resources and mental health assistance to address problems specific to body image[3]. Seek additional support if body image concerns are significantly impacting your sexuality.

Let's tackle unhelpful thoughts about body image that can increase your feelings of anxiety!

"My body isn't good enough", "My body isn't perfect" or "I have physical flaws"

Finding acceptance from yourself and/or a partner is an important first step to addressing concerns about your body:

✓ Speak kindly to yourself about your body
✓ Focus on the parts of your body that you do love
✓ Validate body image concerns by talking openly with a partner about your concerns

Consider how this particular belief about your body is impacting you during sex:

Is it helpful to you? Yes _____ No _____

Does it help you achieve sexual comfort? Yes _____ No_____ Sometimes _____

Is this something that you can easily change? Yes _____ No _____

What benefit does holding onto this belief have for you?

_____

_____

_____

_____

_____

ADHD is related to having a history of self-harm; you may be carrying scars or body damage following self-harm behaviours in your youth or young adult years. These scars are a part of your history. They may help you remember the improvements you have made and the positive journey you have achieved establishing healthier coping strategies. If you are distracted by the scars from your past during sex, find ways to either accept them or budget for scar removal as soon as you can manage. ADHD consequences are part of being an ADHDer. Use self-compassion and self-love to move you towards self-acceptance!

If body concerns are impacting you during sex, talk openly with a partner about how this is changing the way that you engage during sex. If the concern creates issues for you and/or a partner, find ways to problem-solve to address the issue as a team.

✓ Communicate openly about how your body concerns impact you during sex

Ben is struggling as he does not like the moles on his back. When his partner touches his back, it is upsetting to him. Ben hasn't told his partner that this is happening. It distracts him and makes him less interested in sexual play. Ben decides to talk openly to his partner about this issue and see if they can find a solution to this problem together!

For partners: be respectful during these vulnerable discussions. Reassure your partner that their concerns are not dealbreakers for you – if they were dealbreakers, you wouldn't be with them! Remember that this issue is likely going to feel much bigger to your partner than it feels to you.

Review the list of things about your body that you liked from Chapter 4. Post the things that you love about your body somewhere that's visible to you. Continue to remind yourself of your strengths. Focus on self-acceptance.

Challenge this belief with: "My body is a human body", "My body is fine the way it is" or "I will find a partner that finds my body appealing".

This unhelpful thought applies to me:

☐ True
☐ False
☐ Sometimes, not always
☐ Does not apply (N/A)

I will replace this thought with a more helpful thought. My replacement thought will be:

_____

_____

_____

_____

_____

"My penis, my breasts or my vulva is too different (too small, wrong shape, not symmetrical, etc.)"

Many people struggle with the look of their labia/vulva, breasts or penis. When considering your beliefs about your body, it is important to remember that what might be distressing for you about your body, may not necessarily be problematic for others. Penis size and genital quirks (e.g. uneven labia or uneven breasts) are normal parts of a human body. For most people, non-symmetrical body parts are not dealbreakers.

You are human! We all have human bodies! We don't decide the look and size of our body parts. Genitals are all different. Our different shapes and sizes offer unique qualities to ourselves and to a partner.

A particular note about penis size: there are many different genital preferences. For most women, size doesn't offer significant differences in sensations. For some women, smaller is better and more comfortable; for other women, wider or longer may offer different sensations. You simply can't match everyone's preferences, whether it relates to the color of your hair, your height, your complexion or your penis. If you are struggling to find acceptance for your genitals the way they are, talk to a mental health professional for further assistance.

Challenge this belief with: "My body is unique to me!", "Everyone has quirks; my body is not meant to be perfect!" or "My penis works just fine and offers a unique experience, just like everybody else's".

This unhelpful thought applies to me:

☐ True
☐ False
☐ Sometimes, not always
☐ Does not apply (N/A)

I will replace this thought with a more helpful thought. My replacement thought will be:

_____

_____

_____

_____

"What if I smell?" or "What if my body leaks out something other than cum?"

Hygiene concerns can be a large source of sexual anxiety. There are realities that come with sex that are simply the result of being a person, not a machine. As a person, we have various types of fluids and gases that we expel, for example, urine, feces, snot, sweat and farts. These are a normal part of engaging with a human body.

It can be hard to accurately detect whether your body odors could be improved. Find ways to address your hygiene without making assumptions. Ask a partner or a trusted friend if there are any hygiene issues that you need to be aware of. Take the feedback seriously; if your deodorant or a certain hair product doesn't smell good on you, find something different.

At times, concerns about vaginal smells are communicated by a partner. Be open with yourself and your partner about vaginal odor. While it isn't an easy conversation, it will be more beneficial to discuss this together rather than continuing to experience an ongoing level of discomfort during sexual activity. If you are wondering about your vaginal odor, you can check your own scent by squatting and inserting your fingers into your vagina: what do you notice about your scent? Remember, it isn't supposed to smell like nothing, and it isn't supposed to smell like soap! It is your unique scent. What do you think?

If a partner does not identify an issue with your unique odor, drop the worry! If a partner loves the smell of your genitals, great! If you do have concerns about your odor, check with a health care professional to ensure that you don't have an undiagnosed vaginal or yeast infection that requires treatment.

Challenge this belief with: "Smells are normal and natural; I can drop the expectation that I smell like nothing" or "My partner does not identify any problems with my body, so my body is A-Ok!"

This unhelpful thought applies to me:

☐ True
☐ False
☐ Sometimes, not always
☐ Does not apply (N/A)

I will replace this thought with a more helpful thought. My replacement thought will be:

_____

_____

_____

_____

_____

Sexual problems

Difficulties with desire, erections, getting to orgasm, and sexual pain are all labeled sexual disorders. Sexual disorders can take a significant toll on a person's self-confidence. In research, it was found that ADHD was associated with several issues related to sexuality, including sexual function and ADHD, sexual dysfunctions and ADHD, and the sexual side effects of psychostimulants (Soldati, 2020). Some researchers feel that this relationship between ADHD and sexual problems is mediated by anxiety and depression rather than ADHD itself (Abdel-Hamid et al., 2021). Jabalkandi et al. (2019) indicated that males and females with ADHD had more sexual problems than non-ADHDers in all aspects of sexuality; for example, in biological females, there are difficulties with desire, arousal, orgasm, satisfaction, pain and lubrication. For biological males, it's difficulties with orgasm, erectile function, intercourse satisfaction and overall sexual satisfaction. According to Soldati (2020), several brain regions and systems involved in sexual functioning overlap with those found to be involved in ADHD which may explain the increased frequency of sexual problems for people with ADHD. Whatever the cause, ADHD and sexual problems can go together.

Let's explore in more detail the sexual anxieties that can occur as a result of sexual problems!

"I will ejaculate too fast"

Premature ejaculation (PE) can be quite common in ADHD populations. PE is typically occurring if you ejaculate within 30 seconds to one minute of genital stimulation, vaginal insertion and/or if you ejaculate without control. Soydan et al. (2013) reported that in their sample, 42.1 percent of premature ejaculation clients had ADHD – which was defined as ejaculating under a minute once vaginal intercourse began and found a cross section of inattentive (5.3 percent), hyperactive (10.5 percent) and combined (26.3 percent) presentations, with the combined group being more likely to have PE. Bijlenga et al. (2018) note a possible connection between the lack of ejaculatory control and the lack of impulse control in patients with ADHD. Our current knowledge about the ADHD brain doesn't allow us to offer an explanation as to why PE appears to be more prevalent in ADHD populations, but it is noteworthy (Soldati, 2020; Kalejaiye et al., 2017). Neurobiological explanations of this connection are only starting to be explored in earnest.

Practicing ejaculatory control, with the understanding that this may take you some time to master, owing to your ADHD, is key. One very helpful resource is a book by McCarthy & Metz (2004): *Coping with Premature Ejaculation: How to overcome PE, please your partner and have great sex*. This book can be a helpful tool in your efforts to address PE.

Additionally, mind-body connection is essential to managing your response to sexual pleasure and to gain genital control during sex. Switching sexual positions during sex as well as practicing mindfulness exercises on a regular basis can assist you to improve your mind-body connection when you are feeling aroused.

PE has also been related to low levels of Vitamin D as well as other chronic health conditions (Canat et al., 2019). Some medications are reported to improve PE. It is important to get your physical health evaluated as part of your efforts to resolve issues with PE. Discuss your concerns with a health care provider.

Tuckman (2019) indicated that the timing of ADHD medication didn't make a difference regarding people's sexual experiences. However, in theory, your ADHD medication should help you more easily notice your bodily sensations and, as a result, improve your ejaculatory control. There isn't research specifically looking at the question of ejaculatory control and ADHD medications. It may be worthwhile to experiment with the timing of your sexual play and your medication effectiveness to see if ADHD medication can help improve your ejaculatory control during sexual play. PE can be improved and resolved! Work with a sexual therapist to address PE and to gain more information about how you can improve your sexual control.

Challenge this belief with: "I can learn ejaculatory control" or "I will ask for help to resolve this problem and help myself feel more in control of my sexual experience".

This unhelpful thought applies to me:
- ☐ True
- ☐ False
- ☐ Sometimes, not always
- ☐ Does not apply (N/A)

I will replace this thought with a more helpful thought. My replacement thought will be:

_____
_____
_____
_____
_____

"I won't get an erection" or "I won't maintain an erection"

Erectile dysfunction, not being able to get or maintain an erection, is a common source of anxiety. As we have discussed, ADHD and sexual problems can occur together. Erectile problems aren't the end of the world! It impacts one aspect of your sexuality but there are other things that you can do.

Certain medications can create or maintain erectile dysfunction including, at times, ADHD medication. Straterra has been related to sexual problems in some studies (see Soldati, 2020; Adler et al., 2009 & 2006; Upadhyaya, 2015); however, this may or may not be a concern for you. As with all medication attempts, track to see how you respond to the medications that you are taking and make adjustments with the assistance of your health care professional and/or a pharmacist. Pharmacists can be great resources to discuss medication concerns!

Erectile dysfunction can occur for multiple reasons such as undiagnosed, untreated or uncontrolled medical conditions, medications used to treat other physical health conditions, mood disorders (for example, unmanaged depression or anxiety symptoms), relationship problems and/or traumatic incidents. Consult your health care provider, urologist and/or a pelvic floor specialist to explore ongoing problems related to your erections.

While medication is often recommended to resolve erectile issues, ED isn't always caused by physical health problems. Ensure that your psychological health, including the management of symptoms of anxiety, depression and/or traumatic experiences, as well as any relationship concerns, are addressed. Relationship concerns include feelings of anger, irritation, frustration and/or contempt for a sexual partner.

Erections aren't the only way to enjoy sexual touch, and they aren't required for sexual play. Sexual expectations can significantly impact your erections because expectations, either your expectations or your perceived expectations of others, will increase feelings of anxiety. Anxiety and erections don't go together! If you are suffering from sexual anxiety and it's impacting your erections, manage your overall levels of anxiety.

Dealing with ED is best done with the help and support of a partner. If you are in a relationship, ask your partner to work with you to address these concerns. There are useful workbooks to help you address ED such as the book by Metz & McCarthy (2004): _Coping with Erectile Dysfunction: How to regain confidence and enjoy great sex_. This book can be very helpful to explore your symptoms of ED in more detail.

Challenge this belief with: "I am not defined by whether or not I can get an erection" or "There are lots of things that I can do to please a partner without an erection" and "I will ask for help to sort out my physical health needs but, in the meantime, I can still enjoy sexual play!".

This unhelpful thought applies to me:

□ True
□ False
□ Sometimes, not always
□ Does not apply (N/A)

I will replace this thought with a more helpful thought. My replacement thought will be:

_____

_____

_____

_____

_____

"It will go on forever!", "I won't have an orgasm" or "My body won't respond like it should!"

Orgasm problems for people of all genders create significant anxiety. For biological males, ejaculatory issues tend to create significant anxiety and distress. Concerns about not coming, coming too fast or having no control while coming are common. For biological females, not achieving orgasm can also create anxiety. For both men and women with ADHD, achieving orgasm can be difficult!

When one partner takes longer to achieve orgasm, it can feel like sex becomes a long production.

✓ Take the time to enjoy each other
✓ Drop the expectation that sex must end with orgasm or ejaculation
✓ When sex creates anxiety rather than pleasure, stop and transition to another activity
✓ Remember that you can always return to sexual play at another time
✓ Consider whether your sexual play has enough intensity to achieve orgasm
✓ Rule out any medication concerns that may be contributing to this problem

Building a sexual fire of arousal is an important skill. At times, ejaculatory latency can occur when the sexual intensity isn't there.

What are you willing to try to create sexual intensity during solo sex and partnered sex?

_____

_____

_____

_____

Challenge this belief with: "Sex doesn't need to end with an orgasm" or "I can stop even if I haven't ejaculated; experiencing pleasure doesn't require an orgasm".

This unhelpful thought applies to me:

☐ True
☐ False
☐ Sometimes, not always
☐ Does not apply (N/A)

I will replace this thought with a more helpful thought. My replacement thought will be:

_____

_____

_____

_____

_____

"It will hurt"

Pain creates significant anxiety for individuals who have experienced sexual pain during sexual activity. If you are in pain, you can't be in play[4]!

ADHD is more common in populations of children, teens and adults with chronic pain compared to those without chronic pain and in populations at increased risk of inflammatory disease (e.g. asthma, eczema) (Nirouei et al., 2023; Kerekes et al., 2022). ADHD folks may be more represented in people with fibromyalgia, endometriosis and chronic fatigue syndrome (Gao et al., 2020; Karaş et al., 2020; Young, 2020)[5]. In addition, as noted by Jabalkandi et al. (2020) ADHD women reported more problems with sexual pain.

Pain is tricky; it can have a biological cause and it can also occur, as a result of having a sensitive "alarm system" in your brain. In theory, hyperfocus could trigger that alarm. Theories about the ADHD brain and its tendency to be overly sensitive to pain or under sensitive to pain are starting to emerge (Kerekes, 2022). Regardless of the cause, you must address pain. Don't try to grit your teeth and ignore the pain. Simply struggling through the pain won't work and it will make things worse.

Pain can also occur when there is an undiagnosed medical problem at play. Penile pain can occur with unrecognized diabetes or structural issues such as Peyronie's Disease. Penile pain should always be taken seriously. Consult your health care provider if you are experiencing penile pain.

✓ Painful sex is a problem – stop if you are experiencing pain!
✓ Do not try to push through sexual pain

Address pain by doing this:

✓ Consult a sexual therapist specialized in sexual pain
✓ Consult a pelvic floor physiotherapist
✓ Consult a gynecologist/urologist that specializes in sexual pain
✓ Consult your health care provider
✓ Work through specific workbooks and search for professional services aimed at addressing sexual pain[6]

Identify when the pain worsens and notice if/when it tends to get better. Track the patterns to help health care professionals assist you to resolve the underlying issue(s) at play.

Challenge this belief with: "I can do other things that do not cause me pain" or "I will ask for help and sort this out!"

This unhelpful thought applies to me:

□ True
□ False
□ Sometimes, not always
□ Does not apply (N/A)

I will replace this thought with a more helpful thought. My replacement thought will be:

_____

_____

_____

_____

_____

"I can't be spontaneous because I need my medication"

Medications to address sexual issues have gained tremendously in popularity. The upside can be an increased confidence in your sexual response, but the downside can be continued anxiety about sex. Remember that sex can be fun regardless of whether you have an erection.

If you do use medications to facilitate your sexual response, find ways to create some spontaneity despite your medication use. Perhaps you can bring your medication with you and take it earlier in the day or perhaps you can schedule times for sexual play without informing a partner ahead of time that you have a schedule in mind. Get creative about how you can flirt, increase sexual intensity, and engage in sexual conversations with a partner when you are waiting for the medication to kick in. This will likely increase medication effectiveness and be more fun!

Challenge this belief with: "Sometimes we can have sex with medication but other times, I can be spontaneous and have fun without worrying about whether or not I have an erection" or "I can take my medication ahead of time and create sexy fun time while I am waiting".

This unhelpful thought applies to me:

☐ True
☐ False
☐ Sometimes, not always
☐ Does not apply (N/A)

I will replace this thought with a more helpful thought. My replacement thought will be:

_____

_____

_____

_____

_____

_____

_____

_____

_____

_____

"Without an erection, there is no point to sex" or "Without intercourse, there is no point to sex"

Whether intercourse is required or not depends on how you view sexuality. There are many ways to engage sexually. The more flexible your thinking becomes about sex, the more playful your sexuality will be. Relying on intercourse as your only source of sexual pleasure can limit you, particularly if you do not have a partner, if your partner is not available or if your partner's body is not responding the way you would like it to respond. People of all genders can get stuck in this unhelpful thought about sex.

Challenge this unhelpful thought with: "Sex is fun with or without intercourse!" or "Pleasure is experienced in many ways; I will focus on the ways that I find pleasure"!

This unhelpful thought applies to me:

☐ True
☐ False
☐ Sometimes, not always
☐ Does not apply (N/A)

I will replace this thought with a more helpful thought. My replacement thought will be:

_____

_____

_____

_____

_____

Other issues that can create sexual anxiety

There are other issues that can create sexual anxiety, such as problems with self-esteem and self-confidence, concerns with sexual orientation or sexual interests, and a history of sexual trauma. Difficulties in your relationships, problems with your self-concept as well as past traumatic sexual experiences can all impact your comfort in sexual situations[7]. Address the other issues that are impacting your life!

- ☞ Relationship conflicts, attachment disorders, and childhood trauma can all negatively impact your relationships and, subsequently, your sexual functioning
- ☞ Address these underlying concerns with a qualified mental health professional

"I am not loveable; no one will want me"

Attachment problems can create systemic problems in your relationships, including:

✓ Increased conflicts
✓ Loss of trust
✓ Lowered self-confidence
✓ Feeling disconnected
✓ Loss of desire
✓ Feelings of anger and resentment

Increased conflict that arises owing to difficulties with attachment in relationships can create sexual problems. These problems won't simply disappear by addressing your ADHD or your sexuality. Consult a qualified mental health professional to explore issues related to attachment and how these issues may be impacting your relationships and your sexuality!

Challenge this belief with: "I can change and adjust with additional support and self-compassion" or "I will ask for help to address issues related to my feelings of shame".

This unhelpful thought applies to me:

☐ True
☐ False
☐ Sometimes, not always
☐ Does not apply (N/A)

I will replace this thought with a more helpful thought. My replacement thought will be:

_____

_____

_____

_____

_____

"I will be rejected if I initiate sexual play!" or "I am afraid that I will be rejected!"

Rejection sensitivity is a concept that is often discussed in ADHD communities. Fear of rejection is a significant concern for many neurodivergent people. Fear of rejection can keep you stuck and can lead you to avoid partnered sexual activities.

✓ Improve your efforts to manage your emotions
✓ Journal to create reflection time before you react
✓ Increase your mind-body connection with mindfulness/meditation
✓ Exercise daily
✓ Practice positive self-talk
✓ Track your feelings carefully (Right now I feel….)
✓ Use the "How seated am I in my body" scale from chapter 4 to help identify feelings of distress
✓ Practice deep breathing
✓ Use calming scents or essential oils
✓ Objects can serve as reminders such as a special crystal, bracelet, ring or any other meaningful reminders to cue your use of calming skills in the moment
✓ Surround yourself with positive people and community supports
✓ Talk candidly with friends and family about your feelings

Challenge this thought with: "I can manage uncomfortable emotions", "I can take a risk; this partner has my best interests at heart" or "Just because I am told 'no' or 'maybe later', this is not a rejection of me".

This unhelpful thought applies to me:

☐ True
☐ False
☐ Sometimes, not always
☐ Does not apply (N/A)

I will replace this thought with a more helpful thought. My replacement thought will be:

_____

_____

_____

_____

_____

"I am single so there is no point to having sex with myself, developing my sexuality or masturbating"

Sexual engagement is a choice. You can choose what you want or don't want to do. You get to choose how much you want to explore sexual pleasure, regardless of whether you are in a relationship. Developing your sexuality can happen whether or not you have a partner. Your sexuality is yours! It is a part of yourself that you can explore and engage with regardless of your relationship status. It is yours to develop.

There are some benefits to engaging sexually with yourself, whether or not you have a partner:

✓ You will get to know yourself and your body
✓ You will enjoy and experience pleasure
✓ You will engage positively with your body
✓ You will develop sexual experiences that can be shared with a future partner
✓ You will develop sexual knowledge that can be shared with a future partner
✓ You can explore your fantasy world
✓ You can explore play toys and find the one that works best for you
✓ You are creating time to engage in your self-care

Challenge this belief with: "My sexuality is a part of me; it does not depend on my relationship status" or "I am exploring my sexuality for me!"

This unhelpful thought applies to me:

□ True
□ False
□ Sometimes, not always
□ Does not apply (N/A)

I will replace this thought with a more helpful thought. My replacement thought will be:

_____

_____

_____

_____

_____

"I can't say what I am actually sexually interested in; it's taboo!"

The fear that you are interested in something sexual that is not ok, that isn't acceptable, that is somehow problematic or that would not be approved of by your family and friends can create significant and ongoing anxiety. Not wanting to admit to being gay, straight, bi, pan or trans can really impact a person's comfort level with their sexuality.

We don't know why people have certain sexual interests, but we do know that sexual arousal is not something that most people have chosen; they simply have a sexual preference that emerges before or during puberty. If you are struggling with your sexual interests and do not want to admit these to yourself or to others, it is time to talk with a sexual therapist.

Challenge this belief with: "I didn't choose this sexual interest, but it is a part of me. I will ask for help if I can't accept or safely manage my sexual preferences".

This unhelpful thought applies to me:

☐ True
☐ False
☐ Sometimes, not always
☐ Does not apply (N/A)

I will replace this thought with a more helpful thought. My replacement thought will be:

_____

_____

_____

_____

_____

"I don't like feeling uncomfortable emotions, so I will use sex to feel better!"

Some people use sex to feel better when they are anxious or experiencing other emotions such as stress, loneliness, anger, sadness, etc. Using sex to cope with negative emotions, such as stress and tension, may be more frequent in ADHD populations (Soldati, 2021). Managing your emotions, whether it's anxiety, depression or anger, is an important step to engaging more positively with sex. When you use sex to feel better or to manage emotions other than sexual arousal, partners typically will notice and you may receive negative feedback about how you engage sexually with a partner. This is an indication that you may need some assistance to appropriately resolve this issue.

Challenge this belief with: "I will learn to manage my emotions without relying on my sexuality" or "I can handle it! I don't need to use sex to make myself feel better".

This unhelpful thought applies to me:

☐ True
☐ False
☐ Sometimes, not always
☐ Does not apply (N/A)

I will replace this thought with a more helpful thought. My replacement thought will be:

_____

_____

_____

_____

_____

"I need to control how this goes"

Many people with ADHD will use control to mask attention problems. If you control things, you may believe that you won't make mistakes. While that might be true, applying this theory to sex can leave you feeling stuck.

Sexual expectations create anxiety. If you expect that sex MUST go a certain way it will create expectations which will likely increase your anxiety, particularly in situations where things are not going to plan. Rather than giving your fears traction, be curious, ask yourself questions and communicate the problem to others!

✓ Address your fears with information and communication!

How do you feel when you challenge yourself to let go of sexual expectations?

_____
_____
_____
_____
_____

Challenge this belief with: "I can let go; I am safe."

This unhelpful thought applies to me:

□ True
□ False
□ Sometimes, not always
□ Does not apply (N/A)

I will replace this thought with a more helpful thought. My replacement thought will be:

_____
_____
_____
_____

"It will all be too much for me!"

When you are experiencing too much stimulation, sexual interactions can become overwhelming. Too many expectations, demands, sensations and complications can create feelings of overwhelm. Increased sexual intensity can lead to interactions that feel too big, with negative feelings developing as a result.

Too much stimulation can halt desire. It can lead to feeling like sex isn't fun anymore. It's the equivalent of enjoying a smooth canoe paddle on a lake but not enjoying a canoe paddle down a set of rapids that are full of rocks and hazards. Too much stim can create anxiety!

How much is too much? What sexual situations create too much stim for you?

_____

_____

_____

_____

_____

Too much stim means that you are going too fast! When this happens:

✓ Talk to your partner
✓ Slow things down
✓ Discuss expectations
✓ Create a comfortable environment
✓ Dim lights
✓ Reduce sensory stimulations
✓ Ensure that you have provided your clear consent

Challenge this belief with: "I have choice; I can speak with my partner and slow things down"

This unhelpful thought applies to me:

□ True
□ False
□ Sometimes, not always
□ Does not apply (N/A)

I will replace this thought with a more helpful thought. My replacement thought will be:

_____

_____

_____

_____

_____

"What if…" thinking patterns

"What If" thinking can increase fear of new situations. "What if" thinking patterns are a hallmark of anxiety. If you have this habit, you are worrying about potential problems that haven't even occurred yet! As good sex tends to change, grow, evolve, shift and surprise you, being concerned about "what if" can be particularly detrimental in sexual situations.

Fanny is concerned about exploring sexual transitions. She is interested in making sex a bigger priority in her life. Despite this goal, Fanny is very worried about how a partner might respond to her attempts. She wants to try new things but has no idea how they will be received. The anxiety has her in a holding pattern, wanting to change her sexuality, but being too afraid of what might happen when she tries something new.

What thoughts are keeping Fanny stuck?

_____
_____
_____
_____
_____

What would be a more helpful thought for Fanny to remember?

_____
_____
_____
_____
_____

What would you suggest Fanny do?

_____
_____
_____
_____

Communication is one way to reduce anxiety. Knowing what will be happening as well as the general guidelines that we have agreed on, can help. It can help to know the plan. Building trust comes from being with partners that will stick to the plan.

✓ Talk about sex! Individuals and couples who talk more about sex tend to have better sex lives
✓ Communicate clearly about sex; share fantasies as well as likes and dislikes with your partner
✓ Have meetings with a partner to discuss what is going well and what could be improved in your sex life together
✓ Create sexual plans that work for both of you
✓ Allow for spontaneity in the sexual plan if that is important for you or a partner
✓ Manage your ADHD! Put in the effort to appropriately manage your ADHD symptoms

Good sexual skills matter! These can be honed by reading or learning more about sexuality, watching a partner masturbate and asking questions about what they like and dislike as well as exploring new skills that may interest you. To overcome "what if" thinking and fears about the unknown, set yourself up for success!

✓ Take calculated risks
✓ Start small and work your way up
✓ Challenge unhelpful thoughts with more realistic thoughts
✓ Remember the context; this isn't life or death – it's simply sex
✓ Talk to a partner about your goals, what you would like to try and communicate your intentions ahead of time
✓ Find safe partners with whom to try new activities
✓ Ensure that people in your life have good intentions

Sexual validation is another important way to address anxiety in sexual situations. Sexual validation means that you are telling your partner what they are doing well in their sexual efforts. Take time to highlight the good things – things that are going well!

✓ Give your partner cues that they are doing well
✓ Express what you like
✓ Moan, makes encouraging noises to indicate what you like
✓ Move your body to indicate what you are enjoying
✓ Tell a partner what you really enjoyed after sexual play
✓ Leave criticisms and suggestions for another day when you can talk more openly about what is going well and things you might want to adjust in your sexual play

Give your partner clear clues about what you would like and don't assume that they will figure it out without being told! Owning your sexuality and your choice to engage in sex means that you are open to sharing what you want and what you don't want, what your sexual thoughts include and what is fun for you! Give your partner feedback with a focus on sexual validation. Voice words of appreciation to your partner on a regular basis!

I appreciate the following as it pertains to solo sex:

_____

_____

_____

_____

_____

I appreciate the following as it pertains to sex with a partner:

_____

_____

_____

_____

_____

Addressing your overall anxiety, in particular, your anxiety about sex is one way to start creating a space for sexual pleasure in your life!

Bobby was very nervous about sexual play with a new partner. Bobby worried that it wouldn't go to plan, that their partner would be upset with something that was said and that they would not be able to find sexual pleasure, owing to their anxiety. Bobby was freaking out! Throughout the evening, Bobby's anxiety continued to rise. When asked if everything was ok, Bobby lied and said that it was all fine. Eventually, Bobby's anxiety escalated to the point that Bobby could not breathe. Bobby started to sweat profusely. Their partner stopped and questioned what was happening. Bobby bolted, hiding in the bathroom until they were able to catch their breath. Bobby left the bathroom and then quickly left the situation, saying nothing. Bobby felt bad and was very embarrassed. Bobby's date was a very nice person and did not understand what happened.

If you were Bobby what would you do?

✓ Communicate about your level of anxiety ahead of time
✓ Create a plan to manage escalating feelings of anxiety
✓ Stop, take a break from sexual play, and do something else that creates less distress
✓ Don't ignore rising feelings of anxiety; heed the alarm and ask yourself what you need in that moment
✓ Find balance in exploring new situations from a perspective of safety and fun
✓ Engage with a deep breathing or mindfulness app
✓ Ask for help from a mental health professional

Focus on the elements of transition that help create comfort and safety. Allow for enough intensity to keep sex interesting for you. Once you can maintain your attention during sex, sexual play will likely become less anxiety-provoking and more fun!

"I just don't want to have sex"

There are some ADHDers that don't like sex. They will avoid sex, don't want to engage in sex, don't experience desire for sex and would prefer not having sex. Sexual aversion means that you avoid sex, sexual touching, and the idea of having sex is unpleasant to you. Research indicates that ADHD males reported higher levels of sexual aversion and having little desire for sexual contact than non-ADHD males and ADHD females reported more sexual aversion than neurotypical females (Bijlenga et al., 2018). We don't often discuss the fact that ADHD <u>males and females</u> can experience sexual aversion more often than neurotypical folks.

☛ What if I am asexual?
☛ What if I don't want sex?
☛ What if I only want sex within a particular sexual routine or framework?

How has sexual aversion impacted you?

_____

_____

_____

_____

_____

There are many reasons why some people may want to avoid sex. We have talked about hyperfocus, transition problems, sexual problems and pain as some reasons why sex may not be attractive to you. We will discuss sensory concerns, relationship concerns and trauma in upcoming chapters, as these may be other reasons why you might be experiencing a lack of interest in sex. Sometimes, people avoid their sexuality because they feel anxious about sex.

If you identify a link between your anxiety and your lack of sexual interest, addressing anxiety and particularly anxiety about sex is one way to start creating space for sexual pleasure in your life. A great resource to explore anxiety management in detail is Dr. E. Bourne's *Anxiety and Phobia Workbook*, 7th edition (2020). The book *Anchored* by D. Dana (2021) is also very good and aimed at helping you understand how to reduce feelings of tension and anxiety in your body. Self-help books such as those written by Pittman (2015 & 2022) as well as strategies specific to emotional first aid can be helpful resources to help you in your anxiety management journey. There are many resources available online to help you practice deep breathing; one example is Calm with Kyle. In addition, working with a mental health professional to address anxiety can be an important step to improving your sex life!

Solutions for anxiety include:

✓ Deep breathing
✓ Daily exercise
✓ Mindfulness or meditation daily
✓ Challenging anxiety producing thoughts
✓ Positive affirmations
✓ Gratitude
✓ Staying in the present rather than focusing on the past or the future
✓ Remembering your gifts
✓ Planning for success
✓ Essential oils or calming scents to soothe you and encourage you to take a deep breath
✓ Learning various anxiety management strategies
✓ Joining a support group to explore effective anxiety management strategies with others
✓ Seeking additional assistance from a mental health professional

---

Don't forget: Ensure that your ADHD symptoms are being addressed properly!

Biological females and the impact of PMDD on sexual functioning

As discussed in Chapter 1, biological females have specific needs as it relates to ADHD and mood. Premenstrual Dysphoric Disorder (PMDD) is more common in women with ADHD and Autism (Dorani, 2021). PMDD is triggered by hormone changes, which can lead to increased ADHD symptoms (Dorani, 2023). In addition, ADHD medications don't appear to be as effective during these monthly hormone changes.

In females with ADHD, this monthly change can interrupt sexual interest, sexual urges and increase conflicts in relationships, which then can lead to a decrease in sexual satisfaction. There is a moderate association between having PMDD and experiencing postpartum depression after childbirth (Dorani, 2021). In addition, ADHD women report more menopausal and perimenopausal symptoms (Dorani, 2021). Whether you are struggling with postpartum depression or peri-menopausal/menopausal symptoms, consider that you are experiencing hormone-based mood changes. In fact, in recent research, women who have ADHD reported experiencing a two- to three-fold increase in frequency and severity of mood changes during every episode of hormonal change (Dorani, 2021). ADHD women present with unique challenges owing to the impact of hormonal fluctuations on ADHD symptoms (Eng et al., 2024).

Consider the impact of these hormonal mood changes on your sexual play!

✓ You may need to adjust the timing of your sex play to work around hormonal changes
✓ Consider having sex more frequently prior to your premenstrual window
✓ Discuss contraception options with your health care provider that consider the impact of hormonal changes on ADHD symptoms
✓ Use barrier methods of contraception to mitigate pregnancy risk
✓ Communicate clearly about the impact of your hormones on your mood and sexual needs

For Partners: Get curious about your female partner's hormone cycles! Know when their hormones will shift. This can reduce conflicts in the relationship and add compassion to interactions that are more difficult during times of hormonal changes, such as after childbirth, during perimenopause/menopause and during pre-menstrual periods.

> The upside to tracking your partner's menstrual cycle is that you will also know when they are raring to go!

- ☞ Track your PMS cycle (track it yourself with a calendar or use a period app tracker to help you!)
- ☞ If you don't have a menstrual cycle, track your mood to see if there are any patterns that emerge
- ☞ Ask your partner to track your cycle in addition to your own menstrual tracking
- ☞ Additional ADHD medication may be prescribed by your health care provider during hormonal fluctuations to improve your ADHD symptom management
- ☞ Be curious about mood shifts as it relates to your menstrual cycle
- ☞ Be aware that puberty, postpartum and perimenopause/menopause are significantly challenging periods for ADHD women

Medications and sexual functioning

Medication can impact your sexuality. If you are managing your symptoms of anxiety with medication, ensure that this medication does not increase your sexual problems. Review your medications with your physician or with your pharmacist if you are struggling with your sexuality. If your sexual problems began after a medication trial, consult with your physician or your pharmacist to explore alternative options.

- ✓ Talk to your health care providers about the impact of your prescribed medications on your sexuality and your overall health!

What can I do to fix this?

So, what to do in order to address sexual problems when you have ADHD?

- ☞ Maintain and optimize ADHD medication! Medical treatment for ADHD may positively impact sexual functioning (Abdel-Hamid et al., 2021).
  - ✓ Proper diagnosis matters – get diagnosed if you don't have a clear diagnosis
  - ✓ Proper treatment matters – use meds + skills to address your ADHD properly
  - ✓ Skills matter – create the right skill set to address both ADHD and sexual problems
  - ✓ Ensure that you are taking care of your body to address any medical health concerns that may be impacting your sexuality and/or your anxiety levels[8]

☞ Practice new sexual skills!
- ✓ Focus on sexual intensity and sexual transitions
- ✓ Create intensity to obtain and maintain sexual arousal
- ✓ Reduce distractions
- ✓ Communicate what you actually like and want sexually (e.g. threesomes, blowjobs, fantasy role play, dress up – whatever floats your boat!)
- ✓ Ensure sexual novelty
- ✓ Practice being seated in your body to better experience sexual pleasure
- ✓ Practice mindfulness to better anticipate orgasm
- ✓ Improve your sexual skills with practice
- ✓ Consult a local sexual therapist
- ✓ Consult a therapist that knows ADHD and can offer solutions that are tailored to your needs

☞ Manage your overall level of anxiety
- ✓ Deep breathing
- ✓ Daily exercise
- ✓ Mindfulness or meditation daily
- ✓ Identify and change anxiety producing thoughts
- ✓ Positive affirmations
- ✓ Gratitude
- ✓ Stay in the present rather than focusing on the past or future
- ✓ Remember your gifts
- ✓ Plan for success
- ✓ Learn effective anxiety management skills
- ✓ Practice anxiety management skills daily

☞ Ask for help
- ✓ Consult workbooks and self-help books specific to anxiety management
- ✓ Talk to friends or family to obtain more support in applying your anxiety management skills
- ✓ Use a checklist or a journal entry to explore and slow down your anxious feelings
- ✓ Remind yourself daily to apply your skills
- ✓ Seek additional assistance from a mental health professional

There are many reasons why anxiety might be a struggle for you! Learn strategies to manage anxiety. Ensure that there are no underlying physical health concerns and that you are physically healthy, exercise daily and practice deep breathing to calm your body. Focus on maintaining more helpful thoughts rather than anxiety producing thoughts. In addition, it can be helpful to challenge your personal beliefs about the level of safety that you experience in the world and with others. Exploring your personal beliefs about your level of safety in the world can help identify some core beliefs that are getting in your way.

Do I feel safe in the world?

☐   Yes
☐   No
☐   Sometimes

Are others trustworthy?

☐   Yes
☐   No
☐   Sometimes

Can I engage in the world with safety?

☐   Yes
☐   No
☐   Sometimes

What do I need to feel safe in the world?

_____

_____

_____

_____

_____

Creating a positive worldview, a sense of safety and a sense of trust in others can help you manage anxiety in more thoughtful ways. Consult a qualified mental health professional to assist you to explore your worldview, with a goal to decrease your feelings of anxiety and increase your feelings of safety.

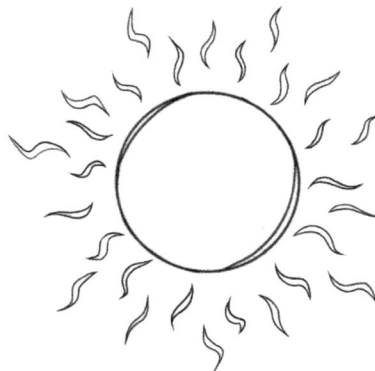

It can be very difficult to admit that you have struggles with your sexuality. You are doing great! Continue to practice your skills, add positive daily habits to better manage feelings of anxiety, and ask for help if you need it.

Let's continue our exploration of factors which may be having an impact on your sexuality!

Working towards my goals

I am afraid! Anxiety is the feeling of fear. Fear is simply one feeling amongst all the other feelings.

✓   I will identify when I am feeling afraid
✓   I will address my fear by identifying it and creating a plan to deal with my fear based on self-compassion, self-kindness and self-love
✓   I will use gratitude to focus on the positives and improve my level of self-acceptance

I have identified the following sexual anxieties:

☐   I am afraid – I won't know what to do or I will do the wrong thing
☐   I am afraid – I am not a good lover; I won't do things right/ I will not satisfy a partner
☐   I am afraid – My mind will drift; I will be thinking about other things, or I will be bored
☐   I am afraid – My body isn't good enough, it isn't perfect; I have physical flaws
☐   I am afraid – My penis, my breasts or my vulva is too different (too small, wrong shape, not symmetrical, etc.)
☐   I am afraid – What if I smell? or What if my body leaks out something other than cum?
☐   I am afraid – I will ejaculate too fast
☐   I am afraid – I won't get or maintain an erection
☐   I am afraid –It will go on forever; I won't have an orgasm, or my body won't respond like it should
☐   I am afraid – It will hurt
☐   I am afraid – I can't be spontaneous because I need my medication
☐   I am afraid – Without an erection or intercourse there is no point to sex
☐   I am afraid – I am not loveable; no one will want me
☐   I am afraid – I will be rejected if I initiate sexual play/I am afraid that I will be rejected
☐   I am afraid – I am single, so there is no point to having sex with myself or developing my sexuality or masturbating
☐   I am afraid – I can't admit to what I like sexually – it's taboo!
☐   I am afraid – I don't like feeling uncomfortable emotions, so I will use sex to feel better!
☐   I am afraid – I need to control how this goes
☐   I am afraid – It will be too much for me!
☐   I am afraid – What if...
☐   I am afraid – So, I just don't want to have sex
☐   Other: _____
☐   Other: _____
☐   Other: _____
☐   Other: _____
☐   Other: _____

I will challenge these sexual anxieties by remembering the following:

_____

_____

_____

_____

✓   I will focus on gratitude by giving attention to the things that I appreciate.
✓   I will use gratitude daily to improve my level of self-acceptance

When I feel afraid, I will remember these things that I love about my body and my sexuality:

_____

_____

_____

_____

I will address my sexual anxieties by doing the following two (2) things to make my life better:

_____

_____

_____

_____

and:

_____

_____

_____

_____

If my sexual anxieties do not improve, I will commit to the following plan:

I will consult with a mental health professional to address my sexual anxieties:

☐   Yes
☐   No

I will consult with a physical health professional to address my sexual anxieties:

☐   Yes
☐   No

I will talk to a friend or safe mentor about my sexual anxieties:

☐ Yes
☐ No

My plan to address my anxiety includes:

_____

_____

_____

_____

_____

Notes

1 To calm your body, see Chapter 4 – What is that feeling? Being in your body to achieve sexual pleasure. In order to ensure that your sexual environment is safe, see Chapter 11 – Neurodivergent Safety: The importance of Sexual and Relationship Safety.
2 Review strategies to address sexual interest in Chapter 5 – What is going on right now? Transition problems! and Chapter 6 – I'm busy! Hyperfocus and pleasure.
3 The book by Dr. Hillary McBride, The Wisdom of Your Body: Finding healing, wholeness and connection through embodied living; can be a helpful resource to explore your relationship with your body in more detail.
4 When discussing sexual pain, we are not talking about consensual activities that may create playful pain, such as BDSM play.
5 There are specific services, apps and workbooks targeting chronic pain. For example, Curable app; Caudill & Herbert (2016) Managing Pain Before It Manages You and Gordon (2020) The Way Out.
6 Ensure that the help you are receiving is specialized to sexual pain. Goldstein et al. (2023) When Sex Hurts is one resource that may be helpful to you.
7 We will discuss sexual trauma in more detail in Chapter 11 – Neurodivergent Safety: The importance of Sexual and Relationship Safety, and we will explore relationship concerns in Chapter 10 – Intimacy… Yikes!
8 Some medical issues can create feelings of anxiety. Talk to a health care professional to rule out physical health disorders which may be impacting your level of anxiety.

References

Abdel-Hamid, M., Basilowski, M., Schönfeld, B, Bartels, C. et al. (2021). Sexual dysfunction in patients with adult attention deficit hyperactivity disorder: A pilot study. The Canadian Journal of Human Sexuality, 30(1), 106–113. https://doi.org/10.3138/cjhs.2020-0036.
Adler, L.A., Barkley, R.A., Newcorn, J.H., Spencer, T.J. & Weiss, M.D. (2007). Managing ADHD in children, adolescents, and adults with comorbid anxiety. The Journal of Clinical Psychiatry, 68(3), 451. https://doi.org/10.4088/jcp.v68n0316.
Adler, L.A., Dietrich, A., Reimherr, F.W. et al. (2006). Safety and tolerability of once versus twice daily atomoxetine in adults with ADHD. Annals of Clinical Psychiatry, 18, 107–113.

Adler, L.A., Spencer, T., Brown, T.E. et al. (2009). Once-daily atomoxetine for adult attention-deficit/ hyperactivity disorder: a 6-month, double-blind trial. *Journal of Clinical Psychopharmacology*, 29, 44–50.

Bijlenga, D., Vroege, J.A., Stammen, A.J.M., van der Rhee K & Kooij, J.J.S. (2018). Prevalence of sexual dysfunctions and other sexual disorders in adults with attention-deficit/hyperactivity disorder compared to the general population. *ADHD Attention Deficit Hyperactivity Disorder*, 10, 87–96.

Bisset, M., Rinehart, N. & Sciberras, E. (2019). Body dissatisfaction and weight control behaviour in children with ADHD: A population-based study. *European Child & Adolescent Psychiatry*, 28(11), 1507–1516. https://doi.org/10.1007/s00787-019-01314-8.

Bourne, E.J. (2020). *The Anxiety and Phobia Workbook* (7th ed.), New Harbinger Publications.

Brotto, L.A. (2018). *Better Sex Through Mindfulness: How Women can cultivate desire*. Vancouver, BC: Greystone Books.

Canat, L., Degirmentepe, R.B., Atalay, H.A., Çakir, S.S., Alkan, I., Çulha, M.G., Ozbir, S. & Canat, M. (2019). Low serum vitamin D is associated with an increased likelihood of acquired premature ejaculation. *International braz j urol: official journal of the Brazilian Society of Urology*, 45(3), 621–628. https://doi.org/10.1590/S1677-5538.IBJU.2018.0887.

Caudill, M. & Herbert, B. (2016). *Managing pain before it manages you*. New York: The Guilford Press.

D'Agati, E., Curatolo, P. & Mazzone, L. (2019). Comorbidity between ADHD and anxiety disorders across the lifespan International. *Journal of Psychiatry in Clinical Practice*, 23, 4, 238–244. doi:10.1080/13651501.2019.1628277.

Dana, D. (2021). *Anchored: How to befriend your nervous system using polyvagal theory*. Boulder, CO: Sounds True.

Dorani, F., Bijlenga, D., Beekman, A., van Someren, E. & Kooij, J. (2021). Prevalence of hormone-related mood disorder symptoms in women with ADHD. *Journal of psychiatric research*, *133*, 10–15. https://doi.org/10.1016/j.jpsychires.2020.12.005.

Eng, A.G., Nirjar, U., Elkins, A.R., Sizemore, Y. J., Monticello, .K.N., Petersen, M.K., Miller, S.A., Barone, J., Eisenlohr-Moul, T.A. and Martel, M.M. (2024) Attention-deficit/hyperactivity disorder and the menstrual cycle: Theory and evidence. *Hormones and Behavior*, 158, 105466, https://doi.org/10.1016/j.yhbeh.2023.105466.

Gao, M., Koupil, I., Sjöqvist, H., Karlsson, H., Lalitkumar, S., Dalman, C. & Kosidou, K. (2020). Psychiatric comorbidity among women with endometriosis: nationwide cohort study in Sweden. *American Journal of Obstetrics and Gynecology*, 223(3), 415.e1–415.e16. https://doi.org/10.1016/j.ajog.2020.02.033.

Garcia-Argibay, M., du Rietz, E., Lu, Y., Martin, J., Haan, E., Lehto, K., Bergen, S.E., Lichtenstein, P., Larsson, H. & Brikell, I. (2022). The role of ADHD genetic risk in mid-to-late life somatic health conditions. *Translational Psychiatry*, 12(1), 152. https://doi.org/10.1038/s41398-022-01919-9.

Goldstein, A., Pukall, C., Goldstein, I. & Krapf, J. (2011). *When Sex Hurts: Understanding and Healing Pelvic Pain. Completely revised and updated*. Da Capo Lifelong Books.

Gordon, A. (2020). *The way out: A revolutionary, scientifically proven approach to healing chronic pain*. New York: Avery Publications.

Gowey, M.A., Stromberg, S.E., Lim, C.S. & Janicke, D.M. (2017). The moderating role of body dissatisfaction in the relationship between ADHD symptoms and disordered eating in pediatric overweight and obesity. *Children's Health Care*, 46(1), 15–33. https://doi.org/10.1080/02739615.2015.1065745.

Jabalkandi, S.A., Raisi, F., Shahrivar, Z., Mohammadi, A., Meysamie, A., Firoozikhojastefar, R. & Irani, F. (2020). A study on sexual functioning in adults withattention-deficit/hyperactivity disorder, *Perspective Psychiatric Care*, 52, 642–648. doi: 10.1111/ppc.12480.

Karaş, H., Çetingök, H., İlişer, R., Çarpar, E. & Kaşer, M. (2020). Childhood and adult attention deficit hyperactivity disorder symptoms in fibromyalgia: associations with depression, anxiety and disease impact. *International Journal of Psychiatry in Clinical Practice*, 24(3), 257–263. https://doi.org/10.1080/13651501.2020.1764585.

Kerekes, N., Lundqvist, S., Schubert Hjalmarsson, E., Torinsson Naluai, Å., Kantzer, A.-K. & Knez, R. (2022). The associations between ADHD, pain, inflammation, and quality of life in children and adolescents – a clinical study protocol. *PLoSONE*, 17(9), e0273653. https://doi.org/10.1371/journal.pone.0273653.

Kooij, J.J.S. (2018). Attention-Deficit Hyperactivity Disorder (ADHD), Intimate Relationships and Sexuality. In Jannini, E.A. & Siracusano, A. (Eds), *Sexual Dysfunctions in Mentally Ill Patients*. Cham: Springer International Publishing, pp. 75–82.

Kooij, J.J.S. (2023). Hormonal sensitivity of mood symptoms in women with ADHD across the lifespan. *European Psychiatry,* 66(S1), S23–S23. https://doi.org/10.1192/j.eurpsy.2023.92.

McBride, H. (2021). The Wisdom of Your Body: Finding healing, wholeness and connection through embodied living. Michigan: Brazos Press.

McCarthy, B.W. & Metz, M.E. (2004). *Coping with premature ejaculation: How to overcome PE, please your partner and have great sex.* Oakland, CA: New Harbinger Publications.

Metz, M.E. & McCarthy, B.W. (2004). *Coping with erectile dysfunction: How to regain confidence and enjoy great sex.* Oakland, CA: New Harbinger Publications.

Nagoski, E. (2021). *Come As You Are: Revised and Updated: The surprising new science that will transform your sex life.* Simon & Schuster Publications.

Nazar, B.P., Bernardes, C., Peachey, G., Sergeant, J., Mattos, P. & Treasure, J. (2016). The risk of eating disorders comorbid with attention-deficit/hyperactivity disorder: A systematic review and meta-analysis. *The International Journal of Eating Disorders*, 49(12), 1045–1057. https://doi.org/10.1002/eat.22643.

Nirouei, M., Kouchekali, M., Sadri, H., Qorbani, M., Montazerlotfelahi, H., Eslami, N. & Tavakol, M. (2023). Evaluation of the frequency of attention deficit hyperactivity disorder in patients with asthma. *Clinical and Molecular Allergy CMA*, 21(1), 4. https://doi.org/10.1186/s12948-023-00185-4.

Orlov, M. (2010). *The ADHD Effect on Marriage: Understand and rebuild your relationship in six steps.* Plantation, FL: Speciality Press/A.D.D. Warehouse, p. 225.

Pittman, C. (2022). *Taming your amygdala: Brain-based strategies to quiet the anxious mind.* PESI Publishing, Inc.

Pittman, C. & Karle, E.M. (2015). *Rewire Your Anxious Brain: How to use the neuroscience of fear to end anxiety, panic & worry.* New Harbinger Publications.

Ravi, P. & Khan, S. (2020). Attention Deficit Hyperactivity Disorder: Association With Obesity and Eating Disorders. *Cureus*, 12(12), e12085. doi:10.7759/cureus.12085.

Soldati, L., Bianchi-Demicheli, F., Schockaert, P., Köhl, J., Bolmont, M., Hasler, R. & Perroud, N. (2020). Sexual Function, Sexual Dysfunctions, and ADHD: A Systematic Literature Review. *Journal of Sexual Medicine*, 17(9), 1653–1664. doi: 10.1016/j.jsxm.2020.03.019.

Soldati, L., Bianchi-Demicheli, F., Schockaert, P., Köhl, J., Bolmont, M., Hasler, R. & Perroud, N. (2021). Association of ADHD and hypersexuality and paraphilias. *Psychiatry Research*, 295, 113638–113638. https://doi.org/10.1016/j.psychres.2020.113638.

Soydan, H., Ates, F., Cuneyt, A., Akyol, I, Basar Semiz, U., Malkoc, E., Yilmaz, O., Basoglu, C. & Vehbi Baykal, K. (2013). Attention-deficit hyperactivity disorder in patients with premature ejaculation: a pilot study *International Urology Nephrology*, 45, 77–81. doi:10.1007/s11255-012-0290-1.

Tuckman, A. (2019). *ADHD After Dark: Better Sex Life, Better Relationship* (1st ed.). Routledge.

Upadhyaya, H., Tanaka, Y., Lipsius, S. et al. (2015). Time-to-onset and -resolution of adverse events before/after atomoxetine discontinuation in adult patients with ADHD. *Postgraduate Medicine*, 127, 677–685.

Van Eck, K., Morse, M. & Flory, K. (2018). The role of body image in the link between ADHD and depression symptoms among college students. *Journal of Attention Disorders*, 22(5), 435–445. https://doi.org/10.1177/1087054715580845.

Young, S., Adamo, N., Ásgeirsdóttir, B. B., Branney, P., Beckett, M., Colley, W., Cubbin, S., Deeley, Q., Farrag, E., Gudjonsson, G., Hill, P., Hollingdale, J., Kilic, O., Lloyd, T., Mason, P., Paliokosta, E., Perecherla, S., Sedgwick, J., Skirrow, C., . . . Woodhouse, E. (2020). Females with ADHD: An expert consensus statement taking a lifespan approach providing guidance for the identification and treatment of attention-deficit/hyperactivity disorder in girls and women. *BMC Psychiatry*, 20(1), 404. https://doi.org/10.1186/s12888-020-02707-9.

Young, S. & Cocallis, K. (2023). A systematic review of the relationship between neurodiversity and psychosexual functioning in individuals with autism spectrum disorder (ASD) or attention-Deficit/Hyperactivity disorder (ADHD). *Neuropsychiatric Disease and Treatment*, 19, 1379–1395. https://doi.org/10.2147/NDT.S319980.

Young, S., Klassen, L.J., Reitmeier, S.D., Matheson, J.D. & Gudjonsson, G.H. (2023). Let's talk about sex… and ADHD: Findings from an anonymous online survey. *International Journal of Environmental Research and Public Health*, 20(3), 2037. https://doi.org/10.3390/ijerph20032037.

Chapter 8

What is that smell?

A word about sensory issues and ADHD

Many neurodivergent individuals struggle with sensory issues. Sensory issues are most often associated with neurodivergent individuals who are diagnosed with Autism Spectrum Disorders (Attwood, 2017); however, it is notable that ADHDers also report experiencing sensory issues (Panagiotidi, 2017; Bijlenga, 2017). While the research is still emerging on this topic, ADHD folks frequently report being impacted by sensory concerns.

Many people don't realize that they are experiencing sensory issues. If sensory concerns are identified, most don't consider how these specific issues also impact their sexuality. There is little, to no, research on the impact of sensory issues on sexuality in neurodivergent individuals (see Aston, 2012 for one example).

Sensory issues are <u>physical reactions</u> that occur as a result of sensations that are experienced by your physical senses. Your senses include smell, taste, hearing, vision and touch as well as your physical position in space and your connection within your body (interoception). Examples of sensory issues may include difficulties with certain smells, sounds, tastes, textures, touches, temperature or even body positions. Sensory issues can lead to you gagging, recoiling, feeling discomfort and avoiding certain activities. You may also experience a feeling of overwhelm when faced with certain sensations.

Sensory concerns may be experienced as being under-responsive to a certain sensation (hyposensitivity) or over-responsive to a certain sensation (hypersensitivity). While sensory issues may improve with time for younger children, they don't necessarily resolve, even with repeated exposure (Bogdashina, 2016).

Sensory reactions are spontaneous reactions from your body. These sensations can't be easily managed by thinking it through; it is more like a reflex. In these situations, mind over body just doesn't work!

DOI: 10.4324/9781003422372-9

Sensory problems during sex might be one reason why some ADHDers don't want to have sex. You may be fearful about experiencing a sensory experience that is unpleasant, whether that is a touch, a smell, a taste or a texture. Soft touch, strong smells or the taste of someone's cum can cause difficulties. Texture examples include that random pubic hair that lands in your mouth or wet kisses with too much saliva. For most people, sensory concerns aren't catastrophic, but for others, they can turn you completely off sex.

Sensitivity to sensations can push you out of your body. It is difficult to stay seated in your body if you are struggling to cope with your physical reaction to certain sensations. Addressing sensory issues, including sensory problems that occur during sex, is an important part of creating a space for fun, joyful and safe sexual pleasure in your life. Identifying and communicating clearly about the sensory issues that are impacting your sexuality is essential to engaging in fun, joyful and enjoyable sexual play!

Let's help you explore sensory issues that may be impacting your sexuality!

Susan doesn't like sex. She isn't really sure why but she tells herself that partnered sex is just not for her. When Susan has tried to engage in partnered sex, it didn't feel good. Something was off. Susan does enjoy solo sex. Sex on her own terms feels better. Susan decided that she didn't need to have partnered sex in her life. When talking with a friend about this problem, her friend reminded her that she never really enjoyed bright lights, she was sensitive to sounds and to the texture of her clothing. As they continued to discuss this issue, Susan identified that during sex, she struggled with feeling overwhelmed by the constant stimulation involving unusual touches, strong smells and bright lights. Once she knew the problem, Susan was able to put together a plan to ease her sensory concerns and communicate her needs to a partner. She has established a fun sexual life for herself!

Sensory issues are best described as that problem that keeps getting in your way and that makes you feel uncomfortable. Often, it is a problem that you can't quite clearly explain to others when they ask you what is wrong.

Some examples of sensory issues include:

- A partner touches you softly and it feels like there are a million small ants crawling up your spine
- Your nose is exposed to a horrible smell that wrinkles your face and you want to retch!
- Your skin crawls at the touch of wet blankets
- The taste of semen makes you gag, and you want to immediately rinse your mouth with mouthwash.
- Bright lights burn into your eyes and distract you
- The idea of kissing makes you want to heave
- Your genitals need a specific touch, in a certain way, at a certain spot, without deviation, in order for you to feel comfortable during sexual play

Other examples of sensory issues can include:

- Clothing tags
- Certain smells
- Certain lighting
- Certain touches
- Textures
- Tastes
- Certain physical activities such as brushing your hair
- Certain physical transitions such as moving your body from one position to another

Sensory issues can impact your sex life!

If you are struggling to identify whether or not sensory issues are getting in your way, take a moment to connect with your body. Find that feeling you can't quite explain when you are having sex. Sensory issues usually provoke a negative or uncomfortable feeling. It may be experienced as a feeling of overwhelm. It's that feeling when something just doesn't feel right in your body. Try to notice <u>when</u> it happens: Is it when you are first touched? During certain sexual activities? Try this exercise:

Take a deep breath and just notice your body.
Breathe
Right now, does your body feel good, bad or neutral?
Touch your body, does your touch feel good, bad or neutral?

Breathe
Notice the lighting, does the lighting feel good, bad or neutral?
If you change the lighting, does your body feel better, worse or neutral?

Take a deep breath, notice the good smells around you
Take a deep breath, do you notice any smells that your body finds unpleasant?

Breathe
Notice which textures are touching your body right now (e.g. blankets, clothing, sheets).
Do these textures feel good, bad or neutral?
Touch your favorite shirt, undies, or some other piece of clothing/material that you like.
What textures does your body enjoy?

Breathe
What do you hear? Are the sounds around you good, bad or neutral?
What sounds help your body feel peaceful and content?

Breathe

What tastes do you notice in your mouth? Are the tastes in your mouth good, bad or neutral?

What tastes does your body like the best?

What tastes does your body react to the strongest?

Journal your observations throughout this exercise here:

_____

_____

_____

_____

_____

Invite a partner to help you and repeat the exercise above. Do you notice any changes when you complete this exercise with a partner?

_____

_____

_____

_____

_____

There are many advantages to identifying the sensory concerns that impact you[1]. While we will discuss various ways to circumvent issues related to sensations, you always have the choice to say no and simply avoid the offending sensory concern. Let's explore various sensations and how these might be creating sensory issues for you!

Clothing, bedding & textiles – those darned textures!

Uncomfortable clothing, clothing tags, itchy fabrics, weird textiles, can all create sensory issues. Rubbing up against a partner's clothing can feel uncomfortable. Expecting yourself to wear itchy or uncomfortable clothing such as scratchy lingerie or tight sexy outfits may not enhance your feelings of sexual pleasure! Honor yourself with textiles that feel good for you.

Comfortable textiles including sheets, towels, clothing and sexy clothing can be found!

✓ Find bedding that gives you sensory pleasure
✓ Don't wear clothing that is uncomfortable or interferes with feelings of pleasure
✓ Add creams, oils or other lubricants to create a barrier between your skin and uncomfortable textiles
✓ Don't wear lingerie if it doesn't feel good to you
✓ Explore textiles that are smooth and comfortable, for example silk, bamboo or other materials
✓ Treat yourself by finding materials that make your skin and body happy!

Wet sheets can be a significant distraction, whether or not you are neurodivergent! For most people, the wet spot and any fluids that get discharged during sex, aren't a ton of fun. The wet spot can be a very uncomfortable and annoying distraction.

Sex blankets are wonderful additions to your bedding in order to address difficulties with the "wet spot"! A sex blanket is a blanket that is designed to get rid of the wet spot. Adding a sex blanket can avoid unnecessary sensory experiences and unnecessary wandering thoughts such as "I have to put a load of laundry in now!"; "Who will be stuck on the spot tonight?" or "Will this wet spot cause odors that will be embarrassing or hard to remove?" These concerns do not have to be a part of your life. Use a blanket, towel or waterproof sex blanket to manage this distraction and banish it from your life!

✓ Buy a sex blanket to deal with sensory issues related to wet blankets and sheets
✓ Have a smaller travel sized sex blanket to take on holidays
✓ Keep a stash of towels nearby to absorb any annoying liquids during sexual play
✓ Have sex in locations that don't involve much clean up such as the bathroom, a closet, hot tub or sauna
✓ Use a warm towel for clean up
✓ Change the sheets, if this isn't overly disruptive to your cuddle time

Touch

It is worth repeating that for many neurodivergent people soft touch is creepy, uncomfortable and simply feels bad! In my clinical experience of all the sensory issues that come up, the most frequent sensory issue identified by ADHDers is related to the intensity of touch.

Tommy really likes sex. Tommy enjoys partnered sex. Unfortunately, Tommy can't handle being touched. Touch is creepy and feels bad! Tommy struggles to articulate this problem. When he tries to involve a sexual partner, he either upsets his partner by jerking away suddenly or avoids sex altogether. Tommy realized that this was a huge problem and has avoided partnered sex. Tommy had a goal of a maintaining a long term relationship so he asked for help! When discussing this problem, Tommy realized that hard touch was fine. If a partner smacked Tommy, grabbed or pushed hard into his body, that touch was ok. In fact, Tommy responded very well when partners gave him blow jobs while grabbing his butt with intensity. Tommy was able to communicate his need for hard touch more clearly to others, stopped upsetting potential partners, and was able to find a long term relationship with a like-minded partner!

> **Hard touch is a common request in the neurodivergent community.**
> **If you prefer hard touch and wish to avoid soft touch, that is perfectly acceptable!**

When soft touch is uncomfortable, explore hard touch. Touch provided with intensity is generally better tolerated (Bogdashina, 2016). Interestingly, this idea was incorporated into the neurodivergent love locutions. The importance of hard touch to help become seated in your body is becoming a common recommendation (Amythest@neurowonderful, May 2021, and *The Five Neurodivergent Love Locutions*, April 19, 2022, Stimpunks. org). Hard touch is often necessary from a sensory perspective, as a way to focus your attention and to provide sufficient intensity during sexual play.

✓ Sensory issues related to soft touch can be resolved by communicating your need for a harder touch
✓ Ask for more intense touch during sexual play
✓ Openly discuss spontaneous reactions that can occur when touch feels uncomfortable (for example, jerking away suddenly). Make it clear to a partner that this reaction is not personal, it is simply a sensation problem
✓ Play with touch to find the type of touch that works for you!

Explore your response to different types of touch, at different times, throughout sexual activity. You may find that touches that bother you in the first part of sexual play don't bother you as much once you are aroused and close to orgasm. Additionally, many biological females identify changes in their physical sensitivity to touch throughout their menstrual cycles. If sensory issues are better or worse at different times, make note of this and communicate this information clearly to a partner.

✓ Play with touch to see what you like and don't like
✓ Communicate your needs for touch clearly to a partner
✓ Track whether sensory issues related to touch change during certain times of your sexual play
✓ Track whether sensory issues related to touch change during certain times of your menstrual cycle

Physical touch can be uncomfortable for reasons that aren't simply the result of a sensory issue but can be connected to experiences of past trauma. We will talk more about trauma and sexual victimization in Chapter 11. In order to distinguish sensory concerns from traumatic events, consider whether your reaction to touch was more pronounced <u>after</u> you experienced trauma or whether these reactions were present before these incidents occurred in your life. Speak with a qualified mental health professional for additional assistance to address this particular concern.

Lighting

Lights can be overwhelming. Some types of light can be more disruptive than others. In addition, light may be more disturbing when you are trying to relax, lying down or trying to transition towards sex. Lighting matters!

Notice how you feel in brightly lit environments. Do bright lights excite you? Do they keep you going? Alternatively, do bright lights overwhelm you? Do bright lights interfere with your ability to relax? Experiment with different types of lighting to see what you like best!

Write your observations about how you react to lighting:

_____

_____

_____

_____

_____

Ways to address sensitivity to light include:

✓ Flameless battery powered candles
✓ Installing dimmer switches in your household
✓ Use floor lamps and table lamps rather than overhead lights
✓ Try various types of lightbulbs with different light color temperatures (e.g. warm or cool)
✓ Consider full spectrum UV lighting if that is helpful to you

✓ Consider eye masks as a playful way to reduce light sensitivity and increase intensity during sex

Ideally, you aren't simply turning off the lights and having sex in the dark. While this strategy can address sensory concerns related to lighting, it can also hinder feelings of intimacy during partnered sex. Of course, if you are engaging in solo sex, having the lights off can be a very effective strategy.

The impact of lighting from screens and/or technical devices can become a problem if you are attempting to watch pornography during sexual play or if there are other screens turned on in the room. In addition to lighting issues, screens can be quite distracting. If computer, tablet or cellphone screens create sensory concerns for you, ensure that all screens, televisions and devices are turned off before you engage in sexual play. Replace visual porn with audio porn if you require more sexual intensity during your sexual play or listen to music from your sexy playlist. Ask for what you need!

Smells

Smell is a sensory issue that is hard to escape. When smells enhance your sexual experience, these can be extraordinarily positive, arousing and impactful. Unfortunately, smells can also interfere with your sexual experience. When this happens, smells can be extremely distracting and downright unpleasant.

There are many smells that can interfere with sexual play. Some smells can be fairly easily adjusted by addressing self-care and hygiene concerns; however, other smells are less easily resolved.

Take note of the usual smells during sex. Which ones create a sensory concern for you?

- ☐ Genital smells
- ☐ Skin smells/body smells
- ☐ Perfumes or certain body products
- ☐ Semen/Cum
- ☐ Hair smells
- ☐ Condom smell
- ☐ Breath/mouth smells
- ☐ Other: _____
- ☐ Other: _____
- ☐ Other: _____

Everyone's genitals smell like their particular brand of perfect! Semen and female ejaculate have a particular smell, taste and texture. Differences in genital smells are normal. If you find that someone's genitals don't smell good to you, consider whether your expectations are reasonable. Are you expecting genitals to smell like nothing, neutral, like flowers or offer an absence of smell? Consider the timing: are their genital odors better or worse at different times of the day? Some people do well with one daily shower while others may need two or even three showers a day to manage body odor. Alternatively, some people have stronger odors that may be caused by an undiagnosed and untreated infection that requires attention. Seek medical attention if you or a partner is struggling with a strong genital odor that does not resolve with regular hygiene.

Sometimes people are more concerned and distracted by their own smell rather than a partner's smell. For example, some women may find that their genitals smell stronger or simply different during their menstrual cycle or if they have had a long, sweaty day. Wafting vaginal smells are typically much more noticeable to you than they are to others. If you are truly concerned about your genital odor, ask a trusted friend for feedback. If others don't smell you, you do not smell, even if you can smell yourself!

Genital smells can be disturbing to some. Practice smelling this scent. Does it get better with time?

- ☐ Yup! I got used to it
- ☐ It's still not great but I can tolerate it now!
- ☐ It's better with some partners but not with others
- ☐ It's never good

Find alternative or competing smells that may help you navigate these sensory issues:

- ✓ Burn essential oils or incense
- ✓ Find a sexy perfume, body spray or a massage oil with a scent that you like
- ✓ Flavored oral sex sprays and blow job gels can offer a competing scent
- ✓ Use mouthwash to create a competing smell in your mouth

Can personal odor change with your diet? It seems that diet can influence scent (Zuniga, 2017); however, there are many other things that can impact how you smell including your genetics, medical concerns, medications and hygiene issues. While adjusting your diet might help, it may not resolve this issue.

Conversations about body odor, genital smells and overall smelly odors can easily lead to hurt feelings. Communicate about scent in ways that are positive and encouraging to a partner. Start by carving out time for a discussion. Advise your partner that you want to bring something up that is delicate and make sure that it is a good time to talk for both of you. Talk about your sensory issues surrounding smells. Identify times when smells were fine and times when you struggled. If the problems with genital odors have persisted without change, discuss the importance of making an appointment with a health care provider to ensure that there are no underlying physical health concerns. Ask your partner for feedback to see if they have any similar concerns with your body odors. Create a plan to address the issue. Finish by validating all the things that you enjoy about having sex with them. Finish with a focus on the good things that make the relationship worthwhile[2].

Openly discuss ways to resolve issues involving smell

✓ Communicate about the smells that you really like
✓ Tell your partner what smells you like and share examples of your favorite scents
✓ Go on a "smell date", find various products that smell in a way that you both like and identify smells that you both dislike
✓ Encourage your partner to use products that create a pleasurable scent
✓ Compliment a partner when they smell nice
✓ Careful not to simply ban certain scents from the household unless everyone agrees, as this may create feelings of resentment
✓ Carefully discuss odors that are challenging to you, own this problem as your sensory issue, not theirs, and find ways to compromise

Taste

What happens when you taste something or someone during sexual play? Does it feel good or bad? The taste of someone's mouth, the taste their skin, the taste of genitals, the taste of ejaculate, the taste during anal rimming as well as the slippery texture of saliva, all have the potential to cause difficulties. Remember that when we are discussing sensory issues, we aren't simply talking about a general dislike ("Well, that wasn't much fun"), we are talking about a sensory reaction that is intense and gets in your way during sex:

☛ Exchanging saliva with another person
☛ Finding a pubic hair in your mouth
☛ Tasting ejaculate (semen, cum from all genders)
☛ Tasting pre-cum and all those bodily fluids that occur prior to orgasm

There are many products available to help manage the taste of bodily fluids during sexual play and particularly for tastes that occur during oral sex. Look for oral sex creams, gels and sprays in flavors that you enjoy. You will also find a selection of oral desensitizing sprays that may help you manage difficulties surrounding taste[3]. Exert caution when using strategies to numb your throat as these could put you at risk of harming yourself if you do not feel pain signals during sex play. Alternatively, salt has often been used to help tame a gag reflex. Simply put salt at the back of your throat to reduce your gag reflex and it also has the benefit of creating a competing taste in your mouth[4]. Whatever option you explore, have fun finding a safe solution that works for you!

✓ Set boundaries about what you are willing to taste and what you are not willing to taste
✓ Focus on the eroticism of the act rather than the specific actions you are engaged in
✓ Distract yourself with an oral spray and/or oral gel with a flavor you enjoy
✓ Consider salt as an alternative or another strong spice/food
✓ Sexual intensity can help you stay focused on sexual pleasure when you are navigating difficulties with taste
✓ Gagging can be sexy during sexual play! There is no need to be embarrassed if this happens to you
✓ If you respond strongly to a taste during sex, don't despair, just laugh, use some mouthwash or breath spray and move on

It can also be helpful to address your physical reactions by using somatic therapies to help calm your nervous system[5]. While you will still likely react to the sensation, going in with a calmer body and a calmer mindset can be helpful:

✓ Try breathing exercises to help create a calm nervous system before starting sexual play
✓ Remind yourself and your body that you are safe
✓ Ensure that you are able to control whether or not you are exposed to unpleasant tastes. Surprises are not helpful in these situations!

Sticky textures

It is hard to mask texture. There are many things that can become sticky during sexual play but often lubes and semen are the top culprits. Avoidance and speedy clean up are good ways to manage texture issues.

There are multiple brands of lube out there. Try as many as you need to find a lube that isn't sticky and one that has a good silky feel for you!

Semen can feel sticky, or it might simply have a texture that you do not enjoy. There isn't much that can be done about the texture of bodily fluids; however, you can keep a warm, wet towel near the bed to wipe off any uncomfortable textures. Condoms and/or underwear can also be a great way to reduce your exposure to sticky textures as it will keep ejaculate contained. Communicate your needs to avoid that uncomfortable sticky feeling if it causes you significant distress.

✓ If you don't like the texture of semen, ask your partner to let you know when they are getting close to ejaculation. If you are in the splash zone, allow yourself to stop, move away and do something else to maintain sexual pleasure
✓ Keep a warm, wet towel close by to help manage sticky or textured bodily fluids
✓ Try different lubes and creams that have a silky feel that you like
✓ Explore the use of condoms and/or underwear to contain sticky fluids

Hygiene

Smells, taste and sticky textures bring us to hygiene. Hygiene is a good way to address sensory issues that are impacting your sexual play. Hygiene and self-care can be a struggle if you are in hyperfocus, if you tend to be forgetful about your hygiene, if you don't schedule regular times to ensure that your basic self-care gets addressed and/or if you have difficulties with sensory issues related to hygiene. It is important to have good hygiene to facilitate your sexual play!

Oral hygiene is particularly problematic and will almost immediately impact sexual play. Basic dental hygiene including flossing daily, brushing your teeth daily and using mouthwash after meals will address most breath issues. If you struggle with halitosis (chronic bad breath that doesn't seem to go away), it is time to go see a dentist or a health care provider to discuss your symptoms in more detail.

If your breath is a concern:

✓ Add a reminder to schedule dentist appointments. Include dentist appointments on your visual whiteboard along with the list of regular chores so that these appointments actually happen
✓ Ensure that you are getting your teeth cleaned regularly (two or three times a year or as recommended by your dentist)
✓ Add a visual reminder on your bathroom mirror or on the back of your front door to remember to brush your teeth
✓ Keep a spare toothbrush in a more convenient location in your home, office or car, particularly if you enjoy having breakfast or coffee before brushing your teeth
✓ Use mouthwash or breath spray for quick breath improvements
✓ Chew gum or use breath mints regularly
✓ Explore products created to address halitosis if these are helpful to you

Body odors can be related to a lack of regular hygiene and self-care. Sometimes, people don't identify the importance of taking regular showers or baths. Other times, people don't wash appropriately because they are focused on watching a show during their shower, distracted by the feeling of the water on their skin or, it might be that you ran out of soap and forgot to buy more! To deal with body odor, water isn't enough. Washing thoroughly includes washing your genitals, perineum and anus. As noted in various social media memes, cleaning between your butt crack is essential, simply wiping the outside of your butt is not enough!

If washing creates a sensory issue for you, let's address that problem! For some people, the transition from being "dry to wet" and "wet to dry" creates a physical transition that is uncomfortable. It may be that transitions when bathing do not feel good, that your skin doesn't like the feeling of soap or that your skin gets overly dry after washing. Whatever the sensory issue you experience before, during or after bathing, be mindful of the importance of hygiene and sex. If taking a shower once or twice a day isn't feasible for you, washing by hand (armpits, genitals, anus, feet and face) is a must!!

Do you <u>dislike</u> transitions into water environments, such as taking a bath or shower?

☐ Yes
☐ Sometimes
☐ No

Do you forget to engage in basic hygiene such as brushing and flossing your teeth or combing your hair?

☐ Yes
☐ Sometimes
☐ No

Things I can do to facilitate my transition into a bath or shower every day include:

☐ Different soap, different products, change your/bathing routine
☐ Warm towel
☐ Adjust the temperature in the room
☐ Remember that this is simply a transition. You will usually feel good once you are in there!
☐ Add a shower chair or other device to make the experience more comfortable and pleasurable
☐ Add safety equipment if you are scared
☐ Allow yourself to bathe with different goals and routines (sometimes it can be short, other times it can be long)
☐ Address any environment problems that bother you about the space such as privacy, mirrors, temperature, etc.
☐ Address any body image concerns that are interfering with your bathing rituals with the help of a qualified mental health professional
☐ Other: _____
☐ Other: _____
☐ Other: _____

Brushing or combing your hair may also create difficult sensations for you. Use conditioners and detanglers to make it easier when brushing your hair. Join social media groups that discuss your specific hair type to help determine the best strategy for your hair care needs.

Let's talk more about difficulties with hair as it relates to your sexuality. Body hair can create sensory issues. Too much hair, not enough hair, pulling hair, brushing hair, prickly hair…. there are many sensations that occur which involve your hair. Some individuals prefer the feeling of smooth skin, skin with absolutely no hair, while others enjoy the feel of hairy bodies. Whatever your preference, sensations problems can occur when body hair is where you don't want it, if it is harder or rougher than you would like, or if it gets pulled or tugged during sexual play.

If having your hair pulled or tugged during sex is unpleasant for you, try wearing hairbands or scarves during sex. Silk pillowcases or silk sheets can also reduce the pull you experience when moving your body.

Reduce sensations involving your hair with:

✓ Hair conditioner, hair oils and/or hair detanglers
✓ Silk pillowcases and sheets
✓ Hair bands, hair ties, hair bonnet or hair scarfs
✓ Regular haircuts
✓ Sex in positions and places that do not involve lying on your back or lying under a partner

The presence of facial hair such as beards, mustaches, and body hair such as hairy arms, backs or genitals can be a source of tickles or sensations that cause discomfort. Talk with a partner about your preferences as it relates to body hair. While hair removal will address your preference for smooth skin, it remains a partner's choice whether or not they would like to have less hair on their body and on what schedule they would prefer to maintain their hair care schedule. If a partner chooses to maintain their facial and/or body hair, navigate these sensory issues by finding compromise through alternative sexual activities.

If you prefer the feeling of a hairless body, there are many ways to achieve this goal including:

✓ Laser hair removal
✓ Electrolysis
✓ Waxing
✓ Hair removal creams

What hygiene issues have you experienced in your relationships, either for yourself or with a partner?

_____
_____
_____
_____
_____

How did you resolve these issues? Did the resolutions work well – why or why not?

_____
_____
_____
_____
_____

What hygiene issues remain to be addressed?

_____

_____

_____

_____

_____

Some hygiene reminders:

✓ Create visual reminders to maintain your hygiene
✓ Make your bathing/bathroom space as comfortable as possible
✓ Add comfortable towels, face cloths and a comfy bathrobe
✓ Add fun pictures, unique items and reminders to make the space fun
✓ Adjust the temperature in the bathroom to suit you
✓ Use a heated towel rack or put your towel in the dryer to warm
✓ Create a body care routine that feels good to you
✓ If necessary, create rewards for yourself when you complete your hygiene

Address any obvious hygiene problems. If a partner hasn't noticed the impact of their lack of hygiene, calmly and compassionately discuss the importance of hygiene as an essential part of making sex playful and fun!

Temperature or "The art of wearing shorts in the winter!"

☛ Does physical touch leave you feeling too hot?
☛ Are you uncomfortable when you feel cold?
☛ Do drafts distract you?

Some people experience specific needs related to their body temperature which interfere in their sexual play. If you tend to be too hot or too cold during sex, adjust the temperature to ensure that your sexual play is not being impacted by the room temperature. You may also want to try different sexual positions that allow you to regulate your body temperature.
   If temperature remains an issue:

✓ Try different types of sheets, blankets and/or mattresses to help regulate temperature more effectively
✓ Install fans or portable heaters
✓ Use warm towels, blankets, ice or cold packs to adjust your body temperature
✓ Play in the water in order to better regulate your body temperature
✓ Play with ice or hand warmers to adjust your body temperature

Don't be afraid to discuss and address your body temperature during sexual play!

Noises

We have discussed how noise can be a distraction during sex. Noises that distract you aren't only difficult because you lose your attention, some noises can also be difficult because of the sensory effect that they create in your body.

Examples of noises that might create sensory reactions include:

- Screeching noises
- High-pitched noises
- Surprising or unpredictable sounds
- Certain words
- Animals in distress
- Sex noises
- Background noises (for example, a certain clock or sound)
- Cellphone notifications

If you find that certain noises are uncomfortable for you, try removing the item that is creating the noise. You may also benefit from adding a competing noise to distract your attention from the sensory disturbing noise (Attwood, 2007). You can try using earplugs that allow noise for the purpose of communication but will dim disturbing or distracting background noises. Experiment with scarves, earmuffs, headphones or earplugs which allow you to filter noise levels based on your environment[6].

It's best for the person who has the issue with noise to block out the sound rather than asking others around them not to be noisy. If a partner tends to be loud during sex, find creative ways to address the problem. When dealing with uncomfortable noises, use communication, noise filters and compromise.

Tongue rings and other paraphernalia

Many other things may create sensory problems for you during sex. For some, body piercings can increase the positive sensations during sex and the intensity of sex. For others, these may create a sensory issue. If body piercings are fun that is wonderful! Otherwise, discuss ways in which you can compromise about specific sensations that distract you.

Some people may struggle with condoms and/or other barrier STI/birth control methods which can create sensory issues. Review Chapter 3 to explore ways to address these concerns in more detail.

If you have certain sensitivities that have not been discussed in this workbook, clearly identify your sensory requirements and discuss these openly with a partner. You may also wish to contact an occupational therapist or a mental health professional for further assistance.

Let's explore the difference between solo sex and partnered sex as it relates to your sensory concerns!

What sensations create problems for you during solo sex?

During solo sex I experience sensory problems related to:

☐ Smells
☐ Touch
☐ Clothing, bedding & textile textures
☐ Lighting
☐ Hygiene
☐ Hair
☐ Sticky/texture
☐ Temperature
☐ Noises
☐ Tastes
☐ Tongue rings and other paraphernalias
☐ Other: _____
☐ Other: _____
☐ Other: _____

Describe any other sensory issues that you notice in more detail:

_____
_____
_____
_____
_____

What sensations create problems for you during partnered sex?

During partnered sex, I experience sensory problems related to:

- ☐ Smells
- ☐ Touch
- ☐ Clothing, bedding & textile textures
- ☐ Lighting
- ☐ Hygiene
- ☐ Hair
- ☐ Sticky/texture
- ☐ Temperature
- ☐ Noises
- ☐ Tastes
- ☐ Tongue rings and other paraphernalias
- ☐ Other: _____
- ☐ Other: _____
- ☐ Other: _____

Describe any other sensory issues that you notice in more detail:

_____
_____
_____
_____
_____

Your sensory issues may vary during sexual activity or they may only occur during one or two specific sexual activities. What do you notice about your sensory experiences based on the sexual environment, for example, who you are having sex with, where you are engaging in sex and what sexual activities you are engaging in?

- ☐ Nothing changes
- ☐ It is better in this context: _____
- ☐ It is worse in this context: _____

Expand on your observations about the contexts where sensory issues are better/less obvious:

_____
_____
_____
_____
_____

Expand on your observations about contexts where sensory issues are worse/more obvious:

_____

_____

_____

_____

_____

Timing may impact whether or not a sensory issue is extremely bothersome or simply annoying for you.

When do sensory issues interrupt your sexual play?

☐ Sensory issues get in my way when I am noticing sexual feelings – I am getting my attention focused on sex, noticing that I am feeling aroused, noticing that my partner is feeling aroused, noticing that now would be a good time to engage in sex

In this phase, sensory issues bother me:

☐ Greatly!
☐ Sometimes
☐ Not at all

☐ Sensory issues get in my way when I am initiating sex – I am getting my clothing off, during the initial sexual touches, during those initial sexual thoughts

In this phase, sensory issues bother me:

☐ Greatly!
☐ Sometimes
☐ Not at all

☐ Sensory issues get in my way when I am engaging in sex – kissing, touching, masturbating, focusing on my body or a partner's body, during sexual play

In this phase, sensory issues bother me:

☐ Greatly!
☐ Sometimes
☐ Not at all

☐ Sensory issues get in my way when I am close to climax – getting close to orgasm, excitement build up pre-orgasm

In this phase, sensory issues bother me:

☐ Greatly!
☐ Sometimes
☐ Not at all

☐ Sensory issues get in my way during cuddle time – time together, holding a partner, talking after sex

In this phase, sensory issues bother me:

☐ Greatly!
☐ Sometimes
☐ Not at all

Take away

Establish a connection to your body and explore how sensations impact you. Identify the sensations that create a concern for you and notice any sensations that are interrupting your sexual play. This is an important step towards improving your level of comfort during sex.

If you find yourself irritated, annoyed or overwhelmed by experiences that others consider to be sensual and fun, that is ok. In fact, it is absolutely fine! Sexual play involves choice. You can choose what sensory sensations to include and which to avoid in your sexual play.

Communicating with others about your sensory needs is an important step. Like pain, simply trying to grit your teeth through sensory issues does not lead to having a happy, relaxed and playful sexual experience. It is important that you choose, when and how you will manage a sensory issue. Focus on setting a positive mindset ahead of time by clearly deciding whether or not this is something that you wish to do.

If you have sensory issues, it can be tempting to simply stop everything, never have sex, never have the relationship you would like to have, and simply do away with it all! While this is a choice that you have, your sexuality is a part of you, and it would be an unfortunate loss. Find compromise in ways that honor your nervous system and yourself!

You may find that your choices about sensory inclusion depend on other factors, for example, your mood, your level of fatigue and/or your comfort level with a partner. If you are a biological female, the intensity of sensory concerns might also vary based on your menstrual cycle. Consider whether you are more tolerant of a sensation at particular times and/or with particular partners.

As an overall rule, you may be able to use intensity of touch and novelty to distract yourself from minor sensory issues. Some states of arousal can make uncomfortable sensations tolerable and maybe even enjoyable. Use sexual intensity to distract your focus and better tolerate discomfort. Exploring ritualized play (for example, kink practices) is one way that people increase intensity and novelty which may distract from sensory concerns.

If you can't work around the sensory issues that bother you, find alternative ways to proceed.

Solo sex while beside a partner (let's call this partnered/solo sex!) is one alternative way to respect your sensory needs and engage in intimacy with a partner. This can involve playful touch, fantasizing together and masturbating side by side. It is a nice way to find compromise and respect each other's needs.

Take the time to breathe and to feel settled in your body prior to starting sexual play. This will help ensure that you are not entering a sexual situation already overwhelmed and fearful before sensory concerns even happen.[7] Your need to reduce sensory sensations may interfere with a partner's need for sexual intensity and sexual novelty. This is where compromise, couples counselling and creativity can be helpful strategies to find an effective resolution.

Dealing with sensory issues

Step 1: Identify the sensation (type of sensation, timing of the sensation, environment when the sensation occurs most often)

Step 2: Drop the expectation that you must simply tolerate it

Step 3: Communicate about the sensory problem, acknowledge it to others

Step 4: Work around it (breathing, acceptance, alternative play, creative options)

Step 5: If you are triggered by a sensory issue during sex, keep a lighthearted attitude and try again, or not

Step 6: Take the time to communicate how to improve the situation for both you and a partner

---

There are resources to help you address sensory concerns including a sensory regulation workbook created by Dr. Neff (neurodivergentinsights.com). There is also information provided by Dr. Olga Bogdashina (www.olgabogdashina.com) as well as additional information and an elearning program provided through the Sensory Processing Disorder foundation's website (www.spdfoundation.net). In addition, somatic based mental health interventions may be of assistance to you.

Sensation seeking

We have been exploring sensory issues that cause concern, but there might be particular sensory experiences that you are seeking during sex. If you prefer experiencing a particular sensation during sex, this may also be a sensory issue. If there is a specific type of blanket, material or perhaps even a ritual that is important to you during sex and this ritual satisfies a sensory concern, take the time to explore this desire in more detail.

- Is the sensation something that can be replicated?
- Does the sensation require another person or does it require solo sex?
- Can you enjoy sex if you do not experience this sensation?
- Is it the only way that you can achieve orgasm?

When certain sensations are required and they interfere with partnered sex, this can leave you quite isolated. Consider the pros and cons of maintaining this particular sensation or ritual into your sexual play. Communicate with a partner and try to find a reasonable compromise. You may also want to consider some of the strategies outlined in the next chapter, Chapter 9, as managing impulsivity may be helpful to slow down your decision making allowing you to further explore the advantages and disadvantages of maintaining this particular sensation in your sexual repertoire. Communicate with a mental health professional for additional assistance.

If this applies to you, answer the following questions.

I am really into <u>this</u> specific sensation during sex:

_____

_____

_____

_____

_____

It's a sensation that I can have:

- ☐ Only with a partner
- ☐ Only during solo sex
- ☐ Can be with or without a partner

It's a sensation that I need to achieve orgasm, I can't have it any other way:

- ☐ Yes, I must have it to achieve orgasm
- ☐ No, I don't need it to have an orgasm

It's a sensation that I can take or leave, I can be flexible about including it or not:

- ☐ Yes, I can be flexible, it isn't a mandatory experience!
- ☐ No, I can't be flexible, I have to have it!

It's a sensation that I can communicate about – I can tell a partner, without feeling shame, guilt or remorse:

- ☐ Yes, I can tell a partner, no problem
- ☐ No, I cannot disclose this to a partner

I want to change this part of my sexuality:

- ☐ Yes
- ☐ No

I will contact a mental health professional for additional assistance:

- ☐ Yes
- ☐ No

I will change this part of my sexuality with the following plan:

_____

_____

_____

_____

_____

The goal of this chapter was to identify sensory issues and communicate these to others in your life. Focus on communicating your needs and finding workarounds for both you and a partner. Discuss your concerns with a mental health professional, an Occupational Therapist and/or brainstorm ideas with sensory groups on social media. Make sex safe, fun and enjoyable!

Let's continue our exploration in the next chapter and examine how impulsivity may be impacting your sexuality!

Working towards my goals

I have identified the following sensory issues:

☐ Smells

    o These smells get in my way: _____

☐ Lighting

    o This type of lighting gets in my way: _____

☐ Noise

    o These noises get in my way: _____

☐ Tastes

    o These tastes get in my way: _____

☐ Textures

    o This type of texture gets in my way: _____

□ Physical touch

o   This type of physical touch gets in my way: _____

□ Body sensations including hair and other body related stuff

o   This type of body sensation gets in my way: _____

□ Temperature

o   This temperature during sex gets in my way: _____

□ Other: _____

□ Other: _____

□ Other: _____

These sensory issues impact me:

□ Always
□ At different times of sexual play
□ At different arousal levels
□ In different sexual environments
□ With different sexual partners
□ Biological females: at certain times in my menstrual cycle
□ Other: _____

If your body does react strongly to certain sensations, what works to settle your body and feel better?

_____

_____

_____

_____

_____

✓   I will work around these sensory issues!

To challenge my difficulty with smell, I will:

_____

_____

_____

_____

_____

To challenge my difficulty with lighting, I will:

_____

_____

_____

_____

To challenge my difficulty with certain noises, I will:

_____

_____

_____

_____

To challenge my difficulty with taste, I will:

_____

_____

_____

_____

To challenge my difficulty with specific textures (e.g. saliva, sticky), I will:

_____

_____

_____

_____

To challenge my difficulty with physical touch, I will:

_____

_____

_____

_____

To challenge my difficulty with hair and other bodily stuff, I will:

_____

_____

_____

_____

To challenge my difficulty with temperature during sex, I will:

_____

_____

_____

_____

To challenge my other difficulties with sensory concerns during sex, I will:

_____

_____

_____

_____

✓ Reach out for help
✓ Join sensory support groups
✓ Talk to a partner about sensory needs in a clear and concrete way
✓ Create a clear and concrete plan to address sensory needs
✓ Calmly seat into my body before sexual play
✓ Talk to an Occupational Therapist specializing in sensory concerns
✓ Talk to a mental health professional for additional assistance

Are there certain sensations that I need to have during sex and that leads me to become isolated and overly engaged in solo sex?

☐ Yes, this applies to me
☐ No, this does not apply to me
☐ I am not sure

In order to manage sensations that I am seeking but that negatively impact my sexual play, I will:

_____

_____

_____

_____

✓ Ask a partner or trusted friends for additional suggestions
✓ Seek mental health assistance as needed

Notes

1 For additional exploration, you may also want to complete The Five Minute Sensory Triggers Checklist by Dr. Megan Anna Neff, Neurodivergent Insights, www.neurodivergentinsights.com.
2 If you want more information about communicating to others about their body odor, there are many online videos to assist you.
3 Caution is warranted if you are using oral anesthetic products to numb your throat. Use only according to the label, be mindful that these products can transfer to a partner and be very cautious not to damage your throat by engaging in activities that are hurting you!
4 I am full of gratitude for my wonderful dentist who, without blinking an eye, was happy to teach me how to tame a gag reflex!
5 EMDR can be a helpful therapeutic strategy to manage feelings of overwhelm and panic when experiencing sensory issues during sex.
6 There are many types of noise filtering headphones currently available on the market including loop earplugs, airpod style headphones as well as over the ear headphones. There are also noise-filtering devices such as white/brown noise machines.
7 Somatic therapies can be helpful to address feelings of overwhelm and anticipatory anxiety related to your sensory reactions. Somatic therapies are aimed at helping reduce nervous system reactivity such as interventions using polyvagal theories, EMDR and somatic experiencing.

References

Amythest@neurowonderful (May 2021) and Stimpunks Foundation (19 August 2022). The Five Neurodivergent Love Locutions, Creative Commons Attribution-ShareAlike 4.0 International license, Stimpunks.org.

Aston, M.C. (2012). Asperger syndrome in the bedroom, Sexual and Relationship Therapy, 27:1, 73–79. doi: 10.1080/14681994.2011.649253.

Attwood, T. (2007). The Complete Guide To Asperger's Syndrome, Jessica Kingsley Publishers: London.

Bijlenga, D., Tjon-Ka-Jie, J.Y., Schuijers, F. & Kooij, J.J. (2017). Atypical sensory profiles as core features of adult ADHD, irrespective of autistic symptoms. *European Psychiatry*, 43, 51–57. https://doi.org/10.1016/j.eurpsy.2017.02.481.

Bogdashina, O. (2016). *Sensory Perceptual Issues in Autism and Asperger Syndrome: Different sensory experiences – different perceptual worlds* (2nd ed.). London: Jessica Kingsley Publishers.

Neff, M.A. (2023). The Five Minute Sensory Triggers Checklist, Neurodivergent Insights. www.neurodivergentinsights.com.

Neff, M.A. (n.d.) Sensory Regulation 101: Crafting your personalized sensory safety plan. www.neurodivergentinsights.com.

Panagiotidi, M., Overton, P.G. and Stafford, T. (2017). The relationship between ADHD traits and sensory sensitivity in the general population. *Comprehensive Psychiatry*. https://doi.org/10.1016/j.comppsych.2017.10.008.

Zuniga, A., Stevenson, R.J., Mahmut, M.K. & Stephen, I.D. (2017). Diet quality and the attractiveness of male body odor. *Evolution and Human Behavior*, 38(1), 136–143. https://doi.org/10.1016/j.evolhumbehav.2016.08.002.

Chapter 9

What have I gotten myself into?

Impulsivity, sex and ADHD

ADHD is frequently synonymous with the word impulsivity. When it comes to impulsivity and sexual decisions, there can be negative outcomes such as STIs, unexpected pregnancies or being in unsafe situations. Too much sex, too much solo sex and sexual engagement with strangers can also be problematic. In contrast, impulsive sexual choices can sometimes lead to meeting partners that you would not have met otherwise, trying sexual activities that are surprisingly positive or finding new communities of like-minded people. Impulsivity can have both negative and positive outcomes in your life.

While ADHD is often associated with impulsive decision making, ADHDers don't always make fast decisions. In fact, some people with ADHD have so much anxiety about their decision making that they become paralyzed when faced with the need to make choices. The irony is that being neurodivergent means you can struggle with sexual anxiety <u>AND</u> engage in impulsive sexual decisions. Both can be true! Impulsivity is a struggle for ADHDers and this struggle can be reflected in their sex lives.

According to the DSM-5-TR, the definition of ADHD impulsivity is "hasty actions that occur in the moment without forethought, which may have potential for harm to the individual" (APA, 2022). They go on to say that impulsivity can occur, "owing to a desire to obtain an immediate reward or an inability to delay gratification". Impulsivity means that you make important decisions without considering the long-term consequences of your decision making (APA, 2022).

> Cindy Purple Hair is trendy and fun. The life of the party. She finds herself thinking about sex every day, most of the day. It's easy to find people that are willing to play with her. She had a STI scare last week. Cindy Purple Hair is starting to wonder if her infatuation with sexual pleasure is too much. There are many chores that she is not completing during the day. Her finances are a mess. She spends lots of time on various social media apps. When she starts counselling, her therapist begins by talking to her about her ADHD and her sexual choices. She is surprised. Cindy Purple Hair had not considered how her ADHD might be impacting her sexuality.

ADHD consequences are often related to impulsive decision making. An ADHD consequence can be an unexpected pregnancy, a tragic car accident, losing a job that you really liked, experiencing bankruptcy, not completing your schooling, having a sexually

DOI: 10.4324/9781003422372-10

transmitted infection or messing up a relationship with someone you love. While there can be positive outcomes following impulsive decision-making, such as getting unexpected opportunities, meeting new friends, finding a fun lover, or having the privilege of raising a cool kid; we will specifically explore the negative impact of impulsivity on your sexuality. If you struggle to transition out of sex and/or make impulsive sexual decisions, this chapter is for you!

Research generally confirms clinical observations that people with ADHD spend more time seeking sexual pleasure. In 2022 Korchia et al. noted that hypersexuality was more common in ADHD samples than in the general population and it is notable that rates of ADHD tend to be higher in populations that are seeking help with sexual addictions (Soldati, 2021). Niazof et al. (2019) found that more ADHDers in their sample reported problematic pornography use than participants without ADHD. Reid et al. (2011) noted in their study that inattentive type features were most prevalent in the ADHD sample of men with hypersexuality. ADHD and hypersexuality was noted to have some association with the inattentive subtype, and perhaps the combined subtype of ADHD, rather than the hyperactive subtype (Soldati, 2021). Moderate associations between ADHD and hypersexuality are generally reported in both men and women (Böthe et al., 2019; Niazof et al., 2019; Hertz et al., 2022)[1].

Sexual eagerness was explored by Tuckman (2019) in more detail. Sexual eagerness was defined by desired sexual frequency, masturbation frequency, use of pornography frequency, feelings about partner's pornography use, history of physical hookups, history of emotional affairs, self-ratings of kinkiness, history of consensual nonmonogamy, desire for consensual nonmonogamy and the desire for a larger repertoire of sexual activities (see Tuckman, 2019 for more details). In his sample, the ADHD group reported more overall sexual eagerness than the non-ADHD group.

There may be biological reasons that would explain the difference in sexual eagerness between people with ADHD and people without ADHD. ADHDers present with differences in their dopaminergic system, which is a system involved in impulse control and executive functioning. According to one theory, these differences in the dopaminergic system may lead directly or indirectly to impulsivity and to differences in reward identification; this could translate to higher sexual desire and higher rates of masturbation (Kasparek, Theiner & Filova, 2015). In addition, there is some research to suggest that sexual arousal may increase dopaminergic function and, as a result, diminish ADHD symptoms (Soldati, 2021). Soldati (2021) theorized that there may also be other reasons why ADHDers struggle with too much sex, including a difficulty staying focused during sex leading to reduced sexual satisfaction and subsequent increase in masturbation as well as the use of sex to cope with emotions, stress and tension, which appears to be more frequent in ADHD populations (Soldati, 2021). When people use sex to cope with uncomfortable feelings, they can become preoccupied with sex over time, eventually increasing their sexual frequency and experiencing symptoms of hypersexuality.

Sexual eagerness may also be related to that feeling of being wired but not tired. That edgy feeling that many ADHDers experience can be uncomfortable. Some ADHDers may use orgasm to deal with feeling edgy. This dependence on using orgasm to calm your body when you feel edgy can lead to hypersexuality.

It is interesting to consider that sexual preoccupation and/or hypersexuality reported by some ADHDers may simply be a byproduct of other difficulties that people with ADHD experience, such as difficulties with transitions, a need for stimulation and an overall tendency to hyperfocus. Any of these ADHD characteristics could lead to getting stuck on a topic, particularly a topic that can be quite satisfying such as sex. Add your unique neuro-biological features (also known as your brain chemistry)[2] and you can anticipate that someone with ADHD may have quite a bit of difficulty with hypersexuality[3]!

When we explore the difficulties that ADHDers express about their sexuality such as difficulties feeling seated in their body, difficulties maintaining focus during sex, being easily distracted during sex and frequently experiencing relationship difficulties, we can expect that solo sex and/or kinky sex (sex with a large amount of sexual novelty and intensity) might be more appealing to someone with ADHD.

Sexual eagerness and/or hypersexuality could be explained by some of the other difficulties that ADHDers report, including:

- Difficulties with transitions
- Need for sexual intensity
- Need for sexual novelty
- Tendency to hyperfocus
- Stimming behaviors
- Differences in brain chemistry

Solo sex and/or kinky sex may be more interesting to people with ADHD because of these struggles:

- Difficulties maintaining focus during sex
- Difficulties feeling seated in the body
- Easily distracted during sex
- Relationship difficulties
- Sexual anxiety

As you can see, there are many reasons why someone with ADHD might struggle with too much sex. Don't assume that hypersexuality is only occurring because of sexual impulsivity. We don't know exactly why hypersexuality is a problem for ADHDers, there are many theories but no conclusion yet. One possibility is this:

Sex is a form of stimming (it is a stim like eating, shopping, passion projects, videogames, etc.)

↓

Sex becomes a hyperfocus (like any other special interest)

↓

Sexual activity increases in frequency and sexual eagerness is high

↓

There is more sexual risk taking (sexual impulsivity)

↓

Sexual consequences occur (yikes!)

Hopefully, more research will emerge exploring these concepts and their connection in the near future. For now, let's look at how impulsivity impacts your sex life!

How often do you have sex, think about sex or engage sexually?

- ☐ Multiple times a day
- ☐ Twice a day
- ☐ Once daily
- ☐ 4–5 times a week
- ☐ 2–3 times a week
- ☐ Once a week
- ☐ Every 2 weeks
- ☐ Every 2–3 weeks
- ☐ Monthly
- ☐ Every 3–4 months
- ☐ Twice a year
- ☐ Yearly
- ☐ Other: _____

Has anyone told you or suggested that you were overly interested in sex?

☐ Yes
☐ No
☐ I don't remember!

Have you had concerns about the intensity of your interest in sex?

☐ Yes
☐ No
☐ Sometimes

What examples come to mind that suggest you are hyperfocused on sex?

_____
_____
_____
_____
_____

What issues may be contributing to you being overly preoccupied with sex:

☐ Difficulty with transitions
☐ Need for sexual intensity
☐ Need for sexual novelty
☐ Hyperfocus
☐ Sex as a stimming behavior
☐ Brain chemistry
☐ Difficulties maintaining focus during sex
☐ Difficulties feeling seated in your body
☐ Easily distracted during sex
☐ Relationship difficulties
☐ Sexual impulsivity
☐ Lonely, bored, unhappy, sad
☐ Sexual problems
☐ Sexual anxiety
☐ Other: _____
☐ Other: _____
☐ Other: _____

Do you experience that wired but not tired feeling:

☐ Yes
☐ No
☐ Not sure

What do you do with that wired but not tired feeling? When I have that edgy feeling I:

- ☐ Exercise (Cardio – hard exercise)
- ☐ Exercise (Stretching – flex exercise)
- ☐ Engage in mindfulness
- ☐ Talk to a friend
- ☐ Eat food
- ☐ Drink alcohol or use drugs
- ☐ Go to sleep
- ☐ Have sex
- ☐ Surf porn
- ☐ Surf social media
- ☐ Try to find a sexual partner
- ☐ Other: _____
- ☐ Other: _____
- ☐ Other: _____
- ☐ Other: _____

What are good ways to address that edgy feeling:

_____
_____
_____
_____
_____

What are unhelpful ways to address that edgy feeling:

_____
_____
_____
_____
_____

> **Noticing that you are stimming is the first step towards change!**
>
> **Change = managing my need for stim more productively**

Let's compare hypersexuality to SEXUAL IMPULSIVITY. Sexual impulsivity is <u>different</u> from hypersexuality. Sexual impulsivity is that quick "yes" response to sexual opportunities. It is saying, "Sure, I'll do that" when a sexual opportunity presents itself without really thinking about it. Sexual impulsivity means that you engage sexually without thinking it through or considering the consequences.

☛ Hypersexuality means that you are always looking for, thinking about or wanting sexual opportunities and your sexual interest creates subjective distress.
☛ Sexual eagerness is a heightened interest and engagement in sexual activity without any subjective distress.
☛ Sexual impulsivity is sexual decision-making that happens too fast; engaging sexually either alone or with a partner, based on a quick decision, and without considering the consequences of that choice.

Joe is on a business trip. Things in his life are going well. He has a wife that he loves, they have fun sex regularly. Their children are getting older, and life is good. Joe is at a bar having a drink with his colleagues. He has some food, engages in good conversation and is chatting with the people at the table beside them. They invite him to a party. Joe says yes right away – Joe loves a party! He has a fun evening, dances, talks to a bunch of new people, learns some cool new things and even makes some new business contacts. One girl had been flirting with Joe all evening; she kisses him, and they have sex. The next day, he is devastated. He isn't quite sure how it all happened or how he will explain things to his wife. He had no intention to cheat, but somehow it happened.

People with ADHD reported higher numbers of sexual partners, higher rates of condomless sex, higher STI diagnoses, higher number of unplanned pregnancies and more emergency contraception use (Rohacek et al., 2022; Margherio et al., 2021). In addition, ADHDers are identified as having more affairs (Tuckman, 2019). These are examples of sexual impulsivity. Sexual impulsivity isn't the only sexual problem that ADHDers face, but it is an important one.

What examples of sexual impulsivity have you experienced?

_____
_____
_____
_____
_____

How has your sexual impulsivity harmed you and/or harmed others?

_____
_____
_____
_____
_____

How has your sexual impulsivity been positive in your life?

_____

_____

_____

_____

_____

On the whole, do you consider your sexual impulsivity to have been a positive or a negative aspect of your life?

_____

_____

_____

_____

_____

Experiencing sexual trauma can increase your use of sex to cope with negative emotions and your overall sexual impulsivity. We will talk more about sexual trauma in Chapter 11. If you are struggling with past or current sexual trauma and this is impacting you today, consult a mental health professional specialized in trauma therapies to assist you!

Let's talk more about what to do if your sexual switch is stuck in the "on" position and you cannot turn it off!

Managing impulsivity can be hard but it IS possible to slow down!

Slowing down your decision-making begins by having some good habits in place.

✓   Mindfulness .... Daily

Your daily mindfulness exercises can include sitting quietly with a hot or cool drink while savoring the flavor or calmly allowing your thoughts to drift in and out without judgement. You may find mindfulness in an environment with less sensory input (such as a sauna, bath or lying under a blanket) or you might enjoy a group meditation or yoga program.

Take a moment <u>each day</u> to sit in gratitude, thanking yourself and others for their positive contributions in your life. Gratitude is important. It helps you slow down and focus on the important people and the meaningful moments in your life.

✓ Deep breathing

Deep breathing helps to slow your body and your brain down. The more you practice deep breathing, the better regulated your nervous system will be and the easier it will be to manage those quick, impulsive thoughts that can get you off track of your goals.

✓ Exercise

Cardio is key! Build up a sweat, move your body, contract your muscles and get active! Exercising daily is an important way to help manage your ADHD symptoms[4].

✓ Sleep

Good sleep habits are key in helping you manage your impulsivity. You know that research showing that when you don't sleep enough, you will overeat the next day[5]? Without sleep, managing impulses is super hard. Set reminders for bedtime, have the Internet turn off at a specific time each day and create a welcoming place to sleep. Ensure that you get a good amount of sleep on a regular basis!

✓ External brains for accountability

External brains are the support people in your life that help slow down your decision making. These people are your brakes. Whether a partner, a friend, a family member, a therapist, a coach, a support group or even a pet, having someone that helps you take the time to question your decision-making is a great way to manage impulsivity. Oftentimes, you may feel frustration or irritation towards the support people in your life, particularly when they encourage you to slow down. Find someone that you will be willing to listen to regardless of their thoughts; make sure it's someone that you can rely on and who has your best interests at heart. It is essential that you trust your accountability partners. Considering an alternative point of view, regardless of whether you take their advice, allows you to slow down your decision-making.

✓ Go outside!

Get outside for some fresh air! Take a walk, go for a hike, build a snowman, drive a snowmobile or sail a sailboat. Getting outside can help you regulate your responses, calm your body and your brain, and help you slow down!

✓ Manage your ADHD with prescribed medications

Effective ADHD medications are shown to drastically improve ADHD symptoms including impulsivity (Hallowell & Ratey, 2022). While there is limited research on this topic, some research does demonstrate a reduction in hypersexuality when stimulants are used for treatment with ADHDers (Kafka & Hennen, 2000).

If you are struggling with impulsivity and the pills aren't working, ask for a medication review. Become an ADHD expert to ensure that you are exploring the best medication options for you and that you can engage in a thoughtful conversation with your physical health provider about your treatment options. Effective medication is an important step in managing your impulsivity. Sexual impulsivity is best managed with proper ADHD medications.

✓   Good stim!

The importance of good stim cannot be overstated. Your need for stimulation is a very good thing. Good stim is essential! Ensure that you are engaged in good, positive and healthy stim to better manage your impulses.

Good stim is:

☛ Beneficial to you and/or others around you
☛ Helps you reach new goals
☛ Expands your sense of self
☛ Creates joy
☛ Fulfilling
☛ Legal

Examples of good stim might be:

✓   Getting things done on your to-do list
✓   Doing something nice for a friend
✓   Creating something
✓   Building something
✓   Starting a new business or a side hustle
✓   Creating a new game or playing a game
✓   Dancing, singing
✓   Exercise
✓   Movement
✓   Time with a pet

What is good stim for you?

_____
_____
_____
_____
_____

Bad stim is:

☛   Negative to you and/or others around you
☛   Conflicts, drama, violence
☛   Stops you in your tracks, it does not allow you to reach your goals
☛   Creates feelings of guilt, shame and despair
☛   Deflating, it leaves you feeling empty and unfulfilled
☛   Creates more negativity
☛   Illegal

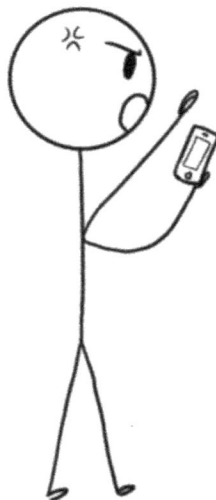

Examples of bad stim might include:

X Starting an argument
X Being negative or saying negative things
X Gossiping about other people
X Affairs
X Drinking or drug use
X Strip clubs or seeking out a sex trade worker
X Social media
X Unproductive daydreams or fantasies

What is bad stim for you?

_____

_____

_____

_____

_____

Mastering impulsivity means that you are willing to get your stim in positive ways, in ways that work better for you. Choose good stim!

✓ Goal setting

Goal setting is important to help manage your impulsivity. Without goals, there is nothing that will encourage you to stop and think twice about your plan, your decisions or your actions. We need goals to achieve specific outcomes. Goals help slow us down.

Create a schedule, a routine or a list of tasks every day. To-do lists will keep you focused on your goals. Maintain a schedule in a way that is effective for you! The more that your scheduling system keeps you on track, the more you will be willing to adhere to your schedule. Random impulsive thoughts will become easier to shake off or they can be added to the list of things to do tomorrow or next month!

☛ Set your intentions for every day, every week, every month and every year
☛ Keep your intentions in a place that is clearly visible to you and to others in order to create accountability for your actions
☛ Have a whiteboard, vision board and/or dream board that you can easily see in your home, in the car and/or at the office to help remind you of your goals
☛ Set clear goals, with specific timelines, tasks and activities required in order to achieve those goals

Goal setting, creating positive intentions and scheduling will help you better manage your impulsivity.

✓ Accountability to yourself

Accountability to yourself is another important way to manage your impulsivity. Accountability can be hard. Find ways to improve your accountability to yourself by doing the following:

- Give yourself a reward for a good job done!
- Use body doubles to help you get things done and stay on track!
- Check in with yourself about your decision-making as well as your progress towards your goals!
- Evaluate how you are feeling about your choices and your progress in life. If you are unhappy with these choices, create a plan to make it different that includes asking for help!
- Write things down. Setting things down in a journal or tracking your choices in writing helps create accountability!

You deserve to reach your goals!

✓ Good people, good food, good environments

You are what you eat. You will become who you hang out with. Clean room, clean mind. All these sayings have one truth in common: your environment matters!

Ensure that the people in your life encourage good decision-making. There are many people who will encourage you to fail. They will encourage you not to try. They will encourage you to give up. Some people do not have your best interests in mind. If you start succeeding, they will remind you about all the reasons why you should stop trying.

- Notice the people who are not helping in your success
- Notice the people who are not reminding you of your goals
- Notice the negative influencers – the people who are not reaching their goals and who encourage you to fail

People who do not encourage you to succeed may be the same people that you would expect to be encouraging, for example, family members, siblings, friends, colleagues, best friends, teachers, etc. Just because someone is supposed to be in your corner, doesn't mean that they actually are! Focus on having good people in your life, people who want to make positive changes in their own lives, people who are making positive changes for themselves and who encourage you to reach your goals.
Food works the very same way. In fact, you can take most of the words above and replace them with the word food!

- Give your body and your brain nourishing, healthy food
- Help your body work its best by making good food choices
- Surround yourself with positive food choices
- Create positive food choices for yourself and for others

Find healthy environments that make you feel good, that are encouraging and that allow you to be your best self. Surround yourself with positivity!

Follow these steps to help slow down your decision making!

Step 1   Identify that you need stim!
Step 2   Find positive sources of stim
Step 3   Keep a <u>visual list</u> of positive stim that you can use daily for inspiration
       Create a jar of fun positive stim options that you can pick from if you run out of ideas in the moment
Step 4   Set goals that are positive for you
       Keep track of your goals with a reminder system, an app or write it down on a whiteboard to help remind you of your goals[6]
       Keep track of your goals with the help of an ADHD coach
Step 5   Adjust when things get stale! Your goals will become less exciting over time and you will want to move on to something else. Create more stim with another level of difficulty, another challenge to strive for or another goal that is similar or altogether different!
Step 6   Manage with medication to better help you navigate your need for stim

Now that we have explored impulsivity, let's focus on a few specific examples of sexual impulsivity that can get you into trouble!

Too much porn use

Porn can be a very positive stim. It can be a fun activity to do alone or with a partner! Porn can also be too much, negative in its content, and you may become dependent on it – needing it prior to having any sexual engagement with yourself and/or with others.

Porn should be like a good wine: lovely, engaging, fun and stimulating. Porn should not be like an alcoholic binge that leaves you feeling burnt out, uninspired, slightly disgusted and uninterested in bonding sexually with another person.

Too much porn can lead to difficulties with your erections and/or your arousal. People report spending so much time masturbating that they need more and more sexual content to get off and reach orgasm. Research supports this observation – there is a moderate correlation observed between hypersexuality and erectile dysfunction during intercourse (Hertz et al., 2022).

Too much porn can leave your partner feeling unimportant, uninvolved and concerned about your pornography use. Sexual partners can feel badly if you <u>need</u> to watch porn prior to engaging in sexual activity with them. When porn becomes a required part of sexual activity, it can lead to hurt feelings and a lack of sexual flexibility.

Too much porn can take you down Internet rabbit holes that encourage sexual discussions, sexual interactions and associations with strangers who may not have your best interests in mind.

Too much porn can lead you to spend hours a day, isolated and alone, while masturbating. You spend your time pushing people away so that you have more time to masturbate. This will leave you withdrawn, lonely, isolated and unfulfilled.

If too much porn is a problem for you, apply the strategies identified in Chapter 5 to transition OUT of sex along with the following:

✓ Limit screen time overall
✓ Use computer blockers and external monitoring software
✓ Limit screen time for your sexual activities online
✓ Set timers for your Internet use
✓ Set a downtime on your router so the Internet can't be used during certain times of the day
✓ Use computer screens in public, never in private
✓ No scrolling online with no specific purpose
✓ Log your urges to use porn so that you can see patterns and find the underlying problems fueling your pornography use
✓ Consider the sexual thoughts that you are creating by watching porn; do they help you achieve positive life goals?
✓ Get additional support from a mental health professional and/or a community support group for sexual addictions such as your local SAA group

External monitoring software and computer blockers are very important to help manage problems with too much porn. External monitoring software are paid services that will block sexual and/or violent content from your devices. These programs can also send accountability reports to your accountability partner[7] who will see exactly where you are going online. This form of online accountability can be quite helpful to manage your urges to use porn. It also helps reduce scrolling without a purpose. Only go online for a specific purpose and then go do something else!

Most internet and cellphone providers offer ways to limit the time that you are online and offer strategies to create automatic downtime for your internet use. There are many different software programs that you can use. Want to avoid watching late into the night? Have your wifi router automatically shut down at 11 pm. While this may be frustrating, it will move you towards more positive sleep habits!

The sexual journal or sex log outlined in Chapter 5 is another important way to manage too much porn! Take note of the intensity of your sexual urges, your use of masturbation, the frequency of your sexual play and the context in which your sexual urges and sexual activities occur. By identifying your patterns of sexual engagement, you will quickly notice unhelpful patterns related to your sexuality and/or your pornography use.

You can create a sexual log or a sexual journal in many ways. You can keep a list on your phone. You can create a checklist. You can write it down in a journal. If using a journal, be careful to not add details that would increase your sexual arousal if you are trying to transition out of sex!

Peanut decided that they needed to have a better handle on their pornography use. They put their laptop in the kitchen and decided to only use it if there was someone else around. They set a downtime for midnight each night so that once the last person in the household went to bed, Peanut did not have access to the Internet. Peanut also kept a log of their urges to use porn. Peanut was able to see that when they were bored, they wanted to go online. They decided to join a pottery class and started tennis lessons. These additional activities, and the friends they made at these events, kept Peanut busy and their urges to use porn went away.

Peanut's sexual log for this week:

Date and time	Urge intensity 0 – no urge 5 – moderate urge 10 – intense, high urge	Masturbation? Sex?	Context? What was I doing at the time?
Wednesday 5 am	8	M	I woke up with an erection, I was feeling stressed about my day
Thursday 4 pm	4	Nope!	I was walking home from work and saw a very attractive person on my way home
Friday 8:30 pm	7	M	I was bored, nothing to do, nothing to watch
Sunday 8 pm	10	S	I was with a casual friend, they asked me to have sex and I wanted to do it
Wednesday 5 pm	7	M	I was heading home and feeling lonely. There wasn't going to be anything to do tonight so I masturbated once I got home

Let's consider your pornography use.

I use porn:

☐   Too much
☐   A reasonable amount
☐   Not at all

I want to address my pornography use by doing the following:

_____
_____
_____
_____
_____

I need help to better manage my pornography use:

☐   Yes!
☐   My friends/family/spouse think that I do
☐   I don't think so
☐   I know that my porn use is ok!

If your family, friends and/or your partner is voicing concerns about your pornography use, consider their observations and carefully assess whether you are using too much porn. If this is a problem for you, consult with a mental health professional to discuss your problems with too much pornography in more detail.

Too much solo sex

Problems with pornography frequently occur in parallel to having too much solo sex. Solo sex is sex that you do alone, without a partner, where you are only focused on yourself and your sexual needs.

Solo sex is just fine! If you are happy with solo sex and it's meeting your needs, there is no problem. Nevertheless, there are some things to consider: are you choosing solo sex because of sensory issues or anxiety issues? Are you choosing solo sex because it is easier than trying to find a partner and face establishing intimacy/vulnerability with another person? Are you choosing solo sex because you are struggling with sexual problems that you have not yet resolved? Is there another reason why you might be uncomfortable and are you using solo sex to avoid an issue or a concern?

Too much solo sex can lead to you feeling isolated and alone. Solo sex may also be happening because you are using orgasm to feel better about other emotions, such as feeling sad, lonely, angry, helpless, powerless or frustrated. As noted earlier, one theory is that sexual eagerness occurs for people with ADHD as a way to cope with emotions (Soldati, 2021). From this perspective, excessive solo sex could be a form of self-soothing, calming yourself down when you are upset. Additionally, it may be that solo sex has become a way to improve your ADHD symptoms, owing to the stim that sex can provide (Soldati, 2021).

- ☐ I use solo sex whenever I am upset
- ☐ I use solo sex when I am bored
- ☐ I refuse invitations to go out with friends/family so that I can engage in solo sex
- ☐ I spend hours a week engaging in solo sex
- ☐ I engage in solo sex every day
- ☐ I lie to others about the amount of solo sex I am having
- ☐ I find myself more dissatisfied, grumpy and unhappy after I engage in solo sex
- ☐ I keep trying to find ways to increase sexual intensity when I am engaged in solo sex
- ☐ I don't engage in exercise or leisure activities so that I have more time for solo sex

There are ways to manage the amount of solo sex you are having. Use the sex log described in the previous section to monitor your use of solo sex.

Other solutions include:

- ✓ Manage your emotions first, then have sex
- ✓ If you have an urge to have sex, consider whether you are trying to manage uncomfortable emotions
- ✓ Have sex for pleasure, not to simply feel better if you are sad, angry, feeling edgy or feeling bored
- ✓ Create more time with friends and family
- ✓ Participate in more community activities
- ✓ Communicate daily with friends, family and/or acquaintances
- ✓ Go for a walk, exercise
- ✓ Ground into your body and work on getting in touch with your body before, during and after sexual pleasure
- ✓ Ensure that you have clear life goals for yourself and work towards those goals
- ✓ Join a community support group as needed

Take the time to clarify your sexual interests clearly to yourself so you can communicate these to a potential partner in the future.

What am I into?

_____

_____

_____

_____

_____

What part of this do I like?

_____

_____

_____

_____

What's the best part of solo sex for me?

_____

_____

_____

_____

What is the worst part of solo sex for me?

_____

_____

_____

_____

I need help to better manage my frequency of solo sex:

☐   Yes!
☐   My friends/family/spouse think(s) that I do
☐   I don't think so
☐   I know that my solo sex use is ok!

If you, your family, friends and/or your partner have concerns about your use of solo sex, carefully assess whether this is a problem for you. Consult with a mental health professional to discuss your problems with too much solo sex in more detail.

Too much partnered sex and misalignments in desired sexual frequency

Partnered sexual problems can occur for the same reasons that are outlined above. Partnered sexual problems are often identified when a partner reports that you aren't all there during sex or you are only "using them" for sex. Take note when you are engaged in sex that feels mechanical, repetitive, a means to an end (only to get off) and/or is occurring too frequently for your partner.

Identify what is driving your sexual urges with the use of your sex log. If you identify problems with your sexuality, refer to the strategies to manage your frequency of sex as identified above. If you do not identify any problems with your sexuality, and a partner is identifying a problem with your sexual frequency, you may be experiencing <u>differences in your desired sexual frequency</u>.

Differences in sexual frequency, differences between your sexual desire and a partner's sexual desire, can create significant problems for many couples. Most often, the ADHD partner is looking for more sex than the non-ADHD partner (Tuckman, 2019).

One way to address this issue is with very clear communication. Often these conversations get sidetracked because, well – communication! Your words, your requests and your goals don't come from a place of sex as pleasure or play. Sex is play, sex is fun, sex is pleasure! Conversations that devolve into fights about sexual frequency without any other context, have lost the point of sexual play!

✓   Address the anger

Often, frequency conversations get stuck because one or both partners are angry. It is important to resolve the relationship issues that are getting in the way of you and a partner finding sexual play together. It is hard to play with someone that you are angry with and it is hard to play with someone who is angry with you! Remember what happens when children are angry: the first shout you will hear on the playground is "I am not playing with you anymore!". This problem extends to us adults as well and impacts our ability to engage in sexual play!

Address the anger. Talk about the anger. Listen. Soothe both your anger and your partner's anger. Ask for help as needed. This is a good time to try some couples counselling or participate in an ADHD relationship program.

✓   Address sexual boredom and/or sexual dissatisfaction

- ☛ Do we both enjoy the sex we are having?
- ☛ Are we both having fun?
- ☛ Are we both getting off and finding pleasure?

Address the lack of fun! Often, frequency conversations come up because one person is having less fun than the other person. If you aren't having fun or your partner isn't having fun, it is impossible to engage in sexual play. Ensure that you are both having fun!

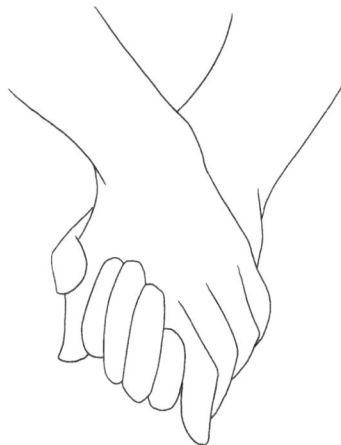

The sexual fun you engage in with a partner should represent you both. Take turns -do the sexual things that you want to do and the things that a partner wants to do. If it isn't your turn this time, remember that next time it will be your turn! Keep track of whose turn it is to ensure that the rotation is fair. Ensure that everyone is getting a fair share of the sexual playbook!

If sex isn't fun for you, talk to a sexual therapist. Explore your own sexuality first, before trying to share it with a partner. Address sexual pain and/or anything else that is getting in the way of sex being a fun activity for you. When you are ready, ask your partner to engage in this process so that they can communicate clearly what they want and need. This leads us to the next part....

✓ Identify and communicate what you actually like

☛ Do I know what I like sexually?
☛ Am I willing to tell my partner what I like?
☛ Do I have an open mind about trying new sexual things?
☛ Am I confident about my sexuality?
☛ Am I allowed to be a fully sexual person?
☛ Do I allow myself to be a fully sexual being?

Arguments about sexual frequency can start when one partner is more flexible, open and curious about sex than another partner. When one partner is assertive and knows what they like, this can be off-putting to the partner who is experiencing more sexual anxiety, particularly if a safe space has not been created in which to discuss sexuality. If you are feeling defensive about your desired sexual frequency, stop, and review the anger section above!

It's ok to assert your sexual needs. It's also ok to talk about your sexual anxiety and your sexual fears. Express your needs and ensure that your partner is also expressing their needs clearly. Just because individual needs are different, doesn't make those needs bad or wrong.

If you do not know your own sexual needs and sexual interests, it is time to work with a sexual therapist to explore sexuality in more detail. If a partner does not communicate their own sexual needs and sexual interests clearly, ensure that you are providing a safe space for conversation. Couples counselling with a qualified mental health professional can help provide a safe environment for these conversations.

✓ Make sex flexible, fun and creative

☛ Is your sexual script flexible?
☛ Is your sexual script creative?
☛ Do you find new ways to pleasure yourself and/or a partner?
☛ Does your sexual script change?

Remember that sex doesn't have to include intercourse. Sex is play! Engaging in Partnered/solo sex together, sex that is occurring together yet physically apart, can be a powerful way to address these difficulties. Ensure that your sexual script is fun and flexible enough to suit you both. Get creative!

✓ Banish sexual shame

- ☛ Do you believe that there is a right way and a wrong way to have sex?
- ☛ Do you engage in sexually shaming comments?
- ☛ Are you stuck on how sex "should" be?
- ☛ Do you judge yourself and others about sexuality?

Sexual shaming happens when you put someone down, whether yourself or others, for having a sexual interest that may be different than what you think it "should" be. Sexual shaming often involves making judgements about other people's sexuality, your partner's sexuality or certain sexual thoughts or fantasies. If you expect sex to be a certain way, to occur at a certain time or to involve specific activities, it may be difficult to talk openly with others about sex.

Conversations about sexual frequency can escalate and become non-productive when sexual shaming occurs. Banish sexual shaming by keeping an open mind, asking questions, and staying curious about what your partner is trying to communicate.

Being sexually eager means that you are interested and curious about sex. Be curious about your sexuality as well as your partner's sexual experience. Bring that curiosity to your partner from a perspective of a fun, playful and exploratory perspective!

If past trauma is limiting sexual scripts and getting in the way of fun and creative sexual play, you can learn to reduce your distress through individual counselling. We will talk more about reducing distress and trauma therapy in Chapter 11.

Sexual differences about desired frequency can be complicated! Differences in sexual frequencies are best addressed through couples counseling with a sexual therapist or a qualified mental health professional.

💣 We will talk more about having hard sexual conversations in the next chapter.

Risky sexual activities

Risky sexual activities involve activities that put you or others at risk and have the potential to damage your physical health, your emotional health, your financial health or your long-term goals.

Risky sexual activities may include:

💣 Sex with strangers
💣 Sex online
💣 Paid sex
💣 Trading sex for other things
💣 Sex with people where there is a large age gap
💣 Sex without contraception
💣 Sex without first communicating your needs to a partner
💣 Sending sexual or naked pictures to strangers or acquaintances
💣 Spending excessive amounts of time or money at strip clubs

What is risky sex for you?

☐ I am engaging sexually with strangers online
☐ I am meeting strangers in person for sex
☐ I am taking sexual risks by avoiding condom use
☐ I am paying for sex or trading drugs/substances for sex
☐ I am making choices that breach my own personal values when I have sex
☐ I am sending people naked pictures of myself

Other ways that I am engaging in risky sex:

_____

_____

_____

_____

_____

What can you do about risky sexual activities?

✓ Use sexual intensity and sexual novelty to reduce your need for risky sex
✓ Use deep breathing to create a gap between a sexual opportunity and agreeing to engage in risky sexual activity
✓ Review the chapters in this workbook to determine how you can increase your sexual intensity and sexual novelty in less risky ways
✓ Focus on sexual variation rather than increasing sexual intensity to address boredom
✓ Manage impulsivity to reduce your spontaneous sexual decisions
✓ Remember your goals
✓ Stay busy with positive stim!

Enthusiastic consent is always essential, and it is particularly important if you have a tendency to engage in risky sexual situations and/or make impulsive sexual decisions. Ensure to obtain enthusiastic consent prior to engaging with a partner. This includes asking for consent before sending a sexual picture, before touching someone, before talking explicitly about sex to a partner, and before engaging sexually with another person.

Enthusiastic consent applies to YOU as well as to the other person. Make sure that you want to engage in sexual activity. When you impulsively say yes, you may change your mind in the first few minutes of physical contact. That is ok! If you change your mind <u>at any time</u>, you can stop. Communicate your desire to stop clearly – both verbally and nonverbally. Say "Stop" clearly and loudly. Shake your head no. Walk away and talk to your partner afterwards to explain what happened in more detail.

Other alternatives to increase sexual novelty and variety can include:

✓ Exploring kink communities
✓ Exploring fetish communities
✓ Meeting like-minded partners and getting to know them before engaging with them sexually

✓ Joining community groups of like-minded people
✓ Meeting people in person rather than engaging sexually with them online
✓ Ensuring that you have enthusiastic consent in all sexual situations, both for yourself and your partner(s)

Are there other activities that would make sex more interesting and that don't involve sexual risk taking?

_____

_____

_____

_____

_____

I want to address my use of risky sex by doing the following:

_____

_____

_____

_____

_____

I need help to better manage my risky sexual choices:

☐ Yes!
☐ My friends/family/spouse think that I do
☐ I don't think so
☐ I know that my sexual activities are ok!

If this problem applies to you, consult with a mental health professional to discuss your problems with risky sex in more detail.

Affairs

Given that ADHDers have more conflicts in their relationships (Wymbs et al., 2021), less sexual satisfaction (Young et al., 2023), more sexual impulsivity (Wymbs et al., 2021) and tend to be more sexually eager (Tuckman, 2019), it would be reasonable to expect that rates of affairs would be higher for ADHD folks. There is limited information about ADHDers and affairs. Extramarital affairs were reported to be higher in some research with ADHD couples (Wymbs et al., 2021). ADHD partners reported a history of having more emotional affairs (Tuckman, 2019). Young et al. (2023) noted a greater number of lifetime affairs for ADHD women. There are many reasons why someone might have an affair. According to Young et al. (2023) ADHDers engaged in affairs, owing to poor impulse control, alcohol disinhibition, sensation seeking and feeling misunderstood by their partner.

This workbook is not focused on affairs, why they happened, what to do when they do happen or how to bounce back from affairs. There are workbooks and resources that can help you understand and deal with affairs[8]. We will talk more about affairs that stem from intimacy and/or relationship issues in the next chapter, but for now, we will focus on affairs that stem from impulsivity.

There are ways to reduce the potential of having an affair:

✓ Manage your alcohol and drug use to better manage your sexual impulsivity
✓ Ensure that you have enough positive stim in your day
✓ Reflect on the role of flirting as stim in your life
✓ React immediately if you notice yourself slipping in your personal values regarding flirting, sexual conversations and the choices that you are making within relationships
✓ Talk about the need for sexual stim
✓ Communicate and integrate sexual intensity, sexual variation and sexual novelty within your relationships

You may decide to maintain open relationships to avoid problems related to affairs. Engaging in consensual non-monogamy (CNM), means that you might be less impacted by affairs; however, if you have a history of affairs, owing to seeking sexual stimulation and/or levels of intoxication, you may breach CNM rules that you have set within your relationships. Whether you are in an open or closed relationship, all relationships have boundaries and agreements.

The need for novelty may contribute to engaging in affairs. Openly discussing ways to expand sexual novelty and coming to an agreement with a partner about how to increase both sexual novelty and sexual intensity in your life is another way to allay concerns about affairs.

Often, flirting can become a source of stim. If you find that flirting creates positive stim for you, explore whether flirting is good stim or bad stim for you. If you don't find flirting helpful to you, replace this form of stim with another stim that feels good and has a greater likelihood of creating positive outcomes in your life.

Substance use

Whether alcohol, cannabis or other drugs, ADHD and intoxicant use can go together. In fact, people with ADHD often struggle with addictions (Kooij et al., 2019).

Addictions impact your sexuality in various ways:

☛ It can create conflicts and multiple problems in your relationships
☛ It can impact your sexual functioning
☛ It can distract you from engaging sexually because you are preoccupied with getting drunk or high
☛ It can lead to incidents of domestic violence
☛ It can lead to incidents of victimization and trauma

Excessive alcohol use can create problems with your erections. Whiskey Dick is a popular term that refers to your erections not working when you are intoxicated. Research indicates that for people with alcohol induced erectile dysfunction, it can take three months of abstinence from alcohol to resolve problems with erections (Karunakaran & Michael, 2022).

Intoxicants, both alcohol and drugs, can negatively impact your ability to manage impulsivity. You are more likely to make impulsive decisions when intoxicated. This involves impulsive decisions such as engaging in affairs (Young et al., 2023) as well as perpetrating domestic violence (Whymbs, 2021).

If you are struggling with problems related to substance abuse, it is essential that you seek help. There are many local resources to help you tame your addictions. Work with an addictions counselor that is well versed in neurodivergence and addictions.

STIs and contraception use

Sexually transmitted infections (STI) rates may be higher in ADHD populations. While some studies did not find any differences, other studies did report differences between ADHD and non-ADHD samples. Young et al. (2023) noted differences between a neurotypical sample and an ADHD sample for both men and women as it relates to STIs. Adolescents and young adults with ADHD were more likely to get an STI later in life than their neurotypical peers. In men, using ADHD medications significantly reduced the risk of obtaining an STI (Young & Cocallis, 2023).

ADHDers have a higher level of unplanned pregnancies (Soldati, 2021). There is also research identifying that women with ADHD are less likely to use contraceptives (Young et al., 2023). We will talk more about ADHD and parenthood in the next chapter. For now, let's examine ways to improve your sexual choices and optimize your sexual health.

What problems do you identify with your sexual health?

- ☐ I avoid condom use
- ☐ I have unprotected sex
- ☐ I have unprotected sex with strangers
- ☐ I have unprotected sex with people who I know have STIs
- ☐ I do not talk about contraception use prior to having sex with someone
- ☐ I do not share the fact that I have an STI with new partners
- ☐ I do not get regularly tested for sexually transmitted infections (STIs)

There are easy ways to reduce your risk:

- ✓ Talk with new partners about their STI history
- ✓ Get checked for STIs regularly[9]
- ✓ Always carry contraception with you
- ✓ Have regular discussions with your health provider about your sexual health
- ✓ Immediately address any symptoms that you notice on your genitals and/or any indications that your physical health is declining
- ✓ Get all available vaccines to help protect yourself and others from STIs
- ✓ Communicate with partners about any STI concerns you have after sexual contact
- ✓ If someone reacts poorly to conversations about maintaining your sexual health, reflect on whether they are a good sexual partner for you

I want to address my risk of STIs and unplanned pregnancies by doing the following:

_____

_____

_____

_____

_____

I need help to better manage my sexual health choices:

☐   Yes!
☐   My friends/family/spouse think that I do
☐   I don't think so
☐   I know that my sexual health choices are ok!

Consult a health professional to discuss your concerns about STIs, unprotected sex and unplanned pregnancies in more detail. If you are worried about your family physician knowing the scope of your sexual activities, talk to another health care provider for assistance.

Give yourself a reward when you prioritize your sexual health! While it may take some getting used to, you can maintain your desired level of sexual adventure while ensuring that your physical health is protected!

The importance of medication

Medications work to improve ADHD symptoms including impulsivity! Stimulant medication is effective to reduce ADHD symptoms (Kooij et al., 2019). If you are struggling in your relationship, in your sexual health or with your sexual impulsivity, it is time to talk with a health care professional to optimize your medication!

✓   Optimize ADHD medications to help you better manage your impulsivity
✓   Work with an ADHD coach to help improve your skills and better manage impulsivity
✓   Create systems of accountability to help manage your impulsivity
✓   Use visual reminders to maintain focus on your goals
✓   Prioritize positive stim on a daily basis

We will explore relationships and intimacy in more depth in the next chapter of our journey!

Working towards my goals

Do I need to address my impulsivity as it relates to sex?

☐   Yes, absolutely
☐   Yes, maybe, perhaps
☐   Not sure
☐   No, probably not
☐   Not, not at all

I will tackle my impulsivity as it relates to:

- ☐ My pornography use
- ☐ Too much solo sex
- ☐ Too much partnered sex
- ☐ Too much risky sex
- ☐ Affairs
- ☐ Substance use
- ☐ STIs/unprotected sex
- ☐ Other: _____
- ☐ Other: _____
- ☐ Other: _____

The best strategy for me to address my sexual impulsivity includes:

_____

_____

_____

_____

_____

I will create accountability to reduce my impulsive sexual choices by:

- ✓ Working with a mental health professional
- ✓ Using a visual whiteboard to remind me of my goals
- ✓ Adding more positive stim in my life
- ✓ Regular exercise
- ✓ Limiting my time online
- ✓ Adding software blockers to my devices
- ✓ Scheduling downtime for my internet use
- ✓ Creating accountability as it relates to my sexual choices

If this plan does not work, I will ask for help by reaching out to:

- ☐ My health care practitioner to optimize my medications
- ☐ A community support group to increase my accountability
- ☐ An ADHD coach to help improve my skills
- ☐ A mental health practitioner to explore my impulsivity in more detail
- ☐ A close friend or family member to increase my level of community support
- ☐ Other: _____
- ☐ Other: _____

Notes

1 There is a difference between hypersexuality, defined as a preoccupation with sexuality that causes distress, and a heightened sexual interest or sexual eagerness which involves being preoccupied with sex but without experiencing any subjective distress. This distinction makes interpreting research conclusions confusing as these terms are frequently interchanged. The concept of hypersexuality <u>requires</u> that a person experiences subjective distress as a result of their sexual preoccupation. If you don't have distress, you would not meet the definition of hypersexuality.
2 See Soldati (2021) for details about brain chemistry, ADHD and sexuality and Kooij (2019) for general information about ADHD brain structures and chemistry.
3 To my knowledge there is no research that explores these concepts as it relates to sexuality and neurodiversity.
4 Always check with your health care professional before adding a new exercise program into your life!
5 See Laurent et al. (2010); Cooper et al. (2018) or Knutson et al. (2007) for details.
6 The Finch app is one example of a goal-directed app but there are many others out there!
7 You decide who your accountability partner will be and you can choose to set up an automatic sharing of your Internet history with them. Ensure that they are consenting to be an accountability partner for you.
8 One excellent resource is the book *After the Affair: Healing the Pain and Rebuilding Trust When a Partner Has Been Unfaithful* (2020), 3rd ed., by Janis Spring.
9 In some areas there are free sexual health checks available to monitor your STI status.

References

American Psychiatric Association (2022). *Diagnostic and Statistical Manual of Mental Disorders*, (5th ed. text revision, DSM-5-TR). https://doi.org/10.1176/appi.books.9780890425787.

Böthe, B., Koos, M., Toth-Kiraly, I., Orosz, G. & Demetrovics, Z. (2019). Investigating the associations of adult ADHD symptoms, hypersexuality, and problematic pornography use among men and women on a largescale, non-clinical sample. *Journal of Sexual Medicine*, 16(4), 489–499. https://doi.org/10.1016/j.jsxm.2019.01.312.

Cooper, C.B, Neufeld, E.V, Dolezal, B.A., & Martin, J.L. (2018). Sleep deprivation and obesity in adults: a brief narrative review, *BMJ Open Sport & Exercise Medicine*, 4 e000392. doi:10.1136/bmjsem-2018-000392.

Hallowell, E.M. & Ratey, J.J. (2022). *ADHD 2.0: New Science and Essential Strategies for Thriving with Distraction--from Childhood through Adulthood*. Ballantine Books, p. 208.

Hertz, P.G., Turner, D., Barra, S., Biedermann, L., Retz-Junginger, P., Schöttle, D. and Retz, W. (2022). Sexuality in Adults With ADHD: Results of an Online Survey. *Frontiers Psychiatry*, 13, 868278. doi: 10.3389/fpsyt.2022.868278.

Kafka, M.P. & Hennen, J. (2000). Psychostimulant augmentation during treatment with selective serotonin reuptake inhibitors in men with paraphilias and paraphilia-related disorders: A case series. *The Journal of Clinical Psychiatry*, 61(9), 664. https://doi.org/10.4088/JCP.v61n0912.

Kasparek, T., Theiner, P. & Filova, A. (2015). Neurobiology of ADHD From Childhood to Adulthood: Findings of Imaging Methods. *Journal of Attention Disorders*, 19, 931–943.

Knutson,K.L., Spiegel, K., Penev, P. & Cauter,E.V. (2007). The metabolic consequences of sleep deprivation. *Sleep Medicine Reviews*, 11(3), 163–178. https://doi.org/10.1016/j.smrv.2007.01.002.

Kooij JJS, Bijlenga D, Salerno L, Jaeschke R, Bitter I, Balázs J, Thome J, Dom G, Kasper S, Nunes Filipe C, Stes S, Mohr P, Leppämäki S, Casas M, Bobes J, Mccarthy JM, Richarte V, Kjems Philipsen A, Pehlivanidis A, Niemela A, Styr B, Semerci B, Bolea-Alamanac B, Edvinsson D, Baeyens D, Wynchank D, Sobanski E, Philipsen A, McNicholas F, Caci H, Mihailescu I, Manor I, Dobrescu I, Saito T, Krause J, Fayyad J, Ramos-Quiroga JA, Foeken K, Rad F, Adamou M, Karunakaran A, Michael JP (2022). The Impact of Abstinence From Alcohol on Erectile Dysfunction: A Prospective Follow up in Patients With Alcohol Use Disorder. Journal of Sexual Medicine, 19(4), 581–589. doi: 10.1016/j.jsxm.2022.01.517.

Korchia, T., Boyer, L., Deneuville, M., Etchecopar-Etchart, D., Lancon, C. & Fond, G. (2022). ADHD prevalence in patients with hypersexuality and paraphilic disorders: A systematic review and meta-analysis. *European Archives of Psychiatry and Clinical Neuroscience*, 272(8), 1413–1420. https://doi.org/10.1007/s00406-022-01421-9.

Laurent, B.J., Romer, M.A., Nougues, P.M., Touyarou, P. & Damien, D. (2010). Acute partial sleep deprivation increases food intake in healthy men. *The American Journal of Clinical Nutrition*, 91(6), 1550–1559. https://doi.org/10.3945/ajcn.2009.28523.

Margherio, S.M., Capps, E.R., Monopoli, J.W., Evans, S.W., Hernandez-Rodriguez, M., Owens, J.S. & DuPaul, G.J. (2021). Romantic Relationships and Sexual Behavior Among Adolescents With ADHD. *Journal of Attention Disorders*, 25(10), 1466–1478. doi:10.1177/1087054720914371.

Niazof, D., Weizman, A. & Weinstein, A. (2019). The contribution of ADHD and attachment difficulties to online pornography use among students. *Comprehensive Psychiatry*, 93, 56–60. https://doi.org/10.1016/j.comppsych.2019.07.002.

Ohlmeier, M., Fitzgerald, M., Gill, M., Lensing, M., Motavalli Mukaddes, N., Brudkiewicz, P., Gustafsson, P., Tani, P., Oswald, P., Carpentier, P.J., De Rossi, P., Delorme, R., Markovska Simoska, S., Pallanti, S., Reid, R.C., Carpenter, B.N., Gilliland, R. & Karim, R. (2011). Problems of self-concept in a patient sample of hypersexual men with attention-deficit disorder. *Journal of Addiction Medicine*, 5(2), 134–140. https://doi.org/10.1097/ADM.0b013e3181e6ad32.

Rohacek, A.M., Firkey, M.K., Woolf-King, S.E. & Antshel, K.M. (2022). Moderation of risks to sexual health by substance use in college students with ADHD. Journal of Clinical Psychiatry, 83(4), e1–e7.

Soldati, L., Bianchi-Demicheli, F., Schockaert, P., Köhl, J., Bolmont, M., Hasler, R. & Perroud, N. (2021). Association of ADHD and hypersexuality and paraphilias. *Psychiatry Research*, 295, 113638. https://doi.org/10.1016/j.psychres.2020.113638.

Spring, J.A. (2020). *After the Affair, Third Edition: Healing the Pain and Rebuilding Trust When a Partner Has Been Unfaithful* (3rd ed.). Harper Publications.

Tuckman, A. (2019). *ADHD After Dark: Better Sex Life, Better Relationship* (1st ed.). Routledge.

Wymbs, B.T., Canu, W.H., Sacchetti, G.M. & Ranson, L.M. (2021). Adult ADHD and romantic relationships: What we know and what we can do to help. *Journal of Marriage and Family Therapy*, 47, 664–681.

Young, S., Bejerot, S., Lehtonen, T., Kustow, J., Müller-Sedgwick, U., Hirvikoski, T., Pironti, V., Ginsberg, Y., Félegyházy, Z., Garcia-Portilla, M.P. & Asherson, P. (2019). Updated European Consensus Statement on diagnosis and treatment of adult ADHD. *European Psychiatry*, February, 56, 14–34. doi:10.1016/j.eurpsy.2018.11.001.

Young, S. & Cocallis, K. (2023). A systematic review of the relationship between neurodiversity and psychosexual functioning in individuals with autism spectrum disorder (ASD) or attention-Deficit/Hyperactivity disorder (ADHD). *Neuropsychiatric Disease and Treatment*, 19, 1379–1395. https://doi.org/10.2147/NDT.S319980.

Young, S., Klassen, L. J., Reitmeier, S. D., Matheson, J. D., & Gudjonsson, G. H. (2023). Let's talk about sex... and ADHD: Findings from an anonymous online survey. *International Journal of Environmental Research and Public Health*, 20(3), 2037. https://doi.org/10.3390/ijerph20032037.

Chapter 10

Intimacy... Yikes!

Ah, intimacy... The word intimacy tends to create confusion. It seems so vague... What exactly are we talking about? Intimacy is the knowledge of ourselves and the knowledge of others. It means knowing, on a deeper level, who we are and who other people are. Intimacy is an emotional closeness[1].

Throughout this chapter, we will discuss intimacy with self – knowing yourself and creating that emotional closeness with yourself, as well as intimacy with others – knowing others and creating that emotional closeness with other people. Both types of intimacy help you feel loved, connected and grounded, within yourself and your community.

We don't create intimacy with everyone. Just because we meet someone doesn't mean that the relationship will grow. Just because someone is in our lives, like a parent, cousin, coworker or spouse, doesn't automatically mean that we have intimacy within these relationships. Intimacy is built; it is created. Intimacy is also maintained. We can get to know someone, know them deeply, profoundly, but if we don't maintain our relationship and the "knowing" of that other person, we can lose the intimacy we once had with them. Intimacy means that initial getting-to-know-you period, but it also includes your efforts to build a relationship and keep it going over time.

We must ALLOW for intimacy. We allow emotional closeness with others and with ourselves[2]. It doesn't just happen; it is something that we open ourselves up to doing. It is possible to live your whole life without sharing who you are with others. It is possible to live your life without truly knowing yourself and/or others.

Abraham is a wonderful person with lots of ideas, creativity and joy. Abraham doesn't easily share thoughts and feelings with others. He focuses on work and doesn't talk about his feelings of loneliness with his friends. Abraham knows many people but they don't know him very well. When thinking about how he might want to improve things for himself, the idea of letting people know his true thoughts and feelings felt too scary. He didn't want to risk people not agreeing with his perspective or not understanding how he felt. He remained quiet. Nothing changed significantly in his life.

Fear of intimacy is increased in folks with ADHD (Hertz et al., 2022). This fear of intimacy appears to be related to several factors. ADHDers seem to perceive intimate situations as being more frightening and report more past issues with intimacy in prior relationships

DOI: 10.4324/9781003422372-11

(Marsh et al., 2015). ADHD folks have a history of poor relationships, divorce and frequent conflicts in relationships (Whymbs, 2021; Marsh et al., 2015). People with ADHD report lower relationship satisfaction (Whymbs, 2021; Kooij, 2018). Spouses of people with ADHD report lower intimacy in their relationships with ADHD folks and lower marital satisfaction than what is reported in neurotypical relationships (Ben-Naim et al., 2017). ADHDers often feel unloved in relationships (Kooij, 2018). Many women with ADHD report feeling like they cannot maintain a long-term relationship (Wallin et al., 2022). In addition, ADHD folks often have a history of victimization and trauma. Given these findings, it isn't surprising that ADHDers may be fearful of intimacy.

It is interesting to note that people with ADHD may be more likely to choose other people who have ADHD as their romantic partners (Whymbs, 2021). Others may do the exact opposite, try to find partners who do not struggle with the same difficulties that they face. Regardless of your choice, hurdles are often experienced in neurodivergent relationships. Learning about ADHD and relationships is one positive way to navigate these hurdles.

Building intimacy with another person assumes that you are engaging in a vulnerable way with someone who is safe. If someone is not safe, or you do not know them well enough to determine your level of safety, it is best to maintain some caution in your level of self-disclosure. Our exploration of intimacy in relationships assumes that you are in safe relationships. If you are not sure whether your relationship is safe or if you know that your relationship is unsafe, <u>please pause</u> and move to the next chapter of this workbook before coming back to explore themes related to intimacy with yourself and others. We will talk more about avoiding victimization in Chapter 11.

Let's explore intimacy in more detail!

Intimacy ingredient #1 – Reciprocity

Building intimacy is a RECIPROCAL experience – this means that individuals who are sharing intimacy together must be willing to share. If someone is not sharing of themselves, there is no intimacy. Intimacy involves equal balance, back and forth!

You may find that you tend to overshare rather than under share. For the teetertotter to work, reciprocity rules need to apply. Balance is needed both ways: sharing of yourself at a similar rate than the other person is sharing of themselves. You may find that you prefer sharing with people who share at the same intensity you do; this is a perfectly acceptable option. Finding balance in your sharing of yourself is a skill that requires practice. Aim for balance in your reciprocity with others!

Am I willing to share information about who I am?

☐ No way, people would not like the real me
☐ Nope, most people won't understand me
☐ No, people will judge me
☐ My words will likely offend or upset someone, so it's best not to share who I am
☐ I will get it wrong. I will say something that isn't right, so there is no point in sharing
☐ I will be embarrassed and feel stupid
☐ Yes, I think that people will like me
☐ Yes, I am a person worth knowing
☐ Yes, people do like me once I give them a chance
☐ Yes, I believe that I will meet someone that is like me if I keep trying!

If you are not sharing your thoughts, feelings and other important aspects of your life, you are not engaging in reciprocal relationships. Hiding your likes, your dislikes, your preferences and your emotions might seem like a good idea in the short-term, and you may avoid feeling rejection or disappointment, but in the long run this may not be the best decision.

> Jackson is trying to be more authentic in relationships with others. The group is talking about where they should eat before leaving for their evening. When asked what Jackson would like to eat, Jackson doesn't reply and just says "Whatever works". Afterwards, Jackson realized that it was a missed opportunity to share with the group. Jackson has decided to be more forthcoming and honest about food preferences next time!

Sharing parts of you doesn't have to be complicated! Take the time to share who you are with someone else. Share your thoughts, beliefs, feelings, dreams, preferences and life goals to build intimacy with others. Take the time to identify your own thoughts, beliefs, feelings, dreams, preferences and life goals to build intimacy within yourself as well!

To improve my level of intimacy,

✓ I will share more about myself including my thoughts, feelings, values, dreams and beliefs with others!
✓ I will seek others who enjoy sharing of themselves!

Intimacy ingredient #2 – Time Management

Creating intimacy and being open with yourself and/or another person starts with having the time to do so! If you have no time in your life that is dedicated to building relationships, it will be hard to improve your level of intimacy. Create time to get to know someone. Create time to connect with yourself. This is an important first step.

Do I create time to get to know people?

- ☐ Yes! People are my first priority, always
- ☐ Sometimes, it depends on what my hyperfocus is driving me to do in the moment
- ☐ Rarely; I often have other tasks and things on my mind
- ☐ Never; I don't want to get to know others

Sometimes people try to build intimacy in ways that do not promote emotional sharing. They spend time with a person, but they do not actually connect, share or reveal parts themselves. Creating intimacy means that you take time to be with someone, <u>AND</u> during that time, you actually share parts of you!

Here are a few things that can help you become closer to someone else:

- ✓ Doing something active together (exercise, projects, renovations/building things together, making music together, playing games together)
- ✓ Talking together
- ✓ Learning together
- ✓ Sex!

Reflect on the reasons why you may want to create the time to build closer relationships with others. How does creating time to connect with others benefit your life?

_____

_____

_____

_____

_____

How will you create time to connect with yourself and others in your life?

_____

_____

_____

_____

- ✓ Schedule time and connecting activities to increase the amount of time available to connect more positively with another person.

There are many ways to improve your time management as it relates to engaging with others in your life.

- ☛ Add socialization reminders to your calendar
- ☛ Create a reminder system to contact specific friends and family every two to three weeks
- ☛ Use texts, emojis or pictures to communicate quickly with people and keep them active in your life

- ☛ Tell people that you are wanting to connect with them and make plans together
- ☛ Ask people to be your body double so that you can connect while getting those chores done!
- ☛ Set aside time to connect with yourself daily and/or in times of heightened stress
- ☛ Reflect back on your activities each month to ensure that you have maintained your relationship goals

✓   To improve intimacy, I will maintain time in my schedule to connect with myself and others regularly

Intimacy ingredient #3 – Emotional Expression

Neurodivergent folks can have unique struggles as it relates to their emotional expression. Finding the right word, keeping your thoughts in order, and communicating your thoughts clearly can be a challenge. This challenge becomes even more difficult when you're in a heightened emotional state. Problems with your emotional expression can interrupt intimacy building.

- ☛ Do I know how I feel?
- ☛ Can I communicate this to others?
- ☛ Will they understand me?

Difficulties with emotional expression means that it can be harder to communicate what you want and what you need. These difficulties can create misunderstandings in relationships and during sexual play.

Alexithymia is a difficulty identifying and communicating your emotions. If you struggle to identify your emotions, rather than pretend that you know how you feel, stop and acknowledge that you do not know. Acknowledging your lack of clarity about your emotions will build more intimacy than trying to identify the emotion in vain.

"I don't know" is a perfectly acceptable response! Talking with partners about your difficulty identifying and sharing emotions can help others realize that you are not avoiding emotional conversations; it's just that emotional knowing is not something that comes easily to you!

Practice identifying and communicating emotions. This is one way to keep improving your connection with your emotions. Your emotions are there, even if it is hard for you to notice them. There is a wonderful app called Animi – Improve Alexithymia/Understand your emotions. This App can help you identify physical sensations and uses a visual representation (an emotional compass) to help you describe your feelings to others. You can also use a feelings wheel or a list of feelings to practice identifying your emotions. If you can't do it, that is completely fine. The more you practice tuning into yourself and simply noticing what is going on in your body, it might become easier.

To practice identifying and sharing my emotions, I will:

✓ Try to connect with my body daily
✓ Ask myself how I am feeling to see if something comes up
✓ Use visual trackers, such as a heart rate monitor or a checklist to explore how my body is reacting each day
✓ Try an emotional identification app such as Animi
✓ Keep a feelings wheel posted somewhere where I can easily see it and refer to it
✓ Keep it simple: Yucky, Not Yucky or OK!
✓ Use visualization, such as an image to get my point across
✓ Create a code word to represent an emotional state and share it with family, friends or partners so that everyone understands its meaning

If the thought of answering the question.... I feel .... or right now I feel.... gives you hives, that is A-OK! Practice sharing your thoughts instead! I am thinking.... is another way to gain understanding about yourself and to share different parts of yourself with others. Sharing your thoughts can help you start to build more intimacy with yourself and others.

The more you share your thoughts, emotions, preferences and life experiences with others, the more intimacy you are building. There are many ways to build intimacy. It starts with SHARING parts of yourself!

Sharing your true self can feel risky! Sometimes it pays off, but sometimes it doesn't. If it doesn't pay off and someone harms us, doesn't care for us in return, doesn't like us or rejects us, the choice to have been vulnerable might feel like it was a bad choice. This simply isn't true! There are people that you will connect with and others that you will not connect with throughout your life. That is ok. It can take time and effort to find the right connections in your life. Creating intimacy is a journey!

Intimacy ingredient #4 – Unmasking Your Neurodiversity

Allowing someone to see your ADHD symptoms is another way to build intimacy. Sharing your symptoms with others includes allowing them to see you jiggle your leg, twirl your hair, chew your tongue, interrupt during conversations and/or hyperfocus on a specific activity. Dropping your social mask and allowing your full ADHD self to shine in the presence of someone else is a powerful way to create intimacy.

I am comfortable having someone see my full ADHD self:

- ☐ Yes
- ☐ No
- ☐ I haven't tried that yet!

My ADHD self is absolutely loveable because:

_____
_____
_____
_____
_____

My ADHD self is unloveable because:

_____
_____
_____
_____
_____

If you truly believe that your ADHD self is unlovable, would others agree with you?

- ☐ Yes
- ☐ No
- ☐ I don't know

Can the things that contribute to your ADHD self being unlovable change?

- ☐ Yes
- ☐ No
- ☐ I don't know

Are you motivated to change these aspects of yourself?

- ☐ Yes
- ☐ No
- ☐ I don't know

Challenge yourself to address these barriers by discussing them with trusted friends, family members and/or with the help of a mental health professional. Loving your entire ADHD self is an important goal. It will help you to start building intimacy with yourself and others!

Let's explore masking in more detail!

Masking means hiding your true self. Masking can be a social requirement, something necessary to fit in, be accepted or as a way to meet your community expectations. Masking can also be something that you impose on yourself for fear that who you really are won't be acceptable to others.

Many neurodiverse individuals have learned to mask to survive. Whether you mask to fit in as a result of social constraints, whether you mask to achieve professional success or whether you mask because it is required for you to be acceptable within your family, social masking can be a barrier to building intimacy with others[3]. Expectations can compel people to hide their true selves. In particular, biological females with ADHD have a tendency to mask to maintain socially appropriate gender norms (Solden, 2012). This interrupts the development of intimacy. Masking can be a barrier to achieving intimacy in your life!

What are the expectations that your community holds for you?

_____

_____

_____

_____

_____

What are the expectations that your family or extended family holds for you?

_____

_____

_____

_____

_____

What are the expectations that you hold for yourself?

_____

_____

_____

_____

_____

How do these expectations contribute to your use of masking in relationships?

_____

_____

_____

_____

_____

Ideally, you are able to meet your own expectations while being your true self. That is a great feeling! However, if you believe that your true self does not align with your expectations or your community's expectations of who you are and what you should be doing, this can be a terrible feeling. Avoiding this feeling can result in hiding who you are including your likes and dislikes in order to meet other people's expectations.

It can be argued that not masking at all isn't a great idea. Without any masking, you might say something impulsively that does not accurately convey your beliefs, values, needs or desires. You can overwhelm people. You may be victimized if you are completely unmasked before getting to know if someone is trustworthy. Having no mask can leave you vulnerable. Boundaries are required in relationships. Boundaries keep you safe. Good boundaries help you maintain your authentic self while respecting both yourself and others. Rather than masking, use boundaries to create safety in relationships.

What are the positive aspects of masking in your life? When I hide who I am, I am able to ...

_____

_____

_____

_____

_____

What are the negatives of masking in your life? When I hide who I am, it harms me because...

_____

_____

_____

_____

_____

To reduce masking in my life:

✓ I will reflect on my use of masking
✓ I will find spaces in my life where I can drop my mask
✓ I will find people in my life who are safe and with whom I can drop my mask
✓ I will allow my mask to drop when I am alone and when I am with trusted people
✓ I will practice being myself

Intimacy ingredient #4 – Sexual Communication

Sexual communication is yet another way to achieve intimacy in relationships. Whether your relationship is with yourself or your relationship is with another person, your sexuality is an important part of you!

Finding your sexual groove is much easier when you are open and honest about your sexual likes and dislikes. Masking can interfere with this process. If you are hiding what you like or don't like sexually, either from yourself or from others, it will be impossible to truly connect with others. You are also likely to feel dissatisfied with your sexual experiences as these will not reflect your true interests. In addition, you may be losing out on a relationship with yourself and/or with others that authentically reflects who you really are, rather than who you think you should be.

As discussed in prior chapters, research demonstrates that people with ADHD use more pornography, are more gender fluid, tend to have same sex and opposite sex partners and have had more sexual experiences involving consensual non-monogamy (Tuckman, 2019; Young & Cocallis, 2023; Hetz et al., 2022; Niazof et al., 2019). In addition, ADHD folks have reported higher number of sexual partners, higher rates of condomless sex, higher STI diagnoses, higher numbers of unplanned pregnancies and more use of emergency contraception (Rohacek et al., 2022; Hetz et al., 2022; Margherio et al., 2021). Regardless of your personal history, you may feel uncomfortable sharing your sexual past with a partner. Your sexual history is unique to you. If you don't share your sexual history with your partner, you lose an opportunity to allow them to fully know the real you!

Are you embarrassed to talk about your sexual history?

☐ Yup! It's too hard to talk about it
☐ Neutral – I don't mind talking about it but it isn't necessary
☐ I am ok with my history and share it openly

Allowing someone to know my sexual history would benefit me because:

☛ I want to be with someone who knows and accepts who I am
☛ I want to acknowledge my life with my partner
☛ I want to explore how to enhance sexual novelty and sexual intensity with my partner
☛ I want others to know me fully
☛ I want both myself and a partner to have choice about what we are wanting and not wanting as part of our relationship
☛ Other: _____
☛ Other: _____

If someone is not accepting of your sexual interests, sexual desires and/or your sexual past, consider whether or not they are a safe partner for you

---

Sometimes, a person's sexuality aligns well with your own, but often there are differences in sexual compatibility, sexual values and/or sexual interests. When there are differences between your sexuality and another person's sexuality, it can feel overwhelming and upsetting. Finding a compromise can be hard.

Sexual shaming can happen when you or a partner, judges or criticizes a person's sexual interests and/or sexual history. Criticisms, judgement and shame can kill communication. When you are building intimacy with a partner, it is important that judgements, criticisms, and shame do not enter the picture. Stop sexual shaming in its tracks![4]

☛ Keep an open mind before automatically saying no to a new sexual experience
☛ Challenge beliefs that are creating barriers for you to be an equal partner in your sexual relationships
☛ Consider what might make the proposed experience enjoyable for you
☛ Communicate your needs, your fears and your concerns respectfully with a partner
☛ Find ways for sexual play to be equitable and fair, respecting both of your needs
☛ Focus on finding the source of your own pleasure and enjoyment so that you can share this information with a partner
☛ Consider the advantages of sharing your sexual thoughts and fantasy life with a partner

Can you remember a time when you shared your sexual likes and dislikes with someone and it was really great and comfortable?

- ☐ Yes!
- ☐ No!
- ☐ I don't know that I have ever shared my sexuality with others

How did that experience feel?

- ☐ Amazing!
- ☐ Good
- ☐ It was ok; we had the same likes and dislikes, so it felt normal
- ☐ Uncomfortable
- ☐ Bad

Can you describe what made the experience feel that way?

_____
_____
_____
_____
_____

Being truthful with others about your sexuality, starts by being honest with yourself. Identifying your likes and dislikes is an important first step. Take the time to identify what you like sexually. This workbook has been a journey of exploration. You have identified your likes, dislikes, tried new things, communicated differently about sex and explored different ways to engage sexually with yourself and/or with a partner. Great job!.

Sometimes, being honest with yourself leads to realizations which can be life changing. If acknowledging your sexual likes and dislikes feels too dangerous, that it would negatively impact your life and/or your current relationships, it is time to talk with a mental health professional to assist you in your journey.

If I am completely honest with myself and true to my personal history about sex, this is what I have enjoyed sexually. This is what I have tried and enjoyed in the past:

_____
_____
_____
_____
_____

If I am completely honest with myself and true to my real feelings about sex, this is what I would like. This is what I am curious to try and/or integrate into my life:

_____

_____

_____

_____

_____

If I am completely honest with myself and true to my personal feelings about sex, this is what I have not enjoyed sexually. This is what I have tried in the past and no longer want in my life:

_____

_____

_____

_____

_____

You may have identified experiences in the lists above that you find difficult to share with others. What are your beliefs about sharing your sexual interests and your sexual history with others?

□ Easy-peasy - I can do it!
□ I can share with some people but not others
□ I can never talk about my true sexuality; it is completely unacceptable

Societal expectations about the number of sexual partners a person has had, or even personal beliefs about what it means to have had a varied sexual history, can lead to a fear of being rejected by a partner or future partners. It can be tempting to simply mask your sexual history as well as your ADHD symptoms.

Do you mask certain aspects of your sexuality?

□ Yes! Always!
□ Yes! In only some situations
□ No!
□ Hell No!

How does masking interfere with your sexuality?

_____

_____

_____

_____

_____

✓ I will openly acknowledge and share my sexual needs/sexual interests to build intimacy with myself and in relationship with others

✓ I will tolerate that my sexual needs/sexual interests won't always be compatible with everyone, and that is ok

✓ I will remain respectful when my sexual interests/sexual needs do not align with other people's sexual interests and needs

We have focused on ways to improve intimacy in relationships. We will now briefly explore intimacy busters: those problems that can disrupt building close relationships with ourselves and with a partner.

Intimacy Busters – Anger and Emotional Dysregulation

Episodes of emotional dysregulation, including strong emotions like anger, rage, jealousy, sadness, despondency or depression, can negatively impact your relationships. All those intense emotions can place you solidly into a negative state. Emotional dysregulation is a symptom of ADHD. It impacts your decision making and your relationships! As we noted earlier, ADHD couples report less relationship satisfaction (Whymbs, 2021) and there are many studies indicating the higher divorce rates within neurodivergent partnerships (Barkley, 2015; Kooij, 2019). Partners of ADHDers struggle to live day in and day out when ADHD symptoms exist within a household (Ben-Naim et al., 2017).

When there is conflict, sex is often the last thing that you think about. This can be particularly true if the fight has damaged your trust and sense of safety in the relationship. While sex can bring that feeling of safety back at times (think post-affair sex or make-up sex), often, someone who is angry with you won't want to have sex with you.

It is worth noting that sex after a conflict can become a form of stimming. If you are seeking stim, you may have a habit of using conflicts to stim and then using post-conflict sex to stim as well! If make-up sex is a form of stimming for you, consider that there are better, healthier, ways for you to find stimulation. This cycle damages your relationship. Dysregulated emotions move you farther away from creating intimacy with others.

Dysregulated emotions are represented by:

☛ Fights, disagreements, conflicts
☛ Breaches of trust
☛ Affairs
☛ Name-calling
☛ Yelling, screaming
☛ Objects being thrown and/or broken
☛ Police being called

How do you feel about your emotional dysregulation and/or your anger?

☐ It's not a big deal! It happens. I apologize and everyone moves on
☐ Everyone gets angry sometimes! My anger is just louder than other people's anger
☐ It's ok, because people yell back. Sometimes you just need to get it out!
☐ I get over it, they will get over it
☐ It is what it is
☐ Other: _____
☐ Other: _____
☐ Other: _____

Consider that these beliefs minimize and normalize poor behaviors. If you believe that it is ok to yell, scream, throw things and/or have a meltdown when you are upset, you are more likely to engage in those behaviors. What are better ways to understand your anger – rather than the beliefs identified above, what would be more helpful alternatives?

_____
_____
_____
_____
_____

Learning to manage your anger is an important skill:

☛ Know your triggers!
  Maintain a clear list of the things that set you off
  Pay close attention to themes of rejection, threats to attachment and feelings of over-whelm as these are often triggers for neurodivergent folks

☛ Communicate your triggers to others
  Make your triggers known so that others can anticipate your reaction to certain situations

☛ Take a time-out
  Time-out <u>before</u> you escalate. This is essential. Go for a walk. Take a cold shower. Stop talking. Take a deep breath. Walk away from the situation

☛ Do something productive during your time-out to calm down!
  Simply taking a time-out isn't always enough. Do your deep breathing, challenge your thinking, talk to a trusted friend or family member, find the hurt/sadness/concern that triggered your initial feeling of upset and allow yourself to feel the sadness underneath, rather than simply feeling the anger

☛ Circle back to talk about the problem/situation when you are feeling more calm and able to discuss things in a more rational way
  If your first attempt to talk calmly does not work, stop, take another time-out and try again later!

☛ Consider whether this is a form of stimming and find other ways to create positive stimulation in your life

If explosive emotions are an issue for you and/or part of your relationships, get help! There are specific couples' counselling programs designed for neurodivergent couples. There are also strategies to manage rejection sensitivity, emotional dysregulation, and impulsivity. Work with a qualified mental health professional to assist you on this journey!

Intimacy Busters – Caregiving

At some point in this workbook, parenthood, babies and children have to be a topic of conversation! Having babies is a great thing! Managing parenthood, partnership and sexuality can be a challenge.

There are many ways that caregiving can impact your life. As you know, ADHDers have a higher frequency of unplanned pregnancies (Rohacek et al., 2022; Hetz et al., 2022). Your lifestyle and your sexual decision-making can impact the number of children that are in your life. Competing demands of parenthood, grandparenthood, caregiving, elder care, foster care, pet care – indeed – caregiving in all its forms, can negatively impact your intimacy with others.

Being a parent is hard! Being an ADHD parent can be particularly challenging. We know that ADHD is a genetic condition, so as an ADHD parent, you are more likely to be raising an ADHD kid (Whymbs et al., 2021). The cycle completes itself.

There are periods in your caregiving relationships when you will need to focus on caregiving more acutely than other times. There are periods in your caregiving when you can make more time for a partner and/or for yourself. Finding balance, in a realistic way, is an essential skill for ADHD parents and caregivers.

☞ Notice if your hyperfocus on household needs are eclipsing your relationship and sexual needs

☞ Communicate about the best ways to create balance

☞ Outline a plan to bring balance into your life

☞ Remain flexible about ways to balance your needs with your caregiving needs

Intimacy Busters – Affairs and Emotional Distance

Jenny and Joe both have ADHD. They come home after their respective days and each plunge into their special interests. When they first met, they discovered that they had the same interest: they both loved the gym. Recently, Joe has hurt himself and stopped going to the gym. Jenny still loves the gym and attends regularly; Joe has started to repair old cars after work. There is no time together anymore. They have lost their connection and feel distant towards each other. Jenny found herself kissing someone at a work event. It was unexpected. She didn't think that she and Joe would have drifted this far apart. Now they are in couples' counselling and trying to work things out.

Affairs don't always occur because of a need for sexual novelty and sexual intensity. Affairs can stem from intimacy issues – not having built or maintained emotional closeness with a partner over time. ADHDers can frequently feel unloved and unsatisfied with the quality of their relationships (Kooij et al., 2018). Creating and maintaining emotional closeness in your relationship is an essential part of keeping affairs at bay.

Some workbooks that can help include Gottman & Silver's book, *The Seven Principles for Making Marriage Work* and M. Orlov's book *The ADHD Effect in Marriage*. There are also workbooks and resources that are specific to dealing with an affair in your relationship. In addition, couples counselling with a mental health specialist can be helpful. There are available resources to assist you to establish a closer, more intimate relationship with a partner!

ADHD partners who were perceived to be putting in more effort to manage their ADHD symptoms were receiving the benefits of a more generous sexual partner (Tuckman, 2019). Just as increasing participation in chores at home is likely to heighten sexual frequency in heterosexual couples, ADHD symptom management can also provide this benefit. In addition, effective problem solving, time management, emotional vulnerability, and effective anger management are all important ways to build more intimacy in your relationships.

The best part of my partnered sexual relationship is…

_____

_____

_____

_____

_____

The stumbling blocks in my partnered sexual relationship include...

_____

_____

_____

_____

The top three things that I want to improve in my partnered sexual relationship are:

1) _____

2) _____

3) _____

Emotional closeness with yourself and with others can feel scary but it can enhance your life in many powerful ways.

To improve your level of intimacy, focus on the following strategies:

✓ Ensure that you have a good level of intimacy with yourself
✓ Ensure that you are attempting to build intimacy with a safe partner
✓ Openly share your likes, your dislikes and your dreams with others
✓ Set aside time to increase the intimacy in your relationships
✓ Communicate about your sexuality openly and honestly
✓ Ensure that you are engaging in a reciprocal sharing of information
✓ Unmask in safe spaces with safe people
✓ Manage emotional dysregulation and other intimacy busters
✓ Set reminders to implement relationship goals
✓ Maintain fun and novelty in your relationships

Great work exploring a hard topic! Let's explore our last chapter together before we transition to working on your plan to better manage the impact of ADHD on your sexuality!

Working towards my goals

I have identified these barriers to intimacy in my life:

- ☐ My time management
- ☐ My emotional expression
- ☐ Masking!
- ☐ Reciprocity
- ☐ Sexual communication
- ☐ Sexual shaming
- ☐ Anger and emotional dysregulation
- ☐ Caregiving
- ☐ Affairs
- ☐ Other: _____
- ☐ Other: _____
- ☐ Other: _____

Here is a list of the important people in my life:

_____
_____
_____
_____
_____

Are these people safe?

- ☐ Yes!
- ☐ No!
- ☐ I am not sure!

I have asked for help to address issues surrounding safety in my relationships:

- ☐ Yes!
- ☐ No!
- ☐ I am not sure that I want to ask for help yet

- ✓ Review the information in the next chapter if you are unsure whether or not your relationships are safe

I will create time for the important relationships in my life by doing the following:

_____
_____
_____
_____
_____

I mask my ADHD symptoms in the following ways:

_____

_____

_____

_____

_____

I will unmask with the following people:

_____

_____

_____

_____

_____

I will unmask in the following ways:

_____

_____

_____

_____

_____

✓   I will openly communicate any difficulties I have identifying and sharing my emotions

I am most comfortable sharing these parts of my sexuality

_____

_____

_____

_____

_____

I am least comfortable sharing these parts of my sexuality

_____

_____

_____

_____

_____

✓   I can talk about sex in safe relationships
✓   I can choose to disclose elements of my sexuality with others to increase the level of intimacy in my relationships
✓   I can use the Sexy Communication Scale to identify my level of sexual interest

These intimacy busters apply to me:

☐ Sexual shaming
☐ Anger and emotional dysregulation
☐ Caregiving
☐ Affairs
☐ Emotional distance
☐ Other: _____
☐ Other: _____
☐ Other: _____

✓ Sexual shaming will be eliminated in all my sexual discussions

I will improve my anger management and/or my emotional dysregulation by doing the following:

_____
_____
_____
_____
_____

✓ I will ask for help if I continue to struggle with my anger management and/or my emotional dysregulation

I love my children and the people that I care for in my life! I will balance my caregiving with my personal needs by doing the following:

✓ I will recognize that I am raising/caretaking a neurodivergent family
✓ I will ask for help and increase my support system
✓ I will optimize my ADHD medications
✓ I will be kind to myself and give myself more self-compassion
✓ I will schedule time for myself and time with a partner
✓ I will find a trusted caregiver to babysit and/or to provide respite care when I need to find balance

Here are other strategies that I will use to improve my intimacy in relationships

_____
_____
_____
_____
_____

Notes

1 Intimacy does not mean sex. Sex is physical and means sexual play! Intimacy is emotional and means emotional closeness. Intimacy requires some vulnerability by letting others know who you are! While some people use the word intimacy to refer to sex, in this context, it does not mean sex.
2 There is a book about intimacy and love that speaks to the need for allowing in relationships. To explore the theme of allowing as a form of love, see D. Richo's book *How to be an adult in relationships* (2021).
3 There is a great book about masking and autism by Devon Price. If you are interested in exploring the theme of masking and neurodiversity in more detail see *Unmasking Autism: Discovering the New Faces of Neurodiversity* (2022).
4 You can disagree with someone's choices or decide that their choices make them an unsuitable partner for you; however, engaging in sexual shaming of consensual sexual activities breaks down opportunity for true communication and encourages the avoidance of important discussions.

References

Barkley, R. (2015). *Attention-Deficit Hyperactivity Disorder: A Handbook for Diagnosis and Treatment* (4th ed.). The Guilford Press.

Ben-Naim, S., Marom, I., Krashin, M., Gifter, B. & Arad, K. (2017). Life With A Partner With ADHD: The moderating role of intimacy. *Journal of Child and Family Studies*, 26, 1365–1373.

Gottman, J. & Silver, N. (1999). *The Seven Principles for Making Marriage Work*. New York: Three Rivers Press.

Hertz, P.G., Turner, D., Barra, S., Biedermann, L., Retz-Junginger, P., Schöttle, D. & Retz, W. (2022). Sexuality in Adults With ADHD: Results of an Online Survey. *Frontiers Psychiatry*, 13, 868278. doi:10.3389/fpsyt.2022.868278.

Kooij. J.J.S. (2018). Attention-Deficit Hyperactivity Disorder (ADHD), Intimate Relationships and Sexuality. In: Jannini EA, Siracusano A (Eds). Sexual Dysfunctions in Mentally Ill Patients. Cham: Springer International Publishing, pp. 75–82.

Kooij, J.J.S., Bijlenga, D., Salerno, L., Jaeschke, R., Bitter, I., Balázs, J., Thome, J., Dom, G., Kasper, S., Nunes Filipe, C., Stes, S., Mohr, P., Leppämäki, S., Casas, M., Bobes, J., Mccarthy, J.M., Richarte, V., Kjems Philipsen, A., Pehlivanidis, A., ... Bolea-Alamanac, B. (2019). Updated European Consensus Statement on diagnosis and treatment of adult ADHD. *European Psychiatry*, 56(1), 14–34. https://doi.org/10.1016/j.eurpsy.2018.11.001.

Margherio, S.M., Capps, E.R., Monopoli, J.W., Evans, S.W., Hernandez-Rodriguez, M., Owens, J.S. & DuPaul, G.J. (2021). Romantic Relationships and Sexual Behavior Among Adolescents With ADHD. *Journal of Attention Disorders*, 25(10), 1466–1478. doi:10.1177/1087054720914371.

Marsh, L.E., Norvilitis, J.M., Ingersoll, T.S. & Li, B. (2015). ADHD Symptomatology, Fear of Intimacy, and Sexual Anxiety and Behavior Among College Students in China and the United States. Journal of Attention Disorders, 19(3) 211–221. doi:10.1177/1087054712453483.

Niazof, D., Weizman, A. & Weinstein, A. (2019). The contribution of ADHD and attachment difficulties to online pornography use among students. *Comprehensive Psychiatry*, 93, 56–60. https://doi.org/10.1016/j.comppsych.2019.07.002

Orlov, M. (2010). *The ADHD Effect on Marriage: Understand and rebuild your relationship in six steps*. Speciality Press/A.D.D. Warehouse, p. 225.

Price, D. (2022). *Unmasking Autism: Discovering the new faces of neurodiversity*. Harmony Press.

Richo, D. (2021). *How to Be an Adult in Relationships: The Five Keys to Mindful Loving*. Shambhala Press.

Rohacek, A.M. Firkey, M.K., Woolf-King, S.E. & Antshel, K.M. (2022). Moderation of risks to sexual health by substance use in college students with ADHD. *Journal of Clinical Psychiatry*, 83(4), e1–e7.

Solden, S. (2012). *Women With Attention Deficit Disorder: Embrace your differences and transform your life*. Introspect Press, p. 515.

Tuckman, A. (2019). *ADHD After Dark: Better Sex Life, Better Relationship* (1st ed.). Routledge.

Wallin, K., Wallin Lundell, I., Hanberger, L., Alehagen, S. & Hultsjö, S. (2022). Self-experienced sexual and reproductive health in young women with Attention Deficit Hyperactivity Disorder: A qualitative interview study, *BMC Women's Health, 22, 289* https://doi.org/10.1186/s12905-022-01867-y

Wymbs, B.T., Canu, W.H., Sacchetti, G.M. & Ranson, L.M. (2021). Adult ADHD and romantic relationships: What we know and what we can do to help, *Journal of Marriage and Family Therapy*, 47, 664–681.

Young, S. & Cocallis, K. (2023). A systematic review of the relationship between neurodiversity and psychosexual functioning in individuals with autism spectrum disorder (ASD) or attention-Deficit/Hyperactivity disorder (ADHD). *Neuropsychiatric Disease and Treatment*, 19, 1379–1395. https://doi.org/10.2147/NDT.S319980.

Chapter 11

Neurodivergent Safety

The importance of Sexual and Relationship Safety

Research identifies, over and over again, that neurodivergent people are at greater risk of being sexually victimized as well as experiencing domestic violence (Young & Cocallis, 2023; Wymbs, & Gidycz, 2021; Gotby et al., 2018; Wymbs et al., 2017; Wymbs, 2021). ADHDers are also at greater risk of being a victim of physical violence (Ghirardi et al., 2023). Despite these facts, there have been limited attempts to address neurodivergent victimization (see Holliday, 2012 and Brown, 2013 for details). It is baffling that, despite research regularly identifying this phenomenon, there are no specific prevention strategies or services for neurodivergent people (Wymbs & Gidycz, 2021).

Sobering statistics about sexual and relationship safety[1]

- ☛ ADHD adults are more likely to be victims of domestic violence
- ☛ ADHD adults are more likely to be victims of rape or attempted rape than adults without ADHD
- ☛ Females with ADHD were at greater risk than males with ADHD for rape or attempted rape victimization
- ☛ More people with ADHD report having experienced any form of sexual victimization compared to a neurotypical control group
- ☛ People with neurodevelopmental disorders (both ASD and ADHD) have an increased risk of childhood sexual victimization
- ☛ Men and women diagnosed with ADHD as children are more likely to be victims of domestic violence as adults
- ☛ Young adults with elevated ADHD symptoms who abuse intoxicants (alcohol or drugs) were at greater risk of perpetrating and/or being victims of domestic violence

We don't know <u>why</u> having ADHD increases your risk of victimization. While there are many factors that may come into play such as family history, substance use, impulsivity, high conflict relationships, being more adventurous, not noticing dangerous situations, being socially isolated, not fitting in, struggling with coordination/motor skills[2] and/or having difficulty communicating effectively, we simply can't say why this is happening more frequently to neurodivergent people.

DOI: 10.4324/9781003422372-12

In this workbook, we will discuss safety strategies for neurodivergent folks, talk about how to recognize grooming and red flags, as well as how to harness the power of social supports to stay safe. We will also discuss ways to address trauma so that if you are victimized, you will be able to get back to being your best self.

Let's explore **Neurodivergent Safety** in more detail!

There are many types of victimization, including:

- sexual victimization
- physical victimization
- bullying
- emotional abuse
- coercive control[3]
- financial abuse
- spiritual abuse
- racism
- gender abuse
- abuse based on sexual orientation
- elder abuse

Abuse can take many forms. The following are examples of how victimization might translate in relationships[4].

PowerControl

POWER & CONTROL   www.whenlovehurts.ca

EMOTIONAL ABUSE

Teasing, Invalidating feelings, Using guilt, Blaming me for everything, Being jealous, Threatening, Withholding affection, Silent treatment, Stalking

INTELLECTUAL ABUSE

Having to prove things to him, Mind games, Demanding perfection, Making me feel stupid, Attacking my ideas and opinions, Manipulation of information, Telling me I'm crazy

SOCIAL ABUSE

Isolating me from my friends and family, Monitoring phone calls or mileage, Dictating who I can see, Preventing me from working

USING CULTURE

Using his culture as an excuse to abuse, Putting down my culture, Forcing me to adopt his cultural practices, Doesn't allow me to participate in mainstream culture

SPIRITUAL ABUSE

Putting down my faith, Cutting me off from my church, Using church and faith to his advantage, Soul destroying behaviour, Using scripture against me

PHYSICAL ABUSE

Blocking exits, Driving too fast, Locking me out of the house, Intimidating me, Punching or kicking me, Spitting on me, Choking me, Hitting me, Restraining me

VERBAL ABUSE

Namecalling, Swearing, Yelling at me, Insulting me, Being condescending, Being sarcastic

SEXUAL ABUSE

Forcing or manipulating sex, Sexual putdowns, Criticizing how I dress, Withholding sex, Comparing me to others, Demanding sex as payment

PETS & PROPERTY ABUSE

Killing or threatening pets, Punching walls and doors, Throwing things, Damaging the vehicle, Smashing and breaking things

USING CHILDREN

Abusing children, Threatening to harm or take children away, Refusing to make support payments, Belittling me in front of my children, Using visitation as leverage

FINANCIAL ABUSE

Calling welfare, Limiting access to money, Making me account for every penny, Controlling the money, Closing bank accounts, Wasting, Creating debt, Taking care of own needs

PSYCHOLOGICAL ABUSE

Intimidating gestures or actions, Threatening suicide, Threatening to kill me, Displaying weapons, Denying he said things, Making light of the abuse, Making me do illegal things, Making me drop charges

Adapted from *When Love Hurts: A Best Practice Guide and Curriculum for Supporting Women with Experiences of Abuse* by Jill Cory and Karen McAndless-Davis. ISBN: 978-0-9686016-2-4

Victimization can be defined by illegal behaviors!

If an action is illegal, you can be pretty sure that it would be defined as being abusive. Knowing what is defined as a crime in your community can help you identify whether someone has engaged in abusive behaviors towards you and/or others.

Societal rules change when it comes to defining what is legal and what is illegal, and these changes can happen quite rapidly. For example, there is now a legal precedent set in Canada that you cannot take off a condom during sexual activity without informing your partner and obtaining their consent (also known as "stealthing"). If consent is obtained for sex with a condom, this consent does not automatically translate to sex without a condom. Disregarding the rules of consent can lead to criminal justice interventions. It is important to stay up to date so that you know what is ok and what is not ok!

Victimization can be defined by distressing situations!

Not all abusive behaviors are criminal in nature. Just because something isn't illegal doesn't mean that it is not harmful. For example, there are uncomfortable sexual experiences that do not breach the criminal code but they leave you feeling distressed. If an experience was uncomfortable, overwhelming or off-putting to you, it still matters and it can be harmful to you regardless of whether it would meet legal criteria for prosecution. Consider your needs irrespective of the legality of the situation. If you are not feeling safe, you can communicate your distress and stop engaging with people who have caused you harm. You matter!

ADHD and victimization

Research identifies that if you have ADHD, you are more likely to experience Post Traumatic Stress Disorder (PTSD) as a result of experiencing traumatic incidents (Gurvits et al., 2000; Biederman et al., 2014)[5]. So, if you have ADHD, you are more likely to be victimized, _and_ you are more likely to experience PTSD as a result of your victimization. This is a dangerous combination for neurodivergent individuals.

> **Being a victim of violence can have a strong impact on you and leave a deep scar!**
>
> **If you are currently a victim of domestic violence including sexual violence, emotional violence or physical violence, it is imperative that you tell someone!**
>
> **Ask for help from a community member, police officer, friend, health care professional or mental health professional!**

ADHDers can be victims of sexual violence but they can also be perpetrators of sexual violence (Soldati et al., 2021). It appears clear that active substance abuse and experiencing childhood abuse, which often co-occurs for people who have ADHD, can increase the risk of perpetrating domestic violence (Wymbs & Gidycz, 2021). There are many factors that impact the perpetration of violence; but, it is noteworthy that research typically demonstrates that ADHD prevalence rates of incarcerated juveniles and adults is much higher than it is for the general population (Baggio et al., 2018). The number of people with ADHD is high in our correctional systems.

The great news is that ADHD treatment can help reduce the risk of domestic violence and sexual violence reoccurring. This means that with proper treatment, which includes proper ADHD treatment, an ADHD offender can make gains to better manage their behaviors, make better choices and reduce their perpetration of violence (Buitelaar et al., 2021; Kafka & Hennen, 2000). People are catching on! In 2023 the London police started to screen everyone on first arrest for ADHD, which is a very positive step forward (City of London Police, 2023).

As previously discussed, a key symptom of ADHD is emotional dysregulation (Barkley, 2015). The combination of emotional dysregulation and rejection sensitivity can create high conflict relationships. As we discussed in the previous chapter, if your difficulties with rejection, perceived rejection or emotional dysregulation lead you to initiate conflicts with others, seek help to address the initial flashpoints that escalate conflicts in your relationships.

Key reminders!

✓ Domestic violence is never ok
✓ Sexual violence is never ok
✓ Adults with ADHD are more likely to be victims of violence
✓ Proper ADHD pharmacological treatment and ADHD education is associated with decreases in intimate partner violence in a sample where the perpetrator had ADHD[6]
✓ If your relationship involves violence of any kind (physical, emotional, financial, sexual as examples) address this problem PRIOR to exploring your sexuality
✓ If violence is occurring in your relationship talk to a mental health provider, a health care provider, a police officer, a friend or a family member for assistance

What can I do about my experiences of victimization?

Solo sex can feel safer if you are a sexual abuse survivor. While this can be a good short-term solution following a traumatic event, over time it can lead to social isolation. Your sexuality is yours. If someone has negatively impacted your sexuality, you are encouraged to address this problem and take your life back!

Mental health interventions are changing rapidly in the provision of effective trauma therapy. We once thought that a memory was a memory and that memories didn't change. This meant that if something happened that was distressing to you, you were stuck with the distress because we could not change the fact that something bad had happened. Memories are much more flexible than we once thought. We can weaken a memory, modify a memory or strengthen our memories (Simon, Gomez & Nade, 2020). The associated learning we obtained from memories can be changed which will lessen the emotional charge of these memories. This appears to be an adaptive mechanism, one of the gifts we have as humans.

Trauma is best defined as a lesson we have learned about ourselves, the world, others or a situation/place/event that was accompanied by a strong emotion. This can be positive, like receiving a reward for a good job done, or it can be negative, like learning that we cannot approach a parent without being criticized or humiliated. <u>We learn things deeply when our learning is accompanied by a strong emotion.</u>

It is important to believe your therapist when they tell you that your emotional distress connected to a memory can be changed. In trauma therapy, you aren't changing the memory and you aren't tricking the brain. You are changing the <u>associated learning</u> which occurred as a result of an event.

In the past, trauma therapy focused on teaching people how to counteract symptoms by learning new ways of functioning that competed with the symptoms that people were experiencing. These strategies did work well; however, often people did not continue to apply the strategies over time. In other words, your gains could disappear if you did not manage your symptoms consistently. For ADHD folks, it can be quite hard to persistently apply effective coping skills to counteract trauma triggers.

Addressing the fundamental issues and beliefs that are triggering your symptoms, rather than managing the symptoms themselves, is the goal. Memory Reconsolidation (MR) is the term used to explain the brain's mechanism for updating previous learning. It allows us to revise or update an existing, acquired neural encoding. This process has been observed to occur for many different types of memory (Ecker & Vaz, 2022). This theory may explain why some therapies work better and more consistently than others to help you feel better.

If you are going to address your past or more recent traumas, work with a therapist using interventions that apply MR theory and strategies as an active part of their interventions. These will likely include: Eye Movement Desensitization and Reprocessing therapy (EMDR), Lifespan Integration Therapy (LI) and Cognitive Reprocessing Therapy (CPT), but there are others[7]. Address the core beliefs and emotional learning that was created by traumatic events. Resolve the symptoms rather than simply managing them.[8] While this work is hard, there is research that demonstrates the effectiveness of these interventions.

Increases in cortisol when remembering a past traumatic event can further consolidate a painful memory. This means that if you simply remember the memory, without changing the negative associations to the memory, this seems to make things worse, not better. By identifying the trigger and calming your body, you can lower your cortisol levels and reduce your stress so that you will be less likely to further deepen the negative emotional load of the distressing memory. This is why many therapists will ask you to calm your nervous system, soothe your body, and breathe as a response to a traumatic memory that occurs outside of a structured trauma therapy session.[9]

Here are some helpful ways to calm your body:

✓ Breathing
✓ Humming
✓ Singing
✓ Relaxing in a warm bath
✓ Using essential oils/soothing scents
✓ Movement such as light stretching, vacuuming the house or tinkering on a project

✓ Doing grounding exercises
✓ Drinking cold water
✓ Telling yourself positive words "I survived", "It is over now", "I am safe right now"[10]
✓ Showing self-compassion, hugs and kindness[11]
✓ Putting your hand on your chest and breathing deeply!
✓ Raising your arms and breathing deeply!

When you wake up from a nightmare about a traumatic incident, do the same thing! Calm yourself in the same way that you calm yourself following a flashback or a trigger in your waking hours.

✓ Visualize taking yourself out of the situation
✓ Give yourself compassion and kindness
✓ Tell yourself helpful thoughts such as "I survived", "It's over now"
✓ Soothe your body and your brain[12]
✓ Deep breathing to calm your body
✓ Notice and engage with the physical space around you (for example, what do you see, what do you hear, what can you touch)

When you are in therapy, it is important to remember the memory when guided to do so by your therapist. If you participate in a therapy session but don't fully connect with the memory when directed to do so by your therapist, you will likely not improve your symptoms.

Ensure that you trust your therapist to keep you safe when you are engaged in trauma therapy. If you don't want to "go there" and don't trust your therapist to take you there safely, it is best to find another therapist. If you arrive for your session and you don't want to remember it or feel it, tell your therapist. If you are feeling anxious coming to therapy, tell your therapist, and keep in mind that this is quite common.

Your job is to calm your body down and then work with a qualified mental health professional to lessen your distress as it relates to traumatic memories. Dealing with trauma requires specific and effective mental health interventions to help you feel less distress about past events.

Given your trauma history, is <u>now</u> a good time for you to address your trauma?

☐ Yes
☐ No
☐ I have no idea!

Given your trauma history, do you want to complete specific trauma work before you address your sexual needs?

☐ Yes
☐ No
☐ Maybe

What strategies can you use to calm your body when you remember a past trauma?

_____

_____

_____

_____

_____

☛ If you need to pause in this workbook to complete your trauma work, that is perfectly ok! Come back to your sexual goals when you feel safer in your body and in your life.

What can I DO to avoid traumatic events?

Most often, victimization happens with people that we know and in situations where there is some form of trust that has been created. Victimization can occur with acquaintances, family members, casual friends, partners and strangers. Let's explore the different types of situations that can lead to victimization. Knowing the characteristics of risky situations can help you manage your risk of being victimized.

Impulsive, dysregulated events: These occur when someone does something to you in a very unpredictable way. It's something that happens quite dramatically. It's a shock because it was unexpected as well as a traumatic. Impulsive events are very hard, if impossible, to see coming.

Grooming: Grooming happens when someone is trying to get you comfortable with an uncomfortable, unsafe, questionable or illegal activity. Grooming is a form of manipulation. Grooming is the slow progression of moving you towards doing something that you don't want to do. It is a very slow and deliberate form of manipulation. Often the bad thing that happens doesn't shock you completely, but it is a surprise, nonetheless. Looking back, you are sometimes able to see that it was not entirely unexpected.

Chaos: These events happen when you are in a chaotic situation or a chaotic environment and something happens to you. The chaos itself promotes the likelihood of getting hurt. Examples can include being intoxicated, being around other people who are intoxicated, getting involved in drug trafficking, going out with strangers or acquaintances that you barely know, participating in large unsupervised gatherings, keeping friends or family members in your life who make unpredictable or harmful choices to themselves and/or others[13]. In these cases, you can see it coming, sort of, but it is the unpredictability of the event/situation or the unpredictability of a person/persons that leads to being harmed. Sometimes when you are in those situations nothing happens, but other times things do happen.

We are often very hard on ourselves when we have been groomed or manipulated into a situation that violated our boundaries. We can also be very hard on ourselves when abuse happens as a result of being in a place of chaos, either with chaotic people or within a chaotic environment. This isn't being fair to ourselves. When someone has a plan that does not value our wellbeing, it isn't our fault. It doesn't happen because you have done anything wrong; it simply happened.

Here are some situations that can increase your risk of being victimized. Do they seem familiar to you?

- ☐ Going off with strangers
- ☐ Being intoxicated in an unsafe place
- ☐ Not noticing someone's sexual interest in you
- ☐ Being misunderstood in your intentions or your communication
- ☐ Not telling friends or family where you are
- ☐ Taking unnecessary risks
- ☐ Assuming that people have your best interest in mind
- ☐ Disregarding a large age difference between you and a partner
- ☐ Disregarding a partner's past harmful behaviors towards others

These situations are not your fault! It is not the fault of your ADHD either! We address these situations by identifying and tracking Red flags, setting and maintaining boundaries, and asking our safe friends and family to help. **Many situations are not preventable.** Balancing your risk-taking, while still having fun, can be one way to stay safe.

Red flags: A red flag is an indicator that someone does not have our best interests in mind. A red flag can be related to their current behaviors or their past behaviors with us or with others. The reason that people will tell you to focus on how someone treats their mom, their children or customer service workers, is because it can tell you how they relate to others.

Here is a list of Red flags that may be helpful to you:

These are RED FLAGS:

- ✓ Someone who treats others poorly
- ✓ Someone who requires alcohol or drug use on a daily, regular, or consistent basis
- ✓ Someone who believes that most victims of abuse lie about their traumatic experiences
- ✓ Someone who will not hear the word "No"
- ✓ Someone who wants to exert control over what you do, who you do it with and when you do it

✓ Someone who encourages you to end close, safe, friendships
✓ Someone who behaves very differently when you are alone with them as opposed to when other people are around
✓ Someone who does not fulfill their responsibilities
✓ Someone who exerts financial control within a relationship
✓ Someone who cannot share power within a relationship
✓ Someone who is unkind or cruel to children and/or animals
✓ Anyone who has hit you
✓ Anyone who has touched you without your consent
✓ Anyone who has had sex with you without your consent
✓ Anyone who engages in bullying you or others
✓ Anyone who tells you that your expressed needs are wrong, bad or inappropriate
✓ Large age differences between yourself and a partner which are minimized, normalized or ignored

Notice if you are:

✓ Minimizing concerns that other people have expressed about your relationship, your safety and/or your partner choice
✓ Becoming isolated from others
✓ Finding excuses to justify or explain someone's bad behaviors towards you
✓ Feeling worse about yourself after talking to a particular person or spending time with them

Red flags that I have identified in the past include:

_____

_____

_____

_____

_____

Red Flags that I need to consider in the future include:

_____

_____

_____

_____

_____

ADHD Safety rules!

✓ Don't expect to remember Red flags!
✓ Create a visual reminder of Red flags
✓ Set phone reminders to remember Red flags
✓ Review your Red flags when you start a new relationship or after a concerning incident that occurred in your relationship with a friend or a partner
✓ Ask a friend or a support person to remind you of Red flags

There are excellent self-help books to help you identify Red flags in relationships, including books by Dr. Stephanie Sarkis (2022) *Healing from Toxic Relationships* and (2018) *Gaslighting: Recognize manipulative and emotionally abusive people – and break free*, as well as books by L. Bancroft (2003) *Why Does He Do That?: Inside the minds of angry and controlling men* and Bancroft & Patrissi (2011) *Should I Stay or Should I Go?: A guide to knowing if your relationship can – and should – be saved.*

Boundaries: A boundary is a rule that you don't want others to cross. It is a rule that involves your own personal beliefs, values, needs, desires or wants. We are all allowed to have boundaries. A list of your personal rights can be found online. It is often referred to as your Personal Bill of Rights[14]. Take a moment now and look up your Personal Bill of Rights in relationships!

We will pause while you go down a quick rabbit hole......

Welcome back!

Know your personal rights and adhere to them! This will ensure that you are holding good solid boundaries for yourself and respecting other people's boundaries too!

There are many workbooks available to help you with assertiveness, boundaries and communication. In the past, many boundary workbooks were geared towards one gender or the other; however the content of most workbooks on boundaries and assertiveness can be useful for everyone.

Some of my favorites include *Boundary Boss* by T. Cole (2021); *Unf*ck your boundaries* by F. Harper (2020), *The Assertiveness Workbook*, 2nd edition, by J. Paterson (2022) and *The Anxiety and Phobia Workbook*, 7th edition, by E. Bourne (2020).

Boundaries are great and very useful, but they only work with people who are willing to accept our boundaries. For people who are unwilling to accept that others have boundaries, different skills are required such as repeating the same message consistently as well as re-evaluating the importance of the relationship in your life and perhaps negotiating the end of certain relationships. Knowing when a relationship has potential and when a relationship offers an unsafe space starts with good communication skills and maintaining boundaries.

You can identify Red flags and you can set boundaries, but sometimes it can feel like your skills seem to evaporate! Knowing Red flags, ensuring that your needs are being met and holding strong boundaries are important. But can you apply these skills when it matters?

Let's make relationship safety, <u>neurodivergent safety</u>!

Being enthralled by a new partner, being overstimulated at the bar, not wanting the night to end – these are all wonderful aspects of being neurodivergent. Sadly, they may also increase your risk of being victimized. This problem can be remedied with reminders! Yes, I know those darned reminders that help you get up on time and help you get to the gym; they can also help you stay safe! Without reminders, we are often caught off guard.

✓ **Set a reminder on your phone or create visual reminders that outline your positive expectations in relationships**

Be clear with yourself about the minimum requirements for you to share your life with someone. Remember what you expect from a loving partner. For example, you can set a reminder or put up a sign that says:

- I am kind and loving. I deserve someone who will be kind and loving to me too!
- Important values such as integrity, honesty and kindness matter!

✓ **Set alarms on your phone when you are going out for the night**

Decide what will be a reasonable time to come home. Then set your alarm! You might decide to stay, but if you do, you will have created a pause in your evening which will allow you to think about whether you still want to be there. For example, my plans for tomorrow and my need for self-care are best served if I start wrapping things up by 11 pm. I will check in with myself at 10:45 pm and again at 12:30 am to see how I am doing, to check my level of intoxication, and to pay close attention to who I am hanging out with. I will set my alarm for 10:45pm, 11:30pm and 12:30am to create a pause for reflection during my evening.

✓ **Be honest with yourself and your close friends if your goal is to go out and have sex**

Often people have a goal to have sex, but they don't articulate it clearly. They hope that they will be "picked up" or that they will find "the one". This leaves you vulnerable to accepting anyone's attention without considering whether you actually want to spend time with them.

- ☛ If you want to have sex, reflect on whether you are going to a safe place to find a casual sexual partner
- ☛ Make a list of safe places where you would feel comfortable going with an unknown sexual partner
- ☛ Let a friend know where you are going and when you expect to be back
- ☛ Ensure that a friend or a family member can track your personal location through your phone
- ☛ Carry condoms and take appropriate measures to ensure your physical safety

✓ **Keep Uber, Lyft or taxi credits on file and ready to use at any time**

It would be great if there were always a friend or a family member available to pick us up, but sometimes we don't call or we don't quite know where we are. Having pre-paid credits with your local transportation company can help you get out of any situation fast, without worrying about how you will pay for your ride!

✓ **Make sure that your phone works**

Carry a portable phone charger so that you always have enough battery life and check your battery levels in case you are separated from your friends.

✓ **If you are drunk, it is time to go home and be with safe people**

Too often, things go sideways when someone is intoxicated as a result of drug or alcohol use. If you are intoxicated, make the decision to go home or go to a safe place with safe people. If you are with others who are intoxicated, it might also be time to go home.

What to do if intoxicated people are in your home? Invest in a door lock so that the party can stay outside your door and unknown or intoxicated people cannot get inside. Alternatively, you can create a plan with loved ones about what to do if people are in your home and won't leave, including where you can go to spend the night to get out of a potentially unsafe situation, such as a hotel, a friend's house or a family member's home.

✓ **Be prepared to say no even if you really want to say yes**

Sometimes, you need to say no when a situation has changed or isn't exactly what you had expected. Learning to say no, and keeping no as an option, always, can be a powerful way to ensure that you are giving yourself a way out of an unsafe situation. Just because you say no once, doesn't mean that you can't say yes, another time!

✓ **Keep visual reminders of problematic interactions in your life**

We alluded to the fact that the issue for neurodivergent people is not remembering "how bad" the last "bad" episode was with a partner, family member or a friend. This seems to be particularly true in situations that include domestic violence and can also occur with unhealthy or toxic friends and/or family members. **Neurodivergent people are vulnerable, in part, because it can be hard to remember "how bad" problem situations have been in the past!**

Remembering is different than forgiving. You can forgive and move on. You can forgive and remember. If you tend to forget bad behaviors and move on, you are more vulnerable and it can surprise you when it happens again. In my clinical experience, once medicated, ADHDers appear better able to see, remember and respond more effectively to patterns of chronic abuse in their relationships.

Here are examples of how to track problematic interactions in your life[15]:

Date & time	What happened?	Context
April 22, 2022	He hit me	I was upset because he criticized me, I started yelling, he told me to stop yelling, I didn't stop, and he hit me
April 23, 2022	He apologized and took responsibility	He said that he would never hit me again
April 30, 2022	We went to couples counselling	We created a plan so that it would not happen again
June 14, 2022	He left my mother's birthday party in a huff, yelling that I was a bitch	He wanted to leave but I wasn't ready to leave the party yet. I wanted to stay
September 1, 2022	He yelled at me	I was making cookies and didn't have time to sit with him. He yelled that I wasn't caring enough, that I was a disaster and that I was hopeless
September 2, 2022	I wanted him to apologize but he didn't	I just moved on and did nothing about it
October 15, 2022	He was so drunk that the cops pulled him over	He was coming home from hanging out with his friends and didn't ask me or anyone else for a ride home

Looking at the patterns above, does this person seem like a good choice for a lifelong partner?

☐ Yes
☐ No
☐ It depends

If your answer is it depends or yes, what features are you focused on?

_____

_____

_____

_____

_____

If this person was very nice to you between these incidents, would that make them a good choice as a lifelong partner?

□ Yes
□ No
□ It depends

If your answer is it depends or yes, what features are you focused on?

_____

_____

_____

_____

_____

Permission-giving thoughts are thoughts that we tell ourselves to make things that are not ok, feel ok. For example, I am very angry, so I yell and scream. It's ok because people will get over it. Is that true?

□ Yes
□ No
□ Maybe

Does this belief mean that I am justified in my actions to yell at people?

_____

_____

_____

_____

_____

Let's consider another example:

Date & time	What happened?	Context
January 15, 2021	Mom was drunk at a party	It was a family event, it was embarrassing, so I left
June 25, 2021	Mom was drunk and called me, she told me that she was disappointed in me	There was no context, I was doing my thing and living my life
July 10, 2021	I sent mom AA information and asked her to attend	She didn't respond to my text
September 15, 2021	Mom got fired and called me to complain	She called her boss an asshole

Date & time	What happened?	Context
December 25, 2021	Mom ruined our holiday family event. She yelled at my sister, she drank too much, my daughter was crying because of the chaos	I decided not to invite mom to any other family gatherings moving forward unless she remained sober for ten months
June 20, 2022	Mom wanted to come to my daughter's birthday party. I calmly explained to her that she could not attend. When she started yelling at me, I ended the phone call	I was proud of maintaining my boundaries
October 1, 2023	Mom texted to tell me that she had been attending AA, had a sponsor and was sober since July 2022. She invited me to participate in family counselling with her to see if we could rebuild our relationship	I told her that I was proud of her and that I would consider her request. I plan to talk with my safe support people before I decide how I want to respond

Whether someone is a family member, extended family member, friend or stranger, abusive behavior remains abusive. For example, abuse is not more acceptable from a parent than it is from a stranger or someone that you met online. The closer people are to you, the harder it can feel to set boundaries, but they still apply[16]!

Date & time	What happened?	Context
November 10, 2023	Cindy S. said that I looked terrible in front of everyone	We were at school
November 10, 2023 – end of day	Cindy S. apologized, she realized that she had hurt my feelings	We are friends again
Things have been good ever since!		

People make mistakes. It's not a huge deal. This visual tracking is not meant for you to ruminate on unfortunate events. Anger, conflicts and problems happen in all relationships! Visual reminders are meant for you to identify abuse in your relationships, including those unending patterns of people saying sorry, doing shitty things and then doing it all over again. It's meant for you to remember, particularly if you tend to forget these events over time. If you notice yourself ruminating on events that you have written down, it is time to talk to a mental health professional for additional assistance.

✓ **On your whiteboard or on a posterboard, write reminders about safety that you need to remember**

Post general reminders about safety. Identify what is safe and what is unsafe in relationships. Be specific and outline what behaviors are unsafe and what behaviors are safe.

You may also want to create a book, journal or a "how to" manual that you review monthly which outlines your key safety rules. This can be particularly helpful if you are navigating an unsafe relationship and/or initiating new relationships. By writing down your rules and reviewing them regularly, you can refresh your memory about the safety plan, the boundaries that you have decided to put in place to ensure your safety and ensure that these rules are not being violated. For example, you might post the following:

Abuse looks like this… Hitting, yelling, coercive control, name calling, forcing sex when I said no

When I am feeling safe and secure it looks like this… I feel good after spending time with the person, I am smiling, my anxiety is low, I am laughing, I am not embarrassed or worried to introduce them to my other friends

Respect for myself looks like this… Allowing myself to say no, taking time for myself, spending time with my other friends, not lending money or giving something away that I want to keep, only having sex if I want to have sex

Respect from others looks like this… Accepting my decision not to participate in an activity, accepting if I say no, showing compassion if I am sad or upset, assuming that I have a positive intention, asking questions and being curious about my thoughts and my experiences, placing value on my thoughts and opinions

Disrespect looks like this… Insulting me in front of my friends or family, putting me down, disregarding my opinions or suggestions, not taking care of my things, not showing appreciation or saying thank you/please, sneering at me/looking down at me, trying to teach me, lack of equal decision making in the relationship

Remember to be clear and specific when you are identifying these reminders!

Let's fill out this grid.

Abuse looks like this:

_____
_____
_____
_____
_____

When I am feeling safe and secure it looks like this…

_____
_____
_____
_____
_____

Respect for myself looks like this...

_____
_____
_____
_____
_____

Respect from others looks like this...

_____
_____
_____
_____
_____

Disrespect looks like this...

_____
_____
_____
_____
_____

✓ **Keep track of how you feel in a relationship!**

If you keep track of how you are feeling in a relationship, you will notice patterns of concern as well as the patterns that demonstrate you can trust someone.

Use an emoji-based app or create your own way to document how you feel in a relationship. If at the end of one month, three months or six months, you mostly have sad emoji faces or angry emoji faces, you may want to reconsider the health of the relationship you are tracking. Alternatively, if at the end of that same time period, you mostly have happy emoji faces or joyful emoji faces, it can remind you that perhaps things are pretty good!

If you identify that you are unhappy in all your relationships, it is time to seek the assistance of a mental health professional to assist you explore your relationships in more detail.

✓ **Create a visual reminder with the important values that you want someone to bring into a relationship**

For example, you can have a reminder that comes up daily asking you these questions:

o   Are they being nice to me right now?
o   How does my body feel?
o   How are my needs being addressed?
o   Am I being nice to them?
o   How am I addressing their needs?

o Do I like them?
o Do I like who I am when I am with them?
o Do I prefer who I become when they are not around?
o How am I using my voice and how is my voice being heard in the relationship?

Take the time to reflect on whether you are contributing to the conflicts in your relationships:

o Am I communicating clearly?
o Am I communicating respectfully?
o Am I able to express my needs and desires while considering their needs as well?
o Am I communicating honestly about what I want, need and expect?
o Am I considering what the other person is telling me or asking for?
o Am I engaging in shaming words or behaviors?

✓ **Create a list of reminders or a "how to" manual that you can follow when you are faced with relationship conflicts and/or relationship drama**

Write down how you want to handle conflicts in your relationships. Create a step-by-step guide. Use this guide when things come up to help you better navigate problems and conflicts in relationships. Include helpful reminders such as your Personal Bill of Rights, key conflict management strategies and a list of your support people. Examples of key conflict management strategies might include take a time out, find some time to talk with my supportive friends, be curious and ask questions to better understand the situation, stay calm and remember that we both have good intentions.

✓ **If you find yourself frequently engaged in impulsive decisions that heighten your risk of victimization, consider that your ADHD symptoms might not be well managed. Address your overall ADHD management!**

If you find yourself continuously risk-taking and impulsive in certain situations and this is putting you at risk, talk to your health provider to discuss how you can optimize your ADHD medication.

Consider working with an ADHD coach to keep you on track and focused on the right goals for you!

Review the goals that you have identified in this workbook and use those goals to move your life in a safe and positive direction.

Here are some additional rules to consider:

1) Learn about boundaries, know your boundaries and do your boundaries work! If you are struggling to set boundaries, ensure that this is a skill you perfect with the help of a mental health professional.

2) Take note of situations where you tend not to notice that people do not have your best interests in mind. Does it happen when you are drunk, out with friends, at night, when the meds have worn off, when you are tired, when you are online, when you are online dating, when you are with old friends or with new acquaintances, etc.?

3) If someone tells you about all the ways that they are great, you may want to be wary. People will show themselves over time, good or bad; it generally does not need advertisement!

4) If someone tells you that they are the problem, that they are chaotic or that they have significant issues – believe them! It is not your job to change them but to believe what they are telling you about their negative traits.

5) If someone tells you who YOU are, be cautious. You don't necessarily need to believe them. Talk with your close friends or family about their impressions to see if there is a consensus.

6) If someone threatens you with any sort of consequence for not dating them, a consequence if you break up with them, if they threaten to commit suicide if you leave or if they are upset that you will not "give them a chance", simply walk away.

7) Your personal rights must be respected in any relationship. Be wary of anyone who does not respect your rights.

8) Being neurodivergent does not make you a shitty partner. It simply makes partnership different! Being different can be a great thing! Remember your ADHD gifts and remind yourself of these every day!

My support people: Support people are people who can help you if you need additional support, want to talk about a situation in more detail or if you are concerned about a situation that is unfolding. Support people can be family, friends, acquaintances, staff at a domestic violence shelter, members of a local support group or spiritual advisors. Support people also include nurses, health care providers, mental health providers, police officers, psychiatric nurses, and social workers. Let's develop your list of support people so that you know who you will turn to if you are concerned about your safety.

My first line: I will call them right away

_____

_____

_____

_____

_____

My second line: I will call them for support and additional backup

_____

_____

_____

_____

_____

My community support people, such as mental health practitioners, spiritual advisors and criminal justice representatives:

_____

_____

_____

_____

_____

✓ Add the first line people to the top in your phone contact list or prioritize them in your contact list
✓ Create a plan to tell your support people where and when you are going out. This might include allowing them to access your location at all times and/or informing them when you might need additional support after a social gathering
✓ Set regular appointments with a mental health professional so that you have access to regular mental health care. If you are doing ok most of the time, set appointments monthly, quarterly, bi-yearly or even yearly. It is a very good idea to ensure that you are maintaining your gains and have a safe space to talk when you need it!

If you do not have support people outside of your paid community support people, such as your ADHD coach, your mental health provider and/or legal authorities, it is a good time to start building a community of like-minded people that you enjoy!

Prevention services for neurodivergent people are severely lacking. This chapter is meant to acknowledge the issue of trauma in neurodivergent relationships, review basic facts about how to protect yourself and know what you can expect from effective mental health treatments. Seek help if you have experienced trauma and/or if you are concerned about your safety in relationships.

You have done fantastic work throughout this workbook! Let's put it all together and create your action plan for moving forward. Creating a healthy, happy, joyful and satisfying sex life is awaiting you! Our journey will end with the next chapter, Chapter 12 – Building your sexual goals!

Working towards my goals

I have been a victim of abuse in my life:

☐ During or throughout my childhood
☐ During or throughout my teen years
☐ As a young adult
☐ During my adult years
☐ During my senior years

I have addressed my trauma history effectively and adequately. I no longer find it physically distressing:

- ☐ True, I did the work, and I am good
- ☐ Not sure; I am not sure how I am feeling about my past
- ☐ Not sure; I have been trying to do the work, but it doesn't feel like anything is changing for me
- ☐ False; I haven't done the work, and I am too afraid to do the work
- ☐ False; I haven't done the work, and I am choosing not to do it at this time

I want to address my history of victimization and will do so with the following plan:

_____

_____

_____

_____

_____

- ✓ I will choose when I want to address my history of victimization and create a timeline that works for me!
- ✓ If my efforts in trauma therapy are not helping me feel better, I will communicate this to my therapist and work on a plan to achieve my goals.

My top 10 Red flags include:

_____

_____

_____

_____

_____

_____

_____

_____

_____

- ✓ On a whiteboard or on a posterboard, I will write reminders about relationship safety that I need to remember.
- ✓ On a whiteboard, in a journal or on a posterboard, I will write my key conflict management strategies

Abuse looks like this… (be clear and specific)
When I am feeling safe and secure it looks like this… (be clear and specific)
Respect for myself looks like this… (be clear and specific)
Respect from others looks like this… (be clear and specific)
Disrespect looks like this… (be clear and specific)

Boundaries that I want to maintain in my relationships include:

_____

_____

_____

_____

_____

✓ My support people are clearly labeled in my contact list, and I know exactly how to reach them
✓ I have talked to them about the fact that I consider them to be my contact people in case of emergency
✓ We have discussed ways that I can offer support to them when they need it too!

My support people include:

_____

_____

_____

_____

_____

✓ I will honour myself by staying safe, asking questions, saying NO and removing myself from unsafe situations
✓ I will honour myself by not blaming myself or my ADHD for my experiences of victimization
✓ I will honour myself by teaching others how they can remain safe if they are a part of the neurodivergent community

Notes

1 All taken from Whyms & Gidycz (2021), Wymbs et al., 2021 and Gotby et al., 2018.
2 See Bejerot et al. (2022) for details.
3 Coercive control happens when someone is engaging in behaviors to purposefully control and limit your behaviors, your options and your choices in order to instill fear and submission. Coercive control limits your freedom!

4 While most information about domestic violence assumes a male perpetrator and a female survivor, this is not necessarily the case. People of any gender can be perpetrators or survivors of domestic violence. This same rule applies to sexual violence.

5 Post-Traumatic Stress Disorder is a mental health diagnosis that has specific criteria. Some people receive this diagnosis following a traumatic incident or a series of traumatic incidents in their lives.

6 Taken from Buitelaar, Posthumus & Buitelaar (2020).

7 There are other resources which can be helpful, for example, the Irest program by R. Miller (2015) and other interventions based on the Polyvagal theory.

8 Memory Reconsolidation is defined as being an experience-driven neurobiological mechanism where complex cellular and molecular processes are triggered and shaped by subjective experiences (Ecker, 2015; Ecker, 2018; Ecker & Vaz, 2022). According to this theory, these subjective experiences can be created within a therapeutic environment which ultimately helps you feel better.

9 Working with your nervous system and helping your body calm down can be very helpful (Antypa et al., 2021). See *Anchored: How to befriend your nervous system using Polyvagal Theory* (2021) by D. Dana for more details.

10 Ensure that the words used are positive and do not contain a negative, for example, use "I am safe" rather than "I'm not in danger".

11 Yes, you can hug yourself! Put your hands on your opposite shoulders and squeeze. You can also put your hand on your chest and apply light pressure while breathing as an alternative exercise.

12 There are many ways to soothe your body and your brain! Look up emotional first aid strategies, grounding strategies as well as anxiety management strategies to find positive ways to help you calm down.

13 This is particularly common for people who experienced childhood abuse owing to the fact that children are powerless to take themselves to a safer place if their environment is chaotic.

14 The Personal Bill of Rights is outlined in Johnson, S. L. (2018), *Therapist's Guide to Clinical Intervention: The 1–2–3's of Treatment Planning*.

15 You can track these reminders on paper, on a whiteboard or create a digital version by using an app or a digital whiteboard. Ensure that you are keeping your log in a private space and that you review it regularly.

16 If you answered that the partner would be a good choice or that it would depend, it's best to talk with a trusted friend, family member or qualified mental health professional to discuss your thoughts in more detail.

References

Antypa, D., Perrault, A.A., Vuilleumier, P., Schwartz, S. & Rimmele, U. (2021). Suppressing the Morning Cortisol Rise After Memory Reactivation at 4 A.M. enhances Episodic Memory Reconsolidation in Humans. *The Journal of Neuroscience*, 41(34), 7259–7266. https://doi.org/10.1523/JNEUROSCI.0096-21.2021.

Baggio, S., Fructuoso, A., Guimaraes, M., Fois, E., Golay, D., Heller, P., Perroud, N., Aubry, C., Young, S., Delessert, D., Gétaz, L., Tran, N.T. & Wolff, H. (2018). Prevalence of Attention Deficit Hyperactivity Disorder in Detention Settings: A Systematic Review and Meta-Analysis. *Frontiers in psychiatry*, 9, 331. https://doi.org/10.3389/fpsyt.2018.00331.

Bancroft, L. (2003). *Why Does He Do That?: Inside the minds of angry and controlling men*. Berkley.

Bancroft, L. & Patrissi, J. (2011). *Should I Stay or Should I Go?: A Guide to Knowing if Your Relationship Can – and Should – be Saved*. Berkley.

Barkley, R. (2015). *Attention-Deficit Hyperactivity Disorder: A Handbook for Diagnosis and Treatment* (4th ed.). The Guilford Press.

Bejerot, S., Ståtenhag, L & Glans, M.R. (2022). Below average motor skills predict victimization from childhood bullies: A study of adults with ADHD. *Journal of Psychiatric Research*, 153, 269–275. https://doi.org/10.1016/j.jpsychires.2022.07.019.

Biederman, J., Petty, C., Spencer, T.J., Woodworth, K.Y., Bhide, P., Zhu, J. & Faraone, S.V. (2014). Is ADHD a risk for posttraumatic stress disorder (PTSD)? Results from a large longitudinal study of referred children with and without ADHD. *The World Journal of Biological Psychiatry*, 15(1), 49–55.

Bourne, E.J. (2020).*The Anxiety and Phobia Workbook* (7th ed.). New Harbinger Publications.

Brown, D. (2013). *The Aspie Girl's Guide to Being Safe with Men: The unwritten safety rules no-one is telling you*. London: Jessica Kingsley Publishers

Buitelaar, N.J.L., Posthumus, J.A., Bijlenga, D. & Buitelaar, J.K. (2021). The impact of ADHD treatment on intimate partner violence in a forensic psychiatry setting. *Journal of Attention Disorders*, 25(7), 1021–1031. https://doi.org/10.1177/1087054719879502.

Buitelaar, N.J.L., Posthumus, J.A. & Buitelaar, J.K. (2020). ADHD in Childhood and/or Adulthood as a Risk Factor for Domestic Violence or Intimate Partner Violence: A Systematic Review.*Journal of Attention Disorders*, 24(9), 1203–1214. https://doi.org/10.1177/1087054715587099.

City of London Police (2023). City of London Police First in the Country to Screen Suspects for ADHD. 10 May.

Cole, T. (2021). *Boundary Boss: The Essential Guide to Talk True, Be Seen, and (Finally) Live Free*. Sounds True Publications.

Dana, D. (2021). *Anchored: How to befriend your nervous system using Polyvagal Theory*. Boulder, CO: Sounds True Publishing.

Ecker, B (2015). Memory Reconsolidation Understood and Misunderstood. *International Journal of Neuropsychotherapy*, 3(1), 2–46. doi: 10.12744/ijnpt.2015.0002-0046.

Ecker, B. (2018). Clinical translation of memory reconsolidation research: Therapeutic methodology for transformational change by erasing implicit emotional learnings driving symptom production. *International Journal of Neuropsychotherapy*, 6(1), 1–92. https://doi.org/10.12744/ijnpt.2018.0001-0092.

Ecker, B. & Vaz, A. (2022). Memory reconsolidation and the crisis of mechanism in psychotherapy. *New Ideas in Psychology*, 66, 100945. https://doi.org/10.1016/j.newideapsych.2022.100945.

Ghirardi, L., Kuja-Halkola, R., Pettersson, E., Sariaslan, A., Arseneault, L., Fazel, S., D'Onofrio, B.M., Lichtenstein, P. & Larsson, H. (2023). Neurodevelopmental disorders and subsequent risk of violent victimization: exploring sex differences and mechanisms. *Psychological Medicine*, 53, 1510–1517. https://doi.org/10.1017/S0033291721003093.

Gotby, V.O., Lichtenstein, P., Langstrom, N. & Pettersson, E. (2018). Childhood neurodevelopmental disorders and risk of coercive sexual victimization in childhood and adolescence— A population-based prospective twin study. *Journal of Child Psychology and Psychiatry*, 59, 957–965.

Gurvits, T.V., Gilbertson, M.W., Lasko, N.B., Tarhan, A.S., Simeon, D., Macklin, M.L., Orr, S.P. & Pitman, R.K. (2000). Neurologic soft signs in chronic posttraumatic stress disorder. *Arch Gen Psychiatry*, February, 57(2), 181–186. doi: 10.1001/archpsyc.57.2.181.

Harper, F.G. (2020). *Unfuck Your Boundaries Workbook: Build Better Relationships Through Consent, Communication, and Expressing Your Needs*. Microcosm Publishing.

Holliday Willey, L. (2012). *Safety Skills for Asperger Women: How to save a perfectly good female life*. Jessica Kingsley Publishers.

Johnson, S.L. (2018). *Therapist's Guide to Clinical Intervention: The 1-2-3's of Treatment Planning (3rd ed.), Practical Resources for the mental health professional*. Academic Press.

Kafka, M.P. & Hennen, J. (2000). Psychostimulant augmentation during treatment with selective serotonin reuptake inhibitors in men with paraphilias and paraphilia-related disorders: A case series. *The Journal of Clinical Psychiatry*, 61(9), 664. https://doi.org/10.4088/JCP.v61n0912.

Kafka, M.P. & Prentky, R.A. (1998). Attention-deficit/hyperactivity disorder in males with paraphilias and paraphilia-related disorders: A comorbidity study. *The Journal of Clinical Psychiatry*, 59(7), 388. https://doi.org/10.4088/JCP.v59n0709.

Miller, R.C. (2015). *The iRest Program for Healing PTSD, A Proven-Effective Approach to Using Yoga Nidra Meditation and Deep Relaxation Techniques to Overcome Trauma*. New Harbinger Publications.

Paterson, R.J. (2022). *The Assertiveness Workbook: How to Express Your Ideas and Stand Up for Yourself at Work and in Relationships* (2nd ed.). New Harbinger Publications.

Sarkis, S.M. (2022). Healing from Toxic Relationships: 10 essential steps to recover from gaslighting, narcissism, and emotional abuse. Hachette Books.

Sarkis, S.M. (2018). Gaslighting: Recognize manipulative and emotionally abusive people – and break free. Da Capo Lifelong Books.

Simon, Gomez & Nade (2020). Sleep's role in memory reconsolidation. *Current Opinion in Behavioral Sciences*, 33, 132–137. doi:https://doi.org/10.1016/j.cobeha.2020.04.001.

Soldati, L., Bianchi-Demicheli, F. Schockaert, P. Köhl, J., Bolmont, M., Hasler & R. Perroud, N. (2021). Association of ADHD and hypersexuality and paraphilias. *Psychiatry Research*, 295, 113638. https://doi.org/10.1016/j.psychres.2020.113638.

Wymbs, B.T., Canu, W.H., Sacchetti, G.M. & Ranson, L.M. (2021). Adult ADHD and romantic relationships: What we know and what we can do to help. *Journal of Marriage and Family Therapy*, 47, 664–681.

Wymbs, B.T., Dawson, A.E., Suhr, J.A., Bunford, N. & Gidycz, C.A. (2017). ADHD Symptoms as Risk Factors for Intimate Partner Violence Perpetration and Victimization. *Journal of Interpersonal Violence*, 32(5), 659–681.

Wymbs, B.T. & Gidycz, C.A. (2021). Examining link between childhood ADHD and sexual assault victimization. *Journal of Attention Disorders*, 25(11), 1612–1622. https://doi.org/10.1177/1087054720923750.

Young, S. & Cocallis, K. (2023). A systematic review of the relationship between neurodiversity and psychosexual functioning in individuals with autism spectrum disorder (ASD) or attention-Deficit/Hyperactivity disorder (ADHD). *Neuropsychiatric Disease and Treatment*, 19, 1379–1395. https://doi.org/10.2147/NDT.S319980.

Chapter 12

Building your sexual goals

This is your plan for change! This chapter is all about **YOUR** plan. You are encouraged to create a sexual plan and outline how you want to improve your sex life, improve your communication about sex, and address the various barriers that you have identified in this workbook. Your sexual plan will help you to openly discuss the advantages and the challenges that ADHD brings to your sex life. Make this plan your own. Ensure that the elements you add are things that you agree with and want to do!

Let's get to work!

MY BODY

> I will move my body by doing the following:
>
> ✓ _____
> ✓ _____
> ✓ _____
> ✓ _____
> ✓ _____

DOI: 10.4324/9781003422372-13

I will love my body by doing the following:

✓ _____

✓ _____

✓ _____

✓ _____

✓ _____

MY ADHD

To manage my ADHD, I will create the following daily expectations:

✓ _____

✓ _____

✓ _____

✓ _____

✓ _____

To manage my ADHD, I will create the following weekly expectations:

✓ _____

✓ _____

✓ _____

✓ _____

✓ _____

To manage my ADHD, I will create the following monthly expectations:

✓ _____

✓ _____

✓ _____

✓ _____

✓ _____

PLAY!

I will add play in my life by doing the following:

✓ _____

✓ _____

✓ _____

✓ _____

✓ _____

✓ _____

MY ENVIRONMENT

I will deal with distracting noises in my environment by doing the following:

✓ _____

✓ _____

✓ _____

✓ _____

✓ _____

I will deal with the lighting in my environment by doing the following:

✓ _____

✓ _____

✓ _____

✓ _____

✓ _____

I will cue myself or a partner to transition towards sexual pleasure with the following WORDS:

✓ _____

✓ _____

✓ _____

✓ _____

✓ _____

I will cue myself or a partner to transition towards sexual pleasure with the following ACTIONS:

✓ _____

✓ _____

✓ _____

✓ _____

✓ _____

I will cue myself or a partner to transition towards sexual pleasure with this type of TOUCH:

☞ _____

☞ _____

☞ _____

☞ _____

☞ _____

HARD and INTENSE TOUCH can be GREAT!

My Sexy Playlist!

I will cue myself or a partner towards sexual pleasure with this music list:

☞ _____

☞ _____

☞ _____

☞ _____

☞ _____

☞ _____

☞ _____

☞ _____

☞ _____

☞ _____

☞ _____

☞ _____

☞ _____

☞ _____

☞ _____

☛ _____

☛ _____

☛ _____

☛ _____

I will use the following scale to express to others how seated I am in my body:

☐   0 – Total shut down, dissociated, not present, gone but not in a good way
☐   1 – Edgy
☐   2 – Can't feel my body, can't feel my toes! Am I breathing?!?
☐   3 – Breathing, I am breathing!
☐   4 – I am here
☐   5 – I am here, and I can feel my body
☐   6 – I am here, and I am IN my body
☐   7 – Peaceful cohabitation with my body
☐   8 – Me and my body are rocking it out, I can feel the flow, it's like magic!

My strategies to become more seated in my body include:

☛ _____

☛ _____

☛ _____

☛ _____

☛ _____

MY SEX LIFE!

I want to make sex an important part of my life because:

✓ _____

✓ _____

✓ _____

✓ _____

✓ _____

I will get my mind and body into my ideal sexual state by doing the following:

✓ _____

✓ _____

✓ _____

✓ _____

✓ _____

I will create sexual novelty in my life by doing the following:

✓ _____

✓ _____

✓ _____

✓ _____

✓ _____

I will create sexual intensity in my life by doing the following:

✓ _____

✓ _____

✓ _____

✓ _____

✓ _____

I will create sexual variation in my life by doing the following:

✓ _____

✓ _____

✓ _____

✓ _____

✓ _____

I will communicate my sexual interest by using The Sexy Communication Scale

My Sexy Communication Scale – Gradients of sexual pleasure

- ☐ 0 – I'm not into it, like absolutely not; I could not pull it off even if I tried
- ☐ 1 – I am not into it, but I am not opposed to sex; it's just not really where I am at right now
- ☐ 2 – I am aware that I am a sexual being, but I have not thought about engaging in sex
- ☐ 3 – I am distracted by other things (tired, hungry, chores, etc.), but I feel that sex could exist if there was space for it
- ☐ 4 – I am thinking about sex on occasion, but I don't have any specific plans or thoughts about doing anything about it
- ☐ 5 – I could have sex or not have sex; I can be moved up the scale or down the scale. I am neutral, but it is an openminded neutral
- ☐ 6 – I am thinking more often about sex
- ☐ 7 – I am thinking more about sex, and I am starting to think about how I might engage in sex
- ☐ 8 – I am thinking about sex, and I have developed a plan to have sex
- ☐ 9 – I really want to have sex; I am excited to have sex
- ☐ 10 – I am there, I am into it, my sexual interest has become a hyperfocus, I could not do anything else right now but have sex. The urge is very strong

I will transition OUT of sex by doing the following:

✓ _____

✓ _____

✓ _____

✓ _____

✓ _____

If I struggle to transition OUT of sex, I will ask for help.

Here is my list of people and/or resources who can help!

☛ _____

☛ _____

☛ _____

☛ _____

☛ _____

I will ensure sexual balance by doing the following:

✓ _____

✓ _____

✓ _____

✓ _____

✓ _____

My anxiety-producing sexual thoughts are:

☛ _____

☛ _____

☛ _____

☛ _____

☛ _____

Challenges or more helpful sexual thoughts for me include:

✓ _____

✓ _____

✓ _____

✓ _____

✓ _____

My sensory concerns include:

☛ _____

☛ _____

☛ _____

☛ _____

☛ _____

I will create a sensory-friendly sexual experience by doing the following:

✓ _____

✓ _____

✓ _____

✓ _____

✓ _____

My unhelpful stims include:

☛ _____

☛ _____

☛ _____

☛ _____

☛ _____

I will create good stim in my life by doing the following:

✓ _____

✓ _____

✓ _____

✓ _____

✓ _____

I will manage my impulsivity, both sexual and otherwise, by committing to do the following:

✓ _____

✓ _____

✓ _____

✓ _____

✓ _____

My life goals include:

Very short-term goals: (4–6 weeks):

_____

_____

_____

_____

_____

Short-term goals (3–6 months):

_____

_____

_____

_____

_____

Moderate term goals (1–3 years):

_____

_____

_____

_____

_____

Long-term goals (3–5 years):

_____

_____

_____

_____

_____

MY NEEDS

My needs in relationships are:

☛ _____

☛ _____

☛ _____

☛ _____

☛ _____

I will honor my need for intimacy by doing the following;

✓ _____

✓ _____

✓ _____

✓ _____

✓ _____

I will share my sexual history, sexual interests and sexual needs with these people

✓ _____

✓ _____

✓ _____

✓ _____

✓ _____

I will stop masking my ADHD symptoms by doing this:

☞ _____

☞ _____

☞ _____

☞ _____

☞ _____

✓ I will communicate more openly about sex!

✓ I will create time for the important relationships in my life

My boundaries are:

☞ _____

☞ _____

☞ _____

☞ _____

☞ _____

Red flags in relationships are:

☞ _____

☞ _____

☞ _____

☞ _____

☞ _____

I will honor my need for safety by doing the following;

✓ _____

✓ _____

✓ _____

✓ _____

✓ _____

Here is the Neurodivergent Sexual Checklist!

✓ Sexual intensity
✓ Sexual novelty
✓ Sexual variation
✓ Sexual transitions towards sex
✓ Sexual transitions out of sex
✓ Neurodivergent atmosphere/ambiance
✓ Sensory friendly sexual experiences
✓ Sexual balance
✓ Sexual communication
✓ Relationship safety
✓ Sexual safety

Things to do to ensure a playful and fun neurodivergent sexual experience include:

☛ Manage sexual distractions
☛ Manage sexual anxieties
☛ Manage impulsivity
☛ Improve interoceptive awareness
☛ Improve intimacy in relationships
☛ Reduce masking in relationships
☛ Address relationship problems
☛ Address trauma and victimization

My top 3 sexual goals are:

✳ _____

✳ _____

✳ _____

Conclusion

Sex can be a complicated and dynamic process. While there are no easy answers, your efforts to explore your sexuality, while considering your neurodiversity, is a positive step forward. ADHD can impact your sex life!

Whether you are using these tools to enhance solo sex or partnered sex, finding creative ways to have fun and playful sex is the goal. Your sexuality is a part of you to be enjoyed. Following pleasure and play is one way to begin identifying your sexual needs and your sexual preferences. Make sexual wellness a lifelong priority!

ADHD is also a lifelong adventure! While ADHD is not always an easy road, it can lead you to experiencing great personal growth and change. There are many gifts that come with having ADHD.

You are encouraged to communicate openly about sex, to identify your sexual likes and dislikes, to address outstanding sexual problems, to practice finding comfort and connection with your body. Finding a balance between solo sex and partnered sex may also be a meaningful goal for you.

Find joy in ensuring that sexual transitions both into sex and out of sex are positive and fulfilling. Manage sexual impulsivity so that you are engaging in safe decision making. Use the tools in this workbook to create a sex life that makes you proud!

It has been a joy to explore these skills with you. You are encouraged to seek the assistance of a qualified mental health professional to address ongoing issues that are impacting you and your sexuality, as well as to continue exploring your neurodivergence.

Good luck on your journey!

DOI: 10.4324/9781003422372-14

Appendix – Additional Resources

Here are some reading and listening resources for you! If you prefer not to read, most of these books are available as audio books. Hopefully, they will provide you with some further rabbit holes to explore!

Attention Deficit Hyperactivity Disorder (ADHD)

Barkley, R. (2021). *Taking Charge of Adult ADHD: Proven Strategies to Succeed at Work, at Home, and in Relationships*, 2nd edition, Guilford Publications.

Hallowell, E. M., & Ratey, J. J. (2021). *ADHD 2.0: New science and essential strategies for striving without distraction from childhood through adulthood*. Random House Publishing Group.

Hiscock, H., & Sciberras, E. (Eds.). (2019). *Sleep and ADHD: An evidence-based guide to assessment and treatment*. Academic Press. Academic Press: San Diego CA.

Solden, S. (2012). *Women With Attention Deficit Disorder: Embrace your differences and transform your life*. Introspect Press, pp. 515.

Solden, S. & Frank, M. (2019). *A Radical Guide for Women with ADHD: Embrace Neurodiversity, Live Boldly, and Break Through Barriers*. New Harbinger Publications.

Tuckman, A. (2013). *Understand Your Brain, Get More Done: The ADHD Executive Functions Workbook*. Specialty Press/A.D.D. Warehouse.

Tuckman, A. (2019) *ADHD After Dark: Better Sex Life, Better Relationship*. Routledge; 1st edition (July 16 2019), 388 pages.

Vincent, A. (2017). *My brain still needs glasses*. Juniper Publishing: California

You can also explore various websites for additional resources, articles and webinars specific to ADHD (one example is www.ADDitudemag.com)

Sexuality

Goddard, A. J. & Brungardt, K. (2015) *Lesbian Sex Secrets for Men*, Plume publishers.

Goldstein, A., Pukall, C., Goldstein, I & Krapf, J. (2023). *When Sex Hurts: Understanding and Healing Pelvic Pain*. Completely revised and updated. Da Capo Lifelong Books.

Kerner, I. (2010). *She comes first: The thinking man's guide to pleasuring a woman*. New York, NY: Harper Collins Publications.

Langford, J. (2016). *Spare me "the talk"!: A girl's guide to sex, relationships, and growing up*. Mercer Island, WA: ParentMap.

Langford, J. (2019). *Spare me "the talk"!: A guy's guide to sex, relationships, and growing up*. Mercer Island, WA: ParentMap.

McCarthy, B. W., & Metz, M. E. (2004). *Coping with premature ejaculation: How to overcome PE, please your partner and have great sex.* Oakland, CA: New Harbinger Publications.

Metz, M. E., & McCarthy, B. W. (2004). *Coping with erectile dysfunction: How to regain confidence and enjoy great sex.* Oakland, CA: New Harbinger Publications.

Morin, J. (2010) *Anal Pleasure & Health: A Guide for Men, Women and Couples.* San Francisco: Down There Press.

Nagoski, E. (2021). *Come As You Are: Revised and Updated: The surprising new science that will transform your sex life.* Simon & Schuster Publications.

Nagoski, E. (2024). *Come Together: The Science (and Art!) of Creating Lasting Sexual Connections.* Ballantine Books.

Tuckman, A. (2019) *ADHD After Dark: Better Sex Life, Better Relationship.* Routledge; 1st edition (July 16 2019), 388pages.

Westheimer, R. K., & Lehu, P. A. (2019). *Sex for dummies* (4th ed.). New Jersey: Wiley & Sons.

Online resources include: Kerly app and OMGYes!

Relationships

Cole, T. (2021). *Boundary Boss: The Essential Guide to Talk True, Be Seen, and (Finally) Live Free.* Sounds True Publications.

Gottman, J. M., & Silver, N. (2015). *The seven principles for making marriage work.* New York: Harmony Press.

Gottman, J. M., & Schwartz Gottman, J. (2022). *The love prescription.* Penguin Books.: London, U.K.

Gottman, J. M., Schwartz Gottman, J., Abrams, D., & Carleton Abrams, J. (2019). *Eight dates: Essential conversations for a lifetime of love.* Workman Publishing Company,: New York p. 224.

Gottman, J. M., Schwartz Gottman, J., Abrams, D., & Carlton Abrams, R. (2016). *The man's guide to women: Scientifically proven secrets from the "Love Lab" about what women really want.* Rodale Books.: Pennsylvania.

Harper, F. G. (2020). *Unfuck Your Boundaries Workbook: Build Better Relationships Through Consent, Communication, and Expressing Your Needs.* Microcosm Publishing.

Hooks, B. (2000). *All About Love: New Visions.* William Morrow Paperbacks.

Orlov, M. (2010). *The ADHD Effect on Marriage: Understand and rebuild your relationship in six steps.* Speciality Press/A.D.D. Warehouse: Plantation, Florida, p. 225.

Orlov, M. & Kohlenberger N. (2014) *The Couple's Guide to Thriving with ADHD.* Specialty Press: Florida.

Paterson, R. J. (2022). *The Assertiveness Workbook: How to Express Your Ideas and Stand Up for Yourself at Work and in Relationships*, 2nd edition, New Harbinger Publilcations: CA.

Pera, G. & Barkley, R. (2008). *Is It You, Me, or Adult A.D.D.?: Stopping the Roller Coaster When Someone You Love Has Attention Deficit Disorder.* Kindle Scribe

Richo, D. (2021) *How to Be an Adult in Relationships: The Five Keys to Mindful Loving.* Shambhala Press.

Tschudi, S. (2012). *A Practical Guide to Understanding your Partner, Improving your Communication and Strenghtening Your Relationship.* New Harbinger Publications.

Wachs, K. M. (2002). *Relationships for dummies.* For Dummies Publications,: New Jersey p. 416.

Weiss, R. (2017). *Out of the doghouse: A step-by-step relationship-saving guide for men caught cheating.* Deerfield Beach, FL: Health Communications, Inc.

Mindfulness and Body Awareness

Dana, D. (2021). *Anchored: How to Befriend Your Nervous System Using Polyvagal Theory.* Sounds True publishers.

Mahler, K, Rothschild, C. & Alma, J. (2019). *My Interoception Workbook: A guide for adolescents, teens and adults.* www.kelly-mahler.com

McBride, H. (2021). *The Wisdom of Your Body: Finding healing, wholeness and connection through embodied living.* Brazos Press: Michigan.

Zylowska (2012). *The Mindfulness Prescription for Adult ADHD: An 8-Step Program for Strengthening Attention, Managing Emotions, and Achieving Your Goals.* Trumpeter Press.

There are many apps for mindfulness, one example is MindfullyADD.com

Mood

Bourne, E. J. (2020). *The Anxiety and Phobia Workbook*, 7th edition. New Harbinger Publications, Oakland, CA.

Burns, D. D. (1981). *Feeling good: The new mood therapy.* New York, NY: Penguin Books.

Dow, M. (2015). *The brain fog fix.* Hay House, Inc.

Greenberger, D., & Padesky, C. A. (2016). *Mind over mood: Change how you feel by changing the way you think* (2nd ed.). New York: Guildford Press.

Hanson, R., & Mendius, R. (2009). *Buddha's brain: The practical neuroscience of happiness, love & wisdom.* Oakland, CA: New Harbinger Publications.

Hayes, S. C. (2005). *Get out of your mind & into your life.* New Harbinger Publications: California.

Jeffers, S. J. (1988). *Feel the fear and do it anyway.* New York: Ballantine.

Miller, R.C. (2015). *The iRest Program for Healing PTSD, A Proven-Effective Approach to Using Yoga Nidra Meditation and Deep Relaxation Techniques to Overcome Trauma.* New Harbinger Publications.

Paterson, R. J. (2016). *How to be miserable.* New Harbinger Publications:California.

Paterson, R. J. (2020). *How to be miserable in your twenties: 40 ways to fail at adulting.* New Harbinger Publications:California

Pittman, C. M. (2022) *Taming Your Amygdala: Brain-Based Strategies to Quiet the Anxious Mind.* Kindle Scribe

Pittman, C. M., & Karle, E. M. (2015). *Rewire your anxious brain: How to use the neuroscience of fear to end anxiety, panic, and worry.* Oakland, CA: New Harbinger Publications.

Siegel, D. (2018). *Aware: The science and practice of presence – The groundbreaking meditation practice.* TarcherPerigee.: New York

Wehrenberg, M. (2008). *The 10 best-ever anxiety management techniques: Understanding how your brain makes you anxious & what you can do to change it.* W.W. Norton Company: New York

Young, J. E., & Klosko, J. S. (1994). *Reinventing your life: The breakthrough program to end negative behavior . . . and feel great again.* Plume.: New York

Sensory Processing Disorder

Dunn, W. (2009). *Living Sensationally: Understanding Your Senses.* Jessica Kingsley Publishers

Heller, S. (2003). *Too Loud, Too Bright, Too Fast, Too Tight: What to Do If You Are Sensory Defensive in an Overstimulating World.* Harper Perennial

Kranowitz, C. S. (2016). *The Out-of-Sync Child Grows Up: Coping with Sensory Processing Disorder in the Adolescent and Young Adult Years.* Penguin.

Kranowitz, C. S., & Newman, J. (2010). *Growing an in-sync child: simple, fun activities to help every child develop, learn, and grow*. Penguin.

Newman, J., & Kranowitz, C. (2012). *Growing in sync children. Teaching Young Children*, 6(1), 7–10.

Zeff, T. (2007). *The Highly Sensitive Person's Companion: Daily Exercises for Calming Your Senses in an Overstimulating World*. Kindle Scribe

Zeff, T. (2004). *The Highly Sensitive Person's Survival Guide: Essential Skills for Living Well in an Overstimulating World*. Kindle Scribe

There are online resources available, one example is STAR Institute Resources (sensory-health.org) and information offered on Dr. Elaine Aron's website and Dr. Neff's website. There are various noise cancelling earplugs available through many different companies, one example is loop earplugs (us.loopearplugs.com) but there are many others.

Childhood Abuse

Levine, P. A. (2010). *In an unspoken voice. How the body releases trauma and restores goodness.* North Atlantic Books,: California p. 384.

Singer, K. (2010). *Evicting the perpetrator: A male survivor's guide for recovery from childhood sexual abuse.* NEARI Press: Vermont.

Van der Kolk, B. A. (2015). *The body keeps the score: Brain, mind, and body in the healing of trauma.* New York: Penguin Books, pp. 445.

Walker, P. (2013). *Complex PTSD: From surviving to thriving.* Azure Coyote Publishing.: California

Pain Management

Bernhard, T. (2010) *How to be Sick: A Buddhist-Inspired Guide for the Chronically Ill and Their Caregivers.* Wisdom Publications: MA.

Caudill, M., & Herbert, B. (2016). *Managing pain before it manages you.* New York: The Guilford Press.

Fernando, P. (2016) *Finding Freedom in Illness. Finding Freedom in Illness: A Guide to Cultivating Deep Well-Being through Mindfulness and Self-Compassion.* Shambhala publisher: Colorado

Goldstein, A., Pukall, C., Goldstein, I & Krapf, J. (2011). *When Sex Hurts: Understanding and Healing Pelvic Pain.* Completely revised and updated. Da Capo Lifelong Books.

Gordon, A. (2020). *The Way Out: A revolutionary, scientifically proven approach to healing chronic pain.* Avery Publications.: New York

Sleep Hygiene

Hauri, P., & Linde, S. M. (1996). *No more sleepless nights.* New York: Wiley.

Hiscock, H., & Sciberras, E. (2019). *Sleep and ADHD: An evidence-based guide to assessment and treatment.* Academic Press.: California

Index

fear of 214–215
masking and 232
reciprocity and 215–216
safe relationships and 215, 231
sexual communication 222–226, 232
sharing of yourself 215–216
time management and 216–218, 231
unmasking your ADHD 219–222, 232
intoxicants, use of 67–68, 70, 208–209,
  247

journal, sexual 93, 198–199, 202

kinky sex 186
kissing 67, 78–79

labia, look of 127–128
lighting
  planning 264
  sensory issues 163–164, 179, 181
  transitions and 79
love languages 79

make-up sex 226
masking 273
  diagnosis and 6
  intimacy and 219–222, 232
  sexual communication and 222
  sexual history 225
masturbation 25
medications
  ejaculatory control 130
  erectile dysfunction 131
  impulsivity 192–193, 210
  maintenance and optimization of 148
  sex and 27–28
  sexual functioning and 148
  for sexual issues 134–135
  timing of sex 41–42
  transitioning out of sex 93
meditation 63
memory, trauma therapy and 239–242
memory reconsolidation (MR) 240
menopausal symptoms 147
mental imagery, using during sex 45–46
mind-body connection 26, 130
mindfulness 63, 130, 191–192, 278
mood lighting 79
moving your body 23, 261
music 39–40, 265–266

neurodivergent people
  differences between 6
  use of term 5
neurodiversity grief 28–29
no, saying 247
noises 38–40, 53
  sensory issues with 172, 179, 181
novelty, sexual 83–84, 85–86, 267

odors
  anxiety and 128–129
  sensory issues with 164–166, 179, 180
open relationships 208
oral hygiene 168
orgasm problems 132–133
overcontrolling 22
overstimulation 141–142

pain
  additional resources 279
  anxiety and 133–134
  management 24
  sexual 52
parenting 114–115, 120
  intimacy and 228–229, 233
partnered sex/relationships
  definition and use of term 2
  problems due to ADHD 12
  sensory issues 173–174
  too much 202–205
  use of term 20
partners
  hyperfocus and 111–112
  talking to 3
penile pain 133
penis size 127–128
perimenopausal symptoms 147
physical health concerns 24–25
physical movement 23–25, 61, 261
physical spaces for sex 37–38, 40–41, 53
physical supports 24
plan, sexual 261–274
play
  adding to life 263
  engagement with self/partner 50
  impact on life 18–19
  increasing 17–18
  sex as 17–18
pleasure sensations
  communication from our bodies 59

For Product Safety Concerns and Information please contact our EU
representative GPSR@taylorandfrancis.com
Taylor & Francis Verlag GmbH, Kaufingerstraße 24, 80331 München, Germany